SECRETS OF ELECTRONIC COMMERCE

A GUIDE FOR SMALL AND MEDIUM-SIZED EXPORTERS

SECOND EDITION

Geneva 2009

ABSTRACT FOR TRADE INFORMATION SERVICES

2009   F-06.06
                                                          SEC

INTERNATIONAL TRADE CENTRE (ITC)
Secrets of Electronic Commerce: A Guide for Small and Medium-Sized Exporters. – 2nd ed.
Geneva: ITC, 2009. x, 196 p.

Guide focusing on Internet-based services with regard to small and medium-sized enterprises (SMEs) – identifies SME issues and constraints related to electronic commerce; explains how to develop an e-commerce strategy and conduct online market research; outlines marketing and online communication techniques; answers questions on legal and financial issues; highlights characteristics of successful websites; deals with technical, policy and country-specific issues; online procurement; describes role of ITC in providing assistance in e-commerce, as well as programmes and services offered by other international bodies; includes bibliographical references.

Subject descriptors: **Electronic Commerce, Marketing, e-Procurement, SMEs.**

English

Palais des Nations, 1211 Geneva 10, Switzerland

Digital image on the cover: © iStockphoto

ITC/P238.E/EC/09-XI   ISBN 978-92-9137-378-9
                                  United Nations Sales No. E.09.III.T.7

Preface to second edition

At the time this book was first published there was still some doubt about the benefits of the Internet as a trading platform. Since then, Internet use has grown at a phenomenal rate and e-commerce is becoming popular in an ever-increasing number of countries.

The topics addressed in this book remain relevant and still seem to cover the questions which business owners and managers would ask. In this edition we have modified the answers to reflect changes in technology and Internet usage and updated the references and links.

Additional information about the books referenced is also available on the Amazon website www.amazon.com.

Acknowledgements

This updated publication was prepared under the overall strategic direction of Aicha Pouye, Director, Division of Business and Institutional Support, and the guidance of Jacky Charbonneau, Chief, Enterprise Competitiveness Section.

Martin Labbé, Online Marketing and Digital Networks Adviser, and Hema Menon, Trade Training Officer were responsible for the technical update of this publication, which was first released in 2001. They identified areas for update and guided the international consultant throughout the process.

Mahmoud Reza Hashemi, Associate Professor at the University of Tehran, researched and updated the contents, particularly reference materials, sources, statistics and recent trends and technically edited the guide on the basis of a preliminary update carried out by Helen Stephenson of Stephenson Consultants.

Natalie Domeisen, as manager of ITC's publications programme, coordinated the publications process and provided valuable comments.

The technical contributions of the following persons are acknowledged with thanks: Paul Kelly, Senior Trade Information Officer, Trade Information Section; Jean-François Bourque, Senior Adviser on Legal Aspects of Foreign Trade; Hong-Siew Lim, Senior Adviser on Enterprise Value Chain Competitiveness.

Sarah McCue was responsible for the design and development of the first edition of this book and its initial concept. She was assisted by Prema de Sousa, who conducted the survey on which this book is based.

The book was edited by Julie Wolf. Leni Sutcliffe also provided editorial support. Isabel Droste and Carmelita Endaya prepared the publication for printing.

Contents

INTRODUCTION

Introductory issues

1.   How is the Internet changing the way business is conducted?

Since 1990s the Internet has grown to become one of the most amazing technological and social accomplishments of the last century. Over a very short time period the Internet has dramatically changed the way business is conducted and continues to do so.

The early pioneers who launched the World Wide Web were not aiming to make money, but within a few years entrepreneurs emerged who convinced United States investors that the pot of Internet gold was just around the corner.

The Internet has altered significantly the way business is conducted in the following ways:

- Lowering the cost of business transactions, especially in the services sector.

- Reducing communication costs through e-mail, Internet telephony (VoIP – Voice over Internet Protocol) and desktop video conferencing.

- Lowering printing and publishing costs.

- Improving the flow of information.

- Providing rapid access to a wide variety of information sources.

- Facilitating collaboration through e-mail, online forums, communities of practice, live online meetings and desktop video conferencing.

- Increasing the coordination of actions, hence facilitating the growth of outsourcing. This has led many companies to move their back-office services, including data processing, customer service, accounting and personnel, to less-expensive offshore locations. This could not have happened without the Internet.

- Facilitating home working. This arrangement, called telecommuting or telework, reduces or eliminates many employment related costs.

- The Internet spreads innovations much more quickly than in the past (in the 1980s, for example, it took an average of 10 years for an innovation in one country to be adopted in another). This also leads to increased competition.

More specifically:

- Buyers can now more easily, and at lower cost, compare prices and services from suppliers anywhere in the world.

- Because of lower search costs, customers who enter markets infrequently are now potentially as well informed about prices and supply as regular suppliers to these markets.

- Research into prices, quality, delivery schedules, product content or components can be carried out on the Internet.

- Customers can more easily specify individual requirements online, permitting customization of products such as cars, computers and CDs.

- It is possible for businesses to maintain one-to-one customer relationships with an unlimited number of customers. This level of customer service has become the standard in online consumer markets. Information on an individual customer is used for marketing, sales and accounts.

- Incentives can be targeted to individuals more effectively than through traditional marketing media (television, catalogue and newspaper advertising).

- Auctions, buyers' cooperatives and barter sites have emerged.

- Buyers are bidding on an unprecedented variety of goods and services. The largest and most well-known auction site is www.ebay.com.

- Buyers are grouping together to obtain quantity discounts.

- Virtual enterprises are reaching customers faster and at a small fraction of the cost of physical stores and sales people.

- Global competition and ease of price comparison mean that many Internet retailers must sustain their business with low price markups.

- Global Internet markets offer new opportunities to small merchants from developed and developing countries, but they also bring global competition into local and niche markets, the traditional outlets for small merchants.

- Online merchants can offer complementary products to customers by cross-selling or up-selling at low cost and even automatically on the basis of data collected online from existing customers on product preferences, purchasing histories, etc. Economic potential is now more closely linked to the ability to control and manipulate information about commercial transactions.

- The Internet is rapidly globalizing most marketplaces and industries.

- The provision of banking, education, consulting, design, marketing and similar services is changing profoundly.

- Local and foreign suppliers are more easily and closely integrated into the supply chain.

- Many small enterprises add to their income by using the e-commerce infrastructure offered by a larger business, such as on the Amazon.com shopping site. Hoping to generate more traffic to their own sites, large Internet companies are enabling small enterprises to set up a website from scratch in a few days, with no technical skill requirement.

- Some build a new website, or expand their list of offered merchandises by advertising the products of another company and providing a link to the company's website. They are in fact acting as middlemen between another company's product or service and its potential customers. They simply advertise on behalf of that company's product by directly or indirectly promoting it on their own website. In exchange they receive a commission or flat fee for any transaction made. In some instances, they may even be paid when no transaction is completed. This new form of Internet-based marketing is referred to as affiliate marketing.

The Internet is only beneficial for a company if it truly creates value for customers or reduces costs. Thus, an Internet-based e-commerce development strategy must coherently integrate the use of the Internet with a company's primary value proposition.

For more information

- Schneider, Gary P. Electronic Commerce. Seventh Edition. Course Technology, a division of Thomson Learning, Inc., 2007.

  This book provides complete coverage of the key business and technology elements of electronic commerce. In Chapter 1, the author describes how companies use the Internet to create new products and services, reduce the cost of existing business processes and improve the efficiency and effectiveness of their operations.

- Affiliate marketing. en.wikipedia.org/wiki/Affiliate_marketing.

  This website provides information and links on the history of affiliate marketing, its advantages and current challenges.

2.   How do companies use the Internet in Europe and North America?

Revenue generated by sales over the Internet has been slowing down recently because of the global economic downturn, but statistics indicate that investing in e-commerce is sustainable and profitable and that it offers prospects for massive upward growth and return on investment (ROI) in the years to come. Some indicators of the adoption of the Internet by companies in Europe and North America are described below.

Europe

According to a survey carried out by European national statistical institutes on usage of information and communication technologies (ICT) by enterprises, the percentage of the total turnover of enterprises from e-commerce via the Internet for the 27 countries of the European Union was 4.7% in 2007. This figure was 9.8% for Ireland, 8.5% for Norway and 7% for the United Kingdom [1].

- *United Kingdom*

A report released by the British Office of National Statistics in February 2009 indicates that Internet retail sales, as a percentage of total retail sales, rose by 13.2% in the United Kingdom. These figures closely match figures issued by the IMRG/Capgemini Sales Index which showed that the year-on-year e-business retail market expanded by 17% in July 2009. This increase was mostly due to online retail sales of clothing, footwear and accessories; electrical goods also performed well [2].

North America

- *Canada*

Although the rate of small firms connected to the Internet is increasing in Canada, they continue to lag behind medium-sized and large firms in terms of both connection rates and the ways in which the Internet is put to use in the business. The overall rate of firms connected to the Internet was 87% in 2007, but small firms (85%) lagged well behind medium-sized and large firms (95% and 99% respectively). However, small firms have been closing the gap in connection rates between themselves and medium-sized and large firms in recent years [3].

Although the proportion of firms selling online has changed very little since 2001, the proportion of small and medium-sized firms that purchase online has doubled. For instance, in 2007, only 7% of small firms sold online, whereas 45% purchased online; for medium-sized firms, 13% sold and 69% purchased online; and for large firms, 22% sold and 74% purchased online. This probably reflects the higher costs associated with setting up operations to sell online compared with the low costs of purchasing online [3].

Small firms that operate in service industries generally have more e-commerce activity than those operating in goods-producing industries. However, small firms have less activity related to e-commerce than medium-sized and large firms across all industries.

Statistics Canada's Survey of Electronic Commerce and Technology (SECT) defines small firms as having fewer than 20 employees, medium-sized firms as having between 20 and 99 employees, and large firms as having 100 employees or more for all industries except manufacturing. The upper limit for the medium-sized category in the manufacturing industry is 499 employees, whereas firms with 500 employees or more are defined as large.

Table 1   Canada: Internet access and use by firm size, 2001–2007 [4]

Internet access and use by firm size		2001	2002	2003	2004	2005	2006	2007
		Percentage of total number of firms						
Internet access	Small	68	73	76	79	79	81	85
	Medium-sized	91	92	94	96	96	96	95
	Large	94	99	97	99	98	99	99
	All firms	71	76	78	82	82	83	87
Own website	Small	24	27	29	32	33	35	36
	Medium-sized	57	62	66	69	70	71	74
	Large	74	77	77	79	82	89	90
	All firms	29	32	34	37	38	40	41
Sell online	Small	6	7	6	7	6	7	7
	Medium-sized	12	13	14	12	10	12	13
	Large	15	16	16	13	16	21	22
	All firms	7	8	7	7	7	8	8
Purchase online	Small	20	29	35	·40	40	42	45
	Medium	30	47	50	59	63	64	69
	Large	52	57	61	62	68	71	74
	All firms	22	32	37	43	43	45	48

- *United States*

In 2007, as in prior years, manufacturers and merchant wholesalers relied far more heavily on e-commerce than retailers or selected service businesses. Business-to-business (B2B) activity accounted for 93% of e-commerce transactions. Manufacturers led all industry sectors, with e-commerce accounting for 35% ($1 856 billion) of total shipments – up substantially for the sixth straight year. E-shipments were 35% of all manufacturing shipments in 2007, higher by 31.2% than in 2006 [4].

From 2002 to 2007, retail e-sales (online B2C sales of the retail industry, including such outlets as Amazon and Walmart) increased at an average annual growth rate of 23.1%, compared with 5.0% for total retail sales. Over 90% of retail e-sales were concentrated in two industry groups – non-store retailers, and dealers in motor vehicles and parts – which accounted for 73% and 19% respectively of the sector's total e-sales.

Nearly all non-store retail e-sales occurred in the electronic shopping and mail-order houses industry group. This group includes: catalogue and mail order operations, many of which sell through multiple channels; retail businesses selling solely over the Internet; and e-commerce units of traditional brick-and-mortar retailers (referred to as "brick and clicks"), with the units operating as separate entities and not engaging in sales of motor vehicles online. The top two merchandise categories, in terms of percentage of online sales, were electronics and appliances, and music and videos, both with 74% [4].

According to a 2008 Ipsos survey (www.ipsos.com) conducted in the United States, Internet operations, far from being an extra 'expense', were in fact boosting businesses' bottom line. Among the businesses surveyed, 64% claimed an increase in sales revenue directly attributed to the Internet while 73% said having a website saved money in administrative costs [2].

For more information

- Eurostat. epp.eurostat.ec.europa.eu.

  Situated in Luxembourg, Eurostat is the Statistical Office of the European Communities. Its task is to provide the European Union with statistics at European level that enable comparisons between countries and regions. Eurostat offers a whole range of important and interesting data that governments, businesses, the education sector, journalists and the public can use for their work and daily life.

- European e-Business Reports. The European e-Business Market Watch. www.ebusiness-watch.org.

  The "Sectoral e-Business Watch" (SeBW) studies the impact of ICT and e-business on enterprises, industries and the economy in general. It highlights barriers to a wider or faster uptake of ICT and identifies public policy changes.

REFERENCES

[1] Information Society Statistics. E-Commerce via Internet. 2009. Eurostat. epp.eurostat.ec.europa.eu.

[2] E-Business Growth Statistics 2009. Internet Business Blog. blog.Internetbusinessesforsale.co.uk/e-business/e-business-growth-statistics-2009.

[3] Statistics Canada. Survey of Electronic Commerce and Technology (SECT). 24 April 2008. www.statcan.gc.ca.

[4] 2007 E-commerce multi-sector report. E-Stats. U.S. Census Bureau. 28 May 2009. www.census.gov/econ/estats/.

3.   What is the level of Internet use by businesses?

Most companies have embraced e-mail, Internet connectivity and FTP (file transfer protocol) to boost overall productivity and as specific tools of efficient communication within and outside the organization. Internet access has become a critical factor in the success of most companies and organizations around the world.

In developed countries the majority of businesses have Internet access for e-mail and access to information; in developing countries the numbers are increasing all the time. In both developed and developing countries e-business continues to develop but at a slower pace.

According to the Information Economy Report 2009: Trends and Outlook in Turbulent Times, published by the United Nations Conference on Trade and Development (UNCTAD), while the number of users has grown five times faster in developing countries than in developed countries, in most developing countries the main purpose of Internet access is to send and receive e-mail, contrasting with usage in the developed world [1]. Few companies in developing countries use the Internet as a marketing tool or to make online transactions. In both developed and developing countries, large enterprises use information and communications technology (ICT), and the Internet in particular, more than small and medium-sized enterprises (SMEs) [1]. This may be a result partly of their greater financial and human resources, and partly of their greater need for such technology. This is in spite of the fact that SMEs have the largest potential for improving productivity by adopting e-business.

An Industry Canada report prepared by Compas (www.compas.ca) states that the level of Internet use increases as the perceived importance of each of the following increases:

- The Internet as an information source.
- Industry and trade associations as an information source.
- E-business as a challenge facing their business.
- Information on new technologies.

Conversely, the level of Internet use decreases as the perceived importance of each of the following increases:

- The media as an information source.
- Suppliers as an information source.
- Information on government services available to business.

Rapid technological progress, for example in wireless technology, and the increasing competitive pressure on companies in the global economy have been important drivers for e-business adoption. However, the pace and direction of related developments differ considerably between industries, and in various countries. Within sectors, opportunities and challenges are different for small firms and for medium-sized and large ones.

The ICT systems of large companies tend to be more powerful and sophisticated than those of small firms. This translates into more intensive and advanced electronic business practices, and a greater potential for exploiting cost-saving opportunities. For business-to-consumer (B2C) e-commerce activities, more small firms have specialized in doing business online, particularly in service sectors. The tourism industry is a good example.

Developing countries

UNCTAD´s Information Economy Report, which has replaced its E-commerce and Development Report since 2005, contains a statistical compilation on ICT use by enterprises in a variety of countries. The 2007-2008 report finds that Internet access by enterprises in developing countries continues to grow, as does the number of employees using the Internet in their daily work [2]. The number of enterprises with websites is also slowly increasing [2].

The report cites a firm-level survey by the World Bank which indicates that service-sector enterprises use websites and computers more than the manufacturing sector, and have a higher proportion of employees who use computers regularly [2].

Some developing countries are not far behind Europe in terms of integrating business processes, according to the UNCTAD report. In Brazil, for example, 36% of enterprises use information technology to manage orders and purchases, with automated linking to several related activities (inventory control, invoicing and payment, production and logistics).

For enterprises in developing countries that are starting to use the Internet, the mere fact of having increased access to information can have immediate positive effects. In Ghana for instance, SMEs that export non-traditional products use the Internet to find information on international best practices and exporting opportunities [2].

New Zealand

In New Zealand, more than 92% of businesses used the Internet in 2008, up from 90% in 2006 and 15% in 2001, according to Statistics New Zealand. Business Operations Survey: 2008 reported that more than 87% of businesses in the country had a broadband Internet connection in 2008, higher than the more than 75% reported in 2006. Over a third of businesses used the Internet to receive orders for goods or services. While almost one in ten New Zealand businesses generated over 10% of their sales through Internet orders in 2006, the number had climbed up to more than 39% by 2008 [3].

Republic of Korea

According to a 2008 report by eMarketer, Japan is the largest market by far for B2C e-commerce in the Asia-Pacific region, and the Republic of Korea ranks second [4].

Sales made over the Internet in the Republic of Korea grew by 22% in 2008, according to a report produced by the Korea National Statistical Office. The report shows that sales and purchases made over the Internet were in excess of US$ 400 billion, a situation largely resulting from the growth in business-to-business (B2B) transactions.

As for the B2B e-commerce transaction value by industry, the transaction value of electricity, gas and water supply skyrocketed by 137.1%, while those of information and communications and of manufacturing showed a downward trend in the second quarter of 2009 compared to the same period in 2008. The transaction values of sports and leisure appliances, agricultural and fishery products, and food and beverages increased by 44.5%, 30.9% and 29.6% respectively from the second quarter 2008. Meanwhile the transaction value of travel arrangement and reservation services fell by 15.2% in 2009 from the second quarter 2008 [5].

REFERENCES

[1] Information Economy Report 2009: Trends and outlook in turbulent times. UNCTAD. 2009. www.unctad.org.

[2] Information Economy Report 2007-2008 – Science and technology for development: the new paradigm of ICT. UNCTAD. 2008. www.unctad.org.

[3] Business Operations Survey. Statistics New Zealand. August 2008. www.stats.govt.nz.

[4] Asia-Pacific B2C E-Commerce: Focus on China and India. eMarketer, Jan 2008. www.emarketer.com.

[5] E-commerce and Cyber Shopping Survey in the Second Quarter and the First Half 2009. Statistics Korea. 2 September 2009. kostat.go.kr.

4. Why is the Internet important for trade?

Internet use is growing faster than the use of any other technology in history. As of 30 June 2009, over 1.67 billion people used the Internet according to Internet World Stats [1].

According to Netcraft's web server survey in September 2009, there were more than 226 million websites online [2].

World Regions	Population (2009 Est.)	Internet Users Dec. 31, 2000	Internet Users Latest Data	Penetration (% population)	Growth 2000-2009	Users % of table
Africa	991,002,342	4,514,400	65,903,900	6.7%	1,359.9%	3.9%
Asia	3,808,070,503	114,304,000	704,213,930	18.5%	516.1%	42.2%
Europe	803,850,858	105,096,093	402,380,474	50.1%	282.9%	24.2%
Middle East	202,687,005	3,284,800	47,964,146	23.7%	1,360.2%	2.9%
North America	340,831,831	108,096,800	251,735,500	73.9%	132.9%	15.1%
Latin America/Caribbean	586,662,468	18,068,919	175,834,439	30.0%	873.1%	10.5%
Oceania / Australia	34,700,201	7,620,480	20,838,019	60.1%	173.4%	1.2%
WORLD TOTAL	6,767,805,208	360,985,492	1,668,870,408	24.7%	362.3%	100.0%

NOTES: (1) Internet Usage and World Population Statistics are for 30 June 2009. (2) Demographic (Population) numbers are based on data from the U.S. Census Bureau. (3) Internet usage information comes from data published by Nielsen Online, by the International Telecommunication Union, by GfK, local Regulators and other reliable sources. (4) Information in this site may be cited, giving the due credit to www.internetworldstats.com. Copyright © 2001– 2009, Miniwatts Marketing Group. All rights reserved worldwide.

(Internet World Stats – Website Directory, www.internetworldstats.com) [1]

The Internet is a powerful tool for trade. Use of the Internet lowers communication costs, reduces the length of time-to-market for goods and services, makes possible the delivery of information in a digital format, reduces transport and distribution costs and allows for more fully integrated and broader business alliances.

The Internet is a growing global trading platform. As Internet technology advances it is likely to be used in almost every conceivable way to exchange information and trade goods and services. Many large firms are building new Internet-based systems for supply chain management and other inventory control.

In addition to selling their products and services, firms are using the Internet to survey customers, supply mass and trade media with information and pictures, submit regulatory compliance documents, manage and track deliveries and manage and transfer funds.

The full impact of the Internet is still to be seen. The Internet has affected the conduct of business, trade patterns, learning and social and political interactions. Industries and firms are increasingly influenced by the applications of the Internet, as are the people who use it for communicating and purchasing.

Small and rural businesses may be among the biggest beneficiaries. By reducing transaction costs, the Internet provides unprecedented opportunities for SMEs to trade across borders. Lower transaction costs also create opportunities for many rural and regional communities to revitalise their economic bases. The Internet can give farmers, small enterprises and communities the ability to present a regional image to the world, and create focal points (or portals) for inquiries about local businesses and their offerings.

For more information

- Information Economy Report 2007-2008 – Science and technology for development: the new paradigm of ICT. UNCTAD. www.unctad.org.

  The Information Economy Report focuses on trends in information and communications technologies (ICT), such as e-commerce and e-business, and on national and international policy and strategy options for improving the development impact of these technologies in developing countries. It replaces the E-commerce and Development Report published by UNCTAD from 2001 to 2004.www.unctad.org. Electronic Commerce Branch, Division for Services Infrastructure for Development & Trade Efficiency.

- International Trade Centre (ITC). www.intracen.org.

  ITC, the technical cooperation agency of UNCTAD and WTO for operational, enterprise-oriented aspects of trade provides a wide variety of online information, and business support services (www.intracen.org/menus/busserv.htm).

- The Role of ICT in Doing Business. By Qiang, C. Z.-W. and others. Information and Communications for Development, Global Trends and Policies, chapter 4. 2006. rru.worldbank.org/documents/other/Chapter4_ICT_in_DoingBusiness.pdf.

- Clark, G.R.G. and Wallsten, S.J. Has the Internet Increased Trade? Evidence from Industrial and Developing Countries. World Bank Policy Research Working Paper 3215. February 2004. www-wds.worldbank.org/external/default/WDSContentServer/IW3P/IB/2004/04/01/000265513_20040401155838/Rendered/PDF/28195.pdf.

- B2B e-Marketplaces: Current Trends, Challenges and Opportunities for SME Exporters in Developing Countries of Asia and the Pacific. International Trade Centre. 2005. www.intracen.org.

=== **REFERENCES** ===

[1] Internet World Stats – Usage and population statistics, www.internetworldstats.com

[2] Netcraft, www.netcraft.com.

5.   What is electronic commerce?

Electronic commerce, also known as EC, e-commerce or ecommerce, consists primarily of the distributing, buying, selling, marketing and servicing of products or services over electronic systems such as the Internet and other computer networks.

The information technology industry might see it as an electronic business application aimed at commercial transactions. It can involve electronic funds transfer, supply chain management, e-marketing, online marketing, online transaction processing, electronic data interchange (EDI), automated inventory management systems and automated data collection systems. It typically uses electronic communications technology such as the Internet, extranets, e-mail, e-books, databases, and mobile phones [1].

E-commerce existed in many forms before the Internet went into wide use and some of these forms still exist.

A commercial transaction can be divided into three main stages: advertising and searching, ordering and payment, and delivery. Any or all of these stages can be carried out on the Internet and are covered by the concept of e-commerce.

Electronic commerce may be categorized by the types of entities participating in the transactions or business processes. Some of the well-known electronic commerce categories are business-to-consumer (B2C), business-to-business (B2B), consumer-to-consumer (C2C) and business-to-government (B2G).

The two categories that are most commonly used are:

- Businesses that sell directly to end-consumers can use online methods to take orders and get paid. This is known as B2C e-commerce. Payment in advance via a secure online system offers more security for the buyer, as a processing company, which agrees to refund the customer if the order is not fulfilled correctly, holds the funds. For larger transactions, the seller may ask for a partial payment in advance with the balance due on delivery. Amazon.com (www.amazon.com) or Walmart.com (www.walmart.com), which sell merchandise to consumers, are good examples of B2C e-commerce.

- B2B e-commerce is for businesses that sell primarily to other businesses. A growing number of trade-related transactions between businesses are taking place online. These systems are often set up between a large business and its suppliers. The business purchasing the services usually establishes the rules and may assist its suppliers in setting up systems to work together electronically. Some companies exclude suppliers that are unable to work with them in this way. The online services that FedEx (www.fedex.com) offers to small businesses are an example of a B2B e-commerce. Sites such as Alibaba (www.alibaba.com) provide an online trade platform for businesses to run B2B.

Online B2B transactions include order management, electronic invoicing and procurement. 'Going online' will allow a company to: process incoming purchase orders and charge orders, send advance shipping notices and invoices, manage buyers' accounts, adjust prices, set user interface preferences and update item availability. In procurement, it helps companies to manage requisitions, catalogue searches and purchase approvals and to place orders.

There are also Internet-based companies that facilitate business to business e-commerce for specific industries. These can be found by searching on the Internet, but before doing business with them, it is best to carry out a background check with business colleagues, their customers, chambers of commerce and trade promotion organizations to determine whether they are effective and reliable.

Some Trade Promotion Organizations provide online B2B services. If these are well organized, these are an excellent choice for small businesses. BuyKorea (www. buykorea.org) is a B2B trade portal operated by the Korea Trade Investment Promotion Agency (KOTRA) and the Government of the Republic of Korea.

E-marketplaces specialize in providing online bidding or auctions, where suppliers can respond to calls for bids from buyers, or buyers can respond to tender offers. ChemConnect (www.chemconnect.com) is an e-marketplace specializing in chemicals, plastics, wire and cable and manufactured goods.

Commercial firms and organizations are increasingly using electronic means to advertise and market goods and services all over the world. Manufacturers and retailers in far-off countries can offer their products or services with information on product capabilities and benefits, content or components, prices, production schedules, delivery terms and payment conditions. This information allows consumers of goods and services, whether they are manufacturers or individuals, to order what they want from the most competitive suppliers.

Business transactions carried out with government agencies online constitute another e-commerce category referred to by some researchers as B2G (in some references B2G transactions are part of B2B and B2C). This may include transactions such as paying taxes, filling forms and updating corporate information. B2G may also include online public procurement or public e-procurement, in which businesses learn about the purchasing needs of agencies and agencies request proposal responses. One such example is the e-procurement site of the state of California (www.eprocure.dgs.ca.gov), or the eTenders website developed by the Department of Finance of the Republic of Ireland (www.etenders.gov.ie).

For more information

- Electronic Commerce: a managerial perspective 2008, *by* Turban, E. *and others*. Prentice Hall; 5th edition. 2007.

  A comprehensive sourcebook on e-commerce; describes what e-commerce is, explains how it is being conducted and managed, and explores its opportunities, limitations and related issues.

- Schneider, Gary P. Electronic Commerce. Seventh Edition. Course Technology, a division of Thomson Learning, Inc., 2007.

  This book provides complete coverage of the key business and technology elements of electronic commerce. In Chapter 1, the author describes how companies use the Internet to create new products and services, reduce the cost of existing business processes and improve the efficiency and effectiveness of their operations.

 **REFERENCES**

[1] Wikipedia, the free encyclopedia. www.wikipedia.org.

6. Why is e-commerce capturing a bigger share of the retail market?

Consumers accepted the e-commerce business model less readily than its proponents originally expected. Even in product categories suitable for e-commerce, electronic shopping has developed only slowly. Several reasons may account for the slow uptake, including:

- Concerns about security. Many people will not use credit cards over the Internet due to concerns about theft and credit card fraud.

- Lack of access in some countries and households to credit cards or other payment methods used for purchasing online.

- Concerns about the speed, reliability and cost of deliveries.

- Concerns about the quality of products purchased online.

- Slow Internet access speeds made online shopping too time-consuming for many people

- Lack of instant gratification with most e-purchases (non-digital purchases). Much of a consumer's reward for purchasing a product lies in the instant gratification of using and displaying that product. This reward does not exist when one's purchase does not arrive for days or weeks.

- The social aspect of shopping. Some people enjoy talking to sales staff, to other shoppers, or to their cohorts: this social reward side of retail therapy does not exist to the same extent in online shopping.

When the Web first became well known among the general public in 1994, many journalists and pundits forecasted that e-commerce would soon become a major economic sector. However, it took about four years for security protocols to become sufficiently developed and widely deployed. Subsequently, between 1998 and 2000, a substantial number of businesses in the United States and Western Europe developed rudimentary websites.

Although a large number of pure e-commerce companies disappeared during the dot-com collapse in 2000 and 2001, many "brick-and-mortar" retailers recognized that such companies had identified valuable niche markets and began to add e-commerce capabilities to their websites. For example, after the collapse of online grocer Webvanin, Albertsons and Safeway both started e-commerce subsidiaries through which consumers could order groceries online.

Few big businesses can afford not to have an Internet site to advertise and sell their wares any more, and it has become second nature for many people to research products, prices and availability online before buying.

According to a report by eMarketer, online retail sales in the United States were estimated at $134.8 billion in 2008 [1]. The U.S. Census Bureau has announced that this value, adjusted for seasonal variation, was $32.4 billion for the second quarter of 2009 [2]. Forrester has estimated that this same number will reach €129 billion by the end of 2009 in Western Europe [3]. According to this report, Business-to-Consumer (B2C) and consumer-to-consumer e-commerce are continuing to grow by double digits annually, in part because sales are shifting away from stores, the number of new online shoppers is rising and online shoppers are less sensitive to adverse economic conditions than the average European consumer.

China is growing even faster, and may have more Internet users than the United States by the end of the decade [4]. Studies show that the Chinese e-commerce market is different than that of the United States and Europe. For example, most Chinese e-commerce sites offer traditional payment methods such as cash on delivery instead of credit card payments [4]. According to statistics from online retail platforms such as Taobao.com and Eachnet.com, the average daily trading volume of Chinese online shops was about RMB 300 million, an increase of 200% from 2007 [5].

Amazon was the top online retailer of the United Kingdom in the last quarter of 2008, followed by Argos, Tesco, Play.com and Marks & Spencer, according to research firm Nielsen Online [6]. The largest store in the United States, Walmart, has one of the largest websites.

So how much does the Internet benefit consumers as well as businesses? One effect is increased competition, due to more effective price comparison. This makes markets more efficient, and in the case of online auction house eBay, creates a marketplace for some goods where none existed before.

But the Internet has another effect – increasing the range of goods available to consumers. The Internet lowers the cost of keeping inventory and storage, and it allows firms to keep in stock items that would not be available offline (for example, the range of books available from Amazon.com).

Finally, the Internet also enables consumers to save time, because purchase and delivery – as well as information – is more quickly available than ever before.

E-commerce is already very big, and it is going to get much bigger. But the actual value of transactions completed online is dwarfed by the extraordinary influence the Internet is exerting over purchases carried out in the offline world. That influence is becoming an integral part of e-commerce, for example:

- One in five customers walking into a Sears's department store in the United States to buy an electrical appliance will have researched their purchase online and most will know what they intend to pay.

- Three out of four people in the United States start shopping for new cars online, even though most end up buying them from traditional dealers. The difference is that these customers come to the showroom with information about the car and the best available deals.

- Half of the 60 million consumers in Europe who have an Internet connection bought products offline after having investigated prices and details online, according to a study by Forrester, a research consultancy.

- In Italy and Spain people are twice as likely to buy offline as online after researching on the Internet. In Germany and the United Kingdom, the two most developed Internet markets, the numbers are evenly split.

- Forrester says that people begin to shop online for simple, predictable products, such as DVDs, and then graduate to more complex items.

- Used-car sales are one of the biggest online growth areas in the United States.

Jeff Bezos, Amazon's founder and chief executive thinks he can sell most things and believes online retailers might capture 10-15% of retail sales over the next decade. This is a significant shift in customer shopping habits. Michael Dell, the founder of Dell, which leads the personal-computer market by selling directly to the customer, has long thought that this massive spending shift will turn many shops into just showrooms. Apple and Sony stores are examples of this new paradigm where stores are designed to display products, in the full expectation that customers will later buy them online.

For more information

- Business Research in Information and Technology (BRINT). www.brint.org.

  BRINT is a content and community portal on business technology management.

- Swerdlow, F. 2009 State of Retailing Online: Marketing Report. www.shop.org/soro.

  Produced in partnership with Forrester Research, Shop.org's 2009 State of Retailing Online is the industry standard of Internet and multi-channel retail research. The comprehensive collection of performance benchmarks is based on data collected directly from retailers, including closely held companies which otherwise do not publicly disclose details about their operations and innovations. In 2008, the first SORO survey collected data from over 125 retailers marketing, merchandising and multichannel issues. The second SORO survey gathered data from 63 retailers about key metrics, profitability, organizational structure, operational issues and the impact of the current economic climate.

REFERENCES

[1] U.S. Online Sales Up. eMarketer. 27 April 2009. www.emarketer.com.

[2] U.S. Census Bureau News, Quarterly retail e-commerce sales 2nd quarter 2009. www.census.gov. For additional information about Census Bureau e-commerce reports visit www.census.gov/retail.

[3] Bracewell Lewis, B. Western European Online Retail And Travel Forecast, 2008 To 2014. Forrester Research. 2009, www.forrester.com.

[4] Freeman Evans, P. Online Chinese Retail: Assessing Opportunities in Chinese eCommerce. 2009. www.forrester.com.

[5] China Online Retail Sales Doubled During Golden Week. ChinaRetailNews.com. 10 October 2008. www.chinaretailnews.com.

[6] Burmaster, A. Bumper Christmas for the most popular retailers online. 13 Jan 2009. uk.nielsen.com.

7.   What industries have been changed most profoundly by e-commerce?

All industries have been changed in some way by e-commerce, many of them profoundly. According to a study in 2003, the best results in terms of efficiency for business-to-business e-commerce involves companies in sectors where information and the speed of its transition have a big impact on business success [1]. The information factor is very important in electronic component and freight services, where usually the high level of competition and information is a main success factor. In addition, in electronics industry the importance of information grows because of rapid improvement in products and services. This generates the need for companies to analyze new information constantly and to always be ready to present new products on the market.

According to the European Commission's e-Business Watch, which monitors e-business trends by sector, the nature, intensity and impact of e-business activity differs widely between sectors, particularly between manufacturing and service industries, as well as between large, medium and small enterprises [2]. Variations depend in particular on the types of products and services that companies offer, the scale of the markets in which they operate and on their marketing strategy, including the choice of distribution channels. E-business activity has reached a high level of intensity, for example, in IT services and automotive, aeronautics and pharmaceutical industries. In manufacturing sectors, the e-business strategies of companies focus on supporting procurement, optimizing supply chain management, integrating with retail and distribution and increasingly on providing the best possible service to customers. In retail, supply chain management is also a key aspect of e-business. Whether and how retailers use e-commerce to sell their goods depends on their business model. In the logistics industry, internal operations are largely based on highly complex ICT systems. In banking, the Internet has transformed the whole sector and become a critical element in the business strategy of banks.

Among the sectors surveyed in 2007 [2]:

- Large companies in the chemical, rubber and plastics products industry are advanced users of ICT and e-business in all business areas. They are increasingly replacing paper-based, manual processes by electronic exchanges.

- In the steel industry, the main impact of ICT is on process efficiency along the value chain. However, the prospects for using e-business in direct e-commerce transactions, such as procurement and sales, are limited.

- In the European furniture industry e-business integration is still underdeveloped between manufacturers and independent distributors. This is due to the characteristics of furniture distribution networks and the complexity of industrial categorization and coding. E-Marketing and e-sales activities towards final customers are still limited in this sector. Those that exist are aimed at providing technical and commercial information rather than actual e-commerce functions.

- The introduction of ICT in the European banking industry has had a significant impact on banks operating with physical branches. Most importantly, the Internet has made it possible for banks to cut costs by offering online banking.

According to the seven manufacturing sectors in the 2005 survey [3]:

- Electronic business activity has reached the highest level of intensity in the automotive, aeronautics and pharmaceutical industries. The large international companies mostly drive the rapid development in these sectors. Supply-chain integration and the streamlining of procurement processes are common objectives in these industries for which e-business solutions are attractive.

- In the pharmaceutical industry, the use of ICT and e-business plays an important role for the process of discovery and development of new drugs and pharmaceutical treatments. Thus, ICT has an impact on R&D efficiency and, thereby, on lowering the competitive pressure.

- In the machinery and equipment industry, electronic business activity has not yet reached the same level of intensity. At first sight, this confirms the findings of the 2003 survey, but developments in this sector have been quite dynamic since then. For example, e-business is increasingly recognized as a useful means of providing customer service.

- The publishing and printing industry has a different e-business profile, as major segments of this sector operate in business-2-consumer (B2C) markets. ICT has a considerable impact on production and internal work processes and customer-facing activities (online publishing, marketing and advertising) are critical. Processes with a high e-business potential such as inventory and supply-chain-management are less critical in this sector.

- The food and beverages sector and the textile and clothing industry were found to be late adopters of ICT compared to the other manufacturing sectors studied.

- In the food and beverages industry, there are signs of increasing e-business activity, mainly in response to structural changes and new requirements. Important issues that promote e-business are food safety and the digital integration of the value chain. RFID (Radio Frequency Identification) based technologies could play an important role in these areas.

- In the textile and clothing industry, there are signs that the use of advanced ICT systems in large companies is in line with adoption rates among large firms from the most advanced manufacturing sectors. Examples are Enterprise Resource Planning (ERP) and Supply Chain Management (SCM) systems. It appears that a significant share of large textile firms have taken the lead towards supply chain integration and online trading with business partners.

- In the construction industry, ICT adoption and e-business activity appears to be very limited. The structure of the industry, which includes many small craft companies, cannot fully explain this gap. An industry with a multitude of standards, technical specifications, labels, and certification marks is not an optimal forum for drawing benefits from electronic business. However, e-business tools have the potential to benefit complex construction projects where there is a need to coordinate a large number of subcontractors.

- The IT services sector is a special case. Although companies in this sector have information technology and e-business as their end product, ICT also plays a significant role in the way that this product is produced, promoted and provided. In this sector the use of ICT and the production of related services are difficult to separate from each other.

- The IT services sector shares a common feature with tourism: in both industries, online channels have become key tools for marketing, communication and interaction with customers. In tourism, online booking and reservation services have been widely accepted among consumers and business travelers, and "e-tourism" has truly taken off."

Internet companies

The biggest revolution of e-commerce has been the rapid growth of Internet based companies and companies that provide the technology underpinning the Internet. Many of the companies of the first e-commerce wave disappeared with the bust of the dot-com bubble in the late 90s, but the ones that remained are the icons of Internet companies – corporations such Amazon, Yahoo, and eBay to name a few. One of the few Internet companies of the second wave that started with the dawn of the 21st century is Google.

Entertainment

The Internet is dramatically changing the entertainment business. The Web is an entertainment medium, a source of music and films for download and a place to purchase entertainment such as music, films, tickets for sporting events and shows, online television and online games. In April 2009, the iTunes App Store (www.itunes.com) set a record with its billionth download, A 2009 report by eMarketer shows that free online gaming sites had 27% more unique visits and 42% more total playing time in December 2008 compared to the same period of 2007 [4].

For more information

- European Sectoral e-business Watch, www.ebusiness-watch.org.

  The "Sectoral e-Business Watch" (SeBW) studies the adoption, implications and impact of electronic business practices in different sectors of the economy. It continues activities of the preceding "e-Business W@tch" which was launched by the European Commission, DG Enterprise and Industry, in late 2001, to support industrial policy, notably in the fields of competitiveness and innovation.

- Standifird , S.S. and Sandvig, J.C. Control of B2B E-Commerce and the Impact on Industry Structure. First Monday. Volume 7, number 11. November 2002. firstmonday.org/issues/issue7_11/standifird/index.html.

REFERENCES

[1] Icasati-Johanson, B., Clegg, C.W., Bennett, S. Increased transparency and trust: comparative case study of e-business in supply chains. Building the Knowledge Economy: Issues, Applications, Case Studies. IOS Press Amsterdam. Bologna. 2003.

[2] The European e-Business Report 2008. 6th Synthesis Report of the Sectoral e-Business Watch. www.ebusiness-watch.org.

[3] Overview of International e-Business Developments, The European e-Business Market Watch. July 2005. www.ebusiness-watch.org.

[4] Traffic Spikes for Ad-Supported Games. eMarketer. www.emarketer.com. 10 February 2009. www.emarketer.com/Article.aspx?R=1006906.

8. What are the common mistakes enterprises make regarding e-commerce?

Some of the common mistakes enterprises make when using e-commerce as a sales and marketing tool are the following:

- Believing that having a website will lead to instant sales.

- Believing that using the Internet is an easy way to make one's business and products known worldwide. A typical search with a search engine such as Google will find hundreds of thousands of matching references; being present on the Web does not necessarily mean being visible.

- Believing that an Internet site will replace other promotional techniques, rather than fit into the firms overall promotional strategy.

- Not spending enough to promote the website, e.g. by using e-mail messaging, registering with all major search engines, direct mailing of notices, updating business cards and letterheads and using print, television and other traditional methods to advertise the website.

- Not spending enough time on the site's content layout and on facilitating navigation. The fastest way to lose potential customers is to make the website difficult to use.

- Designing a site that makes it difficult for customers to identify the advantages of the product or, if the site is used for online transactions, a site that makes it difficult for customers to buy from the firm.

- Not updating the site frequently.

- Believing that a perfect design for the site will automatically lead to sales.

- Not responding within three days or less to e-mailed customer requests for information.

- Believing that intermediaries will automatically disappear with the advent of the Internet. Many manufacturers are not equipped and are not willing to deal with the individual firm or person ordering a product [1].

- Believing that the Internet will level the playing field between small and big businesses. As in traditional business, established brand names and adequate financial resources continue to be major factors for success on the Internet.

- Believing that the risks arising from the use of credit cards will be borne by the buyer. In fact, sellers are obliged to bear the risks and consequences of credit card fraud.

Some business processes may never lend themselves to electronic commerce. For example, perishable foods and high-cost, unique items such as custom-designed jewellery might be impossible to inspect adequately from a remote location, regardless of any technologies that might be devised in the future.

Many products and services require that a critical mass of potential buyers be equipped and willing to buy through the Internet.

Businesses often calculate return-on-investment numbers before committing to any new technology. This has been difficult to do for investments in electronic commerce because the costs and benefits have been hard to quantify. Costs, which are a function of technology, can change dramatically even during short-lived electronic commerce implementation projects because the underlying technologies are changing so rapidly. Many firms have had trouble recruiting and retaining employees with the technological, design, and business process skills needed to create an effective electronic commerce presence [2].

Research performed in Australia in 2004 investigated the pitfalls and challenges of electronic commerce encountered among the top 500 Australian publicly listed companies. Interestingly most of the challenges found in this research paper are still encountered by enterprises contemplating to start an e-commerce [3].

Rank	Challenges
1	Lack of e-commerce knowledge
2	Technology cost
2	Acquiring IT skilled people
2	Lack of e-commerce infrastructure
2	Security
2	Making business known to users
2	Customer service
8	Budget
8	Software compatibility
10	Integrating front-end e-commerce to back-end system
10	Managing change
10	Reliable technology vendor
13	Measuring success
14	Internet service provider reliability
15	Obtaining senior managers' support
16	Employee resistance towards e-commerce
16	Dealing with intermediaries
18	Website issues
19	Reaching customers in rural/regional areas
20	Current e-commerce legislation

For more information

- Small Business Bible. www.smallbusinessbible.org.

  Small Business Bible is a site intended to guide budding and experienced entrepreneurs who plan to start a new home-based business or a small business firm. It helps small business owners to understand the intricacies of how to handle business online and in person.

- Ecommerce-Guide. www.ecommerce-guide.com.

  Ecommerce-Guide provides information, advice, guides, links to other sites, and discussion forums.

- McCue, S. Farce to Force: Building Profitable E-Commerce Strategies (Hardcover). South-Western Educational Pub. 2006.

REFERENCES

[1] Datta, P. Intermediaries as Value Moderators in Electronic Marketplaces. Thirteenth European Conference on Information Systems, 26-28 May 2005. aisel.aisnet.org/ecis2005/35/.

[2] Schneider, Gary P. Electronic Commerce. Seventh Edition. Course Technology, a division of Thomson Learning Inc., 2007.

[3] Kuzic, J. and McKay, J. Pitfalls of Electronic Commerce in Large Corporations. European Conference on Information Systems. 2004. aisel.aisnet.org/ecis2004/88.

9. What Internet-based services provide assistance to SMEs on e-commerce?

Numerous online programmes and services have been developed to help SMEs to sell their products and services electronically at home and abroad. Some examples are given below, but there are many more.

Government sites are particularly good. Their primary purpose is to promote e-business and help SMEs in their own country, but much of the information provided is a useful resource for businesses anywhere in the world.

- SME Toolkit. www.smetoolkit.org. The SME Toolkit is a programme of the International Finance Corporation (IFC), a member of the World Bank Group, and is available in multiple languages through local partners around the world. It promotes sustainable private sector investment in developing countries. Through its website, SMEs can access business resources, training, information and links to various free online training, and website builder software. Contents related to e-commerce are available at: www.smetoolkit.org/smetoolkit/en/category/966/E-Commerce.

- Industry Canada. www.ic.gc.ca. The Industry Canada website provides various business tools and resources for e-commerce (www.ic.gc.ca/eic/site/ic1.nsf/eng/00148.html). In addition it contains information on companies, statistics, financing, innovation, research, regulations and standards, sustainability and environment, as well as trade and investment.

- Business Link. www.businesslink.gov.uk. The Business Link, in partnership with Business Gateway in Scotland and Invest Northern Ireland, supports new and existing SMEs by providing information, advice and tools on IT and e-commerce
(www.businesslink.gov.uk/bdotg/action/layer?r.s=tl&r.lc=en&topicId=1073861197).

- Australian e-business guide. www.e-businessguide.gov.au. This e-businessguide website provides information and resources about e-business for small businesses in Australia and for those who advise them. It is an initiative of the Australian Government. It provides advice, tools and case studies.

- Small Business NSW. www.smallbiz.nsw.gov.au. Small Business NSW is the New South Wales Government information website for people starting, running or growing a small business. The website talks about the various aspects of the use of information and communication technology for SMEs, such as e-marketing (www.smallbiz.nsw.gov.au/run/marketing/market/pages/e-marketing.aspx), e-commerce (www.smallbiz.nsw.gov.au/run/it/pages/ecommerce.aspx) and e-business (www.smallbiz.nsw.gov.au/run/it/pages/ebiz.aspx).

- GoOnline. www.go-online.gr. The GoOnline programme is part of the European GoDigital initiative. The go-online.gr portal is in Greek and has been developed to supplement training programmes and familiarize Greek SMEs with the potential offered by the new technologies.

Universities also provide information

- Access eCommerce. www.access-ecom.info. The objective of the University of Minnesota's Access eCommerce is to enhance rural development through electronic commerce. It offers training material and tutorials online, in hard copy, as well as through videos.

- SBDCNet. sbdcnet.org/SBIC/e-com.php. The Small Business Development Center National Information Clearinghouse (SBDCNet) aims to meet the information needs of the SBDC community in the United States. Through its E-Commerce section it provides a variety of resources to establish and run a successful e-commerce site. SBDCNet is funded by the U.S. Small Business Administration and the University of Texas at San Antonio.

- Center for Research in Electronic Commerce. cism.mccombs.utexas.edu. Since its establishment in 1998 at the University of Texas at Austin, the McCombs School Center for Research in Electronic Commerce (CREC) has served as an incubator for breakthrough research blending business and computer science.

Commercial organizations provide free guides to attract people to their sites.

- Business Owner's Toolkit. www.toolkit.cch.com. Business Owner's Toolkit has more than 5,000 pages of free cost-cutting tips, step-by-step checklists, real-life case studies, start-up advice, and business templates for small business owners and entrepreneurs.

Technical papers

- ECIS Papers. is2.lse.ac.uk/asp/aspecis. This provides a complete list of the papers issued by the European Conference on Information Systems (ECIS) from 1993 to 2008 as well as electronic copies of all papers.

Portals provide a list of links to other useful sites.

- SmartBiz. www.smartbiz.com. SmartBiz provides resources for small businesses and start-ups through its forums, white papers, blogs and links to outside services.

International or regional organizations

- UNCTAD. www.unctad.org. UNCTAD's annual Information Economy Report focuses on ICT trends, such as e-commerce and e-business, and on national and international policy and strategy options for improving the development impact of these technologies in developing countries. It replaces the E-commerce and Development Report published by UNCTAD from 2001 to 2004.

Europe's Information Society e-Thematic portal. ec.europa.eu/information_society/tl/ecowor/ebusiness/index_en.htm. The Information Society Portal provides a unique entry point for all European Commission policies and activities related to the information society. Its "Economy and the world of work" section has information on e-business and SMEs.

Magazines on e-commerce and technology

- CIO Magazine. www.cio.com. CIO provides technology and business leaders with insight and analysis on information technology (IT) trends and a keen understanding of IT's role in achieving business goals.

- E-Commerce Times. www.ecommercetimes.com. E-Commerce Times is one of the several e-business and technology news sites published by the ECT News Network in the United States.

Trade promotion organizations

Some trade promotion organizations provide online business-to-business (B2B) services: if they are well organized, these are an excellent choice for small businesses.

- HKTDC. www.tdctrade.com. The Hong Kong Trade Development Council (HKTDC) helps SMEs to expand their international trade by providing information on marketing opportunities, business matching services, market intelligence and SME development programmes.

E-marketplaces

E-marketplaces specialize in providing online bidding or auctions, where suppliers can respond to calls for bids from buyers, or buyers can respond to tender offers. Be very careful about giving away confidential company information online. Only use such services after verifying that the e-marketplace is a bona fide company, and that any information you supply will be secure, kept confidential and used only for the purpose for which it was provided.

- One reliable source of information on e-marketplaces is eMarket Services (www.emarketservices.com). This is a non-profit project funded by the trade promotion organizations of Canada, Ireland, Norway, the Netherlands and Spain. Its mission is to make it easier for companies to use e-marketplaces to find new customers and suppliers for their international business. It offers a directory of e-marketplaces around the world, case studies and industry reports.

Online markets

An online market brings together a number of online shops on the same website, often from the same sector. It hosts your online shop and processes payments for you. Some specialize in particular products; others are targeted at particular types of customers. You maintain and update your own shop within the marketplace, but most of the administration is done for you. These are a very good option if they are well established, efficiently run, already trading successfully and offer low costs for the merchant.

Many Internet service providers offer online market facilities, as do specialist companies. If you sell to a particular trade or industry, the relevant trade association may be able to put you in touch with a dedicated marketplace. For SMEs in developing countries, the best options are online marketplaces operated by trade promotion organizations, non-profit organizations, or well-established and trusted private companies.

Large, well-established e-commerce sites

Large e-commerce sites such as Amazon and eBay allow other businesses to sell their goods through their sites. Amazon (www.amazon.com) has different options for companies wishing to do business through the Amazon site, such as 'Sell on Amazon' where you can sell your products on Amazon.com, 'Fulfilment by Amazon' where Amazon.com handles the shipment of the products that you sell. For a complete list of Amazon.com services for businesses, refer to www.amazon.com/gp/seller-account/mm-landing.html?ld=AZSOAviewallMakeM. Businesses as well as individuals can offer goods for sale on auction sites such as eBay (www.ebay.com).

Web hosting

Please refer to question 26: "Where should I host my website?"

Translation

Please refer to question 22: "How do I get my website translated accurately?"

Services for specific industry sectors

Please refer to question 15: "Where can I access market research on my sector?"

Part I

USE THE INTERNET TO IDENTIFY OPPORTUNITIES AND ENGAGE WITH PARTNERS

Online market research

10. How is the Web organized to disseminate information?

This answer is in two parts, the first dealing with the organization of the Web, and the second with the dissemination of information.

The Web is not formally organized, and no central regulatory or other authoritative body controls the information made available on the Web, or how it is presented. However, although there is no one place to apply to for registering a site, information on the Web can be retrieved by those looking for it, and be made retrievable by those providing it.

On the demand side, people looking for information make use of search engines, directories, advertising, personal recommendations, topic-specific portals and occasionally unsolicited e-mail to find relevant sites.

On the supply side, those wishing to make information available to others should:

- Ensure that their websites are listed, and properly ranked with indexing search engines such as Google and with web directories such as Yahoo.

- Advertise in printed or online product-specific magazines.

- Use low-cost or no-cost promotion in newsgroups, or by selectively and responsibly using e-mail and newsletters, or by asking clients online to recommend you to friends (and providing some small incentive for such recommendations).

(See also question 35: "How do I drive traffic to my site?" and question : "How do I get my products listed prominently by the major search engines?"

For more information

- Web search engines. en.wikipedia.org/wiki/List_of_search_engines.

  This website presents a short history and a list of search engines. It also describes how search engines work. Finally it offers references for further reading.

- SearchEngineWatch.com. www.searchenginewatch.com.

  SearchEngineWatch provides tips and information about searching the Web, analysis of the search engine industry and help to website owners trying to improve their ability to be found in search engines.

- Mostafa, J. Seeking Better Web Searches. Scientific American. February 2005. www.sciamdigital.com.

11.   What are some Internet directories of sources of information for e-market research?

Given the huge amount of information now available on the Internet, the biggest problem is finding relevant information on the subject you are interested in. For this reason it is a good idea to start from a website which provides links to related sites. Some examples are given below. For more specific information, a search with a search engine such as Google, Yahoo or Bing on the topic of interest will usually find some sites providing directories.

- Internet Public Library. This is a good source of links to other sites. www.ipl.org.

- United Nations Business Directory Online. www.devbusiness.com. The Business Directory lists websites of companies and consulting firms involved in international business.

- European Association of Directory and Database Publishers. www.eadp.org.

- Financial Times Research Centre. www.ft.com/research/marketresearchfinder. MarketResearch.com is a continuously updated collection of market research papers. It offers more than 250,000 market research reports from over 650 leading global publishers.

- Free Management Library. www.managementhelp.org. The library provides access to comprehensive resources on leadership and management, as well as links to related sites.

- Small Business Information. sbinformation.about.com. About.com's Small Business Information is a well-organized collection of business-related information. International Trade Centre. www.intracen.org. The ITC website offers a wide range of business information, guides, tools and links.

- ITC Online Library System. www.intracen.org/tirc. The ITC Library is a good source of trade information. The Web Index provides references and direct links to a selection of websites covering various aspects of international trade such as: country profiles, market access conditions, contact information and market news.

- Infobel.com. www.infobel.com/teldir. Infobel.com is a free online telephone and business directory.

- European Business Directory. www.europages.com. This is available in 25 languages, displays information on over 1.5 million companies from 35 countries and is freely accessible.

- Google Directory. www.google.com/Top. The Google directory is a comprehensive directory of businesses organized by topic into categories.

- A search in Wikipedia (www.wikipedia.org) or Answers (www.answers.com) on a specific industry or product may also bring up some useful references.

Service communities. These include portals such as Ei (Engineering Information), available at www.ei.org. This portal gives online search assistance and guidance, contact information on engineering experts, and technical and business information. The latest industry research is provided on www.globalspec.com, the engineering search engine.

Product portals. An example is the Asian and Pacific Coconut Community's site, www.apccsec.org, which publishes a newsletter and other documents, gives details of conferences, advertises training events, consultancies and market promotion services offered by the organization.

Country/regional portals. An example is Small Business NSW (www.smallbiz.nsw.gov.au). Small Business NSW is the New South Wales Government information website for people starting, running or growing a small business.

12. Where can I find information on trade shows in my product line?

Many trade organizations use the Internet to post the agenda of their trade events. For worldwide searches, the following sources offer opportunities with free online access:

- World Chambers Network. www.worldchambers.com. WCN portal provides access to 14,000 registered Chambers of Commerce and Industry (CCI) that in turn represent over 40 million member businesses worldwide. It also lists trade shows and events

- Allworld Exhibitions. www.allworldexhibitions.com. Allworld Exhibition's member companies currently organize 150 international exhibitions throughout the world and are one of the top organizers by revenue in the Asian Exhibition Market according to a report by the Trade Fair Industry in Asia 3rd Edition 2007.

- BizTradeShows.com. www.biztradeshows.com. BizTradeShows.com is a portal powered by IndiaMART, that bridges the gap between the organizer and the target audience, i.e. exhibitors, sponsors and visitors. BizTradeShows.com's directory of trade fairs and business events provides exhaustive coverage of exhibitions, trade shows and expositions, conferences and seminars for various industries worldwide.

- Tradeshow Week. www.tradeshowweek.com. In addition to its editorial on trade shows, it has a searchable trade show directory.

13.   Where can I find information on what my competition is doing?

Primary sources

The most important primary sources of information on what your competition is doing are trade journals on your area of business. Journals usually provide updates of the state of the market (domestic and/or international) for your product or service, as well as company news, analyses and profiles.

Examples of industry trade journals are given below.

- Metal Bulletin   www.metalbulletin.com

- Food and drink industry   www.william-reed.co.uk

- Food and drink federation   www.fdf.org.uk

- Coffee   www.coffeereview.com

The Internet Public Library is a good source of links to other sites www.ipl.org.

A search in Wikipedia (www.wikipedia.org) or Answers (www.answers.com) on a specific industry or product may also bring up some useful references.

Look at their websites

Use a search engine such as Google, Yahoo, or Bing to find websites for competing products.

Check business-to-business (B2B) trade portals such as:

- www.go4worldbusiness.com
- www.fita.org
- www.asiatradehub.com

Your trade development organization can also be a useful source of information, particularly if it carries out sectoral studies. It may also be the depository for publicly available annual reports of individual companies, which provide important information on what a company is doing.

Secondary sources

Reference databases can be of real value, as they list primary sources of information which have been analysed and indexed, thus making it much easier to find specific information through the use of search keywords.

Some examples of pay-to-use online databases are listed below. These are provided by DIALOG's DataStarWeb. Dialog provides up-to-date company and industry intelligence covering nearly 500,000 companies worldwide as well as market share and sales figures, business directories and financials on 14 million United States and international companies. Dialog offers access to business journal news and analysis, First Call consensus estimates, consumer marketing data, corporate chronologies and histories, press releases, stock quotes and more. Business information is provided by such sources as Dun & Bradstreet, Standard & Poor's, Frost & Sullivan, SEC filings and the Thomson Financial and Gale Group content used by financial institutions around the world. The subscription-based services range from automatic alerts delivered to you via e-mail, ftp, or postal delivery, to a command-driven solution for more experienced searchers who prefer access via the Internet.

- PTSP – Gale Group PROMT. PTSP is a multi-industry database with abstracted information on companies, products and markets. Available from: ds.datastarweb.com/ds/products/datastar.

- INDY – Gale GroupTrade & Industry Database. INDY is a full-text database with information on companies, products, marketing and other subjects. Available from: ds.datastarweb.com/ds/products/datastar.

Business periodicals such as the *Financial Times* (published daily) and *The Economist* (published weekly) also contain company and market information. Their respective websites are www.ft.com and www.economist.com.

For more information

- Dialog. www.dialog.com.

  The Dialog online-based information services help organizations across the globe to seek competitive advantages in such fields as business, science, engineering, finance and law. Dialog offers organizations the ability to retrieve data from more than 1.4 billion unique records of key information, accessible via the Internet or through delivery to enterprise intranets.

- The Federation of International Trade Associations (FITA). www.fita.org.

  The FITA Global Trade Portal is the source for international import/export trade leads, events, and links to 8,000 international trade (export import) related websites.

14.   Where can I obtain information on foreign markets?

Before you start delivering your products overseas you need to have sound knowledge of your target markets. You will need to research local laws or regulations relating to the import of your products. You will also have to take into account trading practices and trade barriers, or anything that could hinder you from exporting your goods.

You should look for an answer to the following questions:

- Do you need an export licence to export your products?
- Are the items you are planning to export allowed into the country you are sending them to?
- Do you need an import licence?
- Are there any special restrictions or controls applying to the products you are planning to export?
- Are you or your customer liable for any harm caused by the imported items?
- Are there laws applicable in the country of origin that must be adhered to?
- Do you have to notify customs and excise or complete a specific declaration?
- Do you have to pay duties?

Each country has its own rules and requirements for imports. The rules include:

- Customs tariffs
- Documentation requirements
- Licensing
- Shipping terms
- Methods of payment

A great deal of country-specific information is available on the Internet. Governments, national standards institutes and international organizations are starting to find it easier and cheaper to disseminate official documents via the Internet than to mail printed publications. The best places to look for information on foreign markets are on the following websites:

- Government websites:
  You may find government websites from the following sources:

  - University of Michigan Library. www.lib.umich.edu/government-documents-center/explore.
    The Government Document Center of the University of Michigan Library.
  - AdmiNet. www.adminet.com. AdmiNet aims to be a centre delivering general information about governmental authorities and public services.

- Chambers of commerce and importers associations

  - World chambers network. www.worldchambers.com. WCN portal provides access to 14,000 registered Chambers of Commerce and Industry (CCI) that in turn represent over 40 million member businesses worldwide. It lists trade shows and events.
  - The International Trade Centre www.intracen.org.

- Transport service providers
  In addition to providing information about their own services, many transport service providers are beginning to include general and country-specific information for shippers and online tools on their sites, some examples are:

  - UPS.   www.ups.com.
  - FedEx.   www.fedex.com.
  - DHL WorldwideExpress. www.dhl.com.
  - TNT.   www.tnt.com.
  - Parcelforce Worldwide.   www.parcelforce.com

- Embassies
  You should search the Web for the website and contacts of the embassy of the country you are exporting to. Embassypages.com (www.embassypages.com) is a directory of diplomatic and consular missions around the world.

- International organizations
  The followings are some of the relevant international organizations that offer export information:
  - World Trade Organization. www.wto.int.
  - International Trade Centre. www.intracen.org. ITC provides extensive business-related information and links to other information
  - ITC International Trade Forum magazine. www.tradeforum.org. International Trade Forum is the magazine of the International Trade Centre. It focuses on trade promotion and export development, as part of ITC's technical cooperation programme with developing countries and economies in transition. The magazine is published quarterly in English, French and Spanish.
  - Informed Trade International. www.itintl.com. Informed Trade International is an import/export compliance community devoted to US Customs import and export practices.
  - The Market Access Database. mkaccdb.eu.int. The Market Access Database is a free, interactive, service providing information about market access conditions in non-EU countries.

- Libraries
  ITC Online Library System. www.intracen.org/tirc. ITC Library is a good source of trade information. The Web Index provides references and direct links to a selection of websites covering various aspects of international trade such as: country profiles, market access conditions, contact information, and market news.

- Trade promotion organizations
  - Austrian Trade. www.advantageaustria.org. Austrian Trade is the official Austrian Foreign Trade Promotion Organization.
  - TPOnet.www.tpo-net.com. TPOnet, the virtual community of the World Conference of Trade Promotion Organizations, is an electronic forum for the exchange of information by and for trade promotion organizations. TPOnet (www.tpo-net.com) is hosted and managed by the International Trade Centre (ITC).

Country-specific market information is also available from the following sources:

- **CIA World Fact Book**, annual publication. Central Intelligence Agency. Available free at www.cia.gov/cia/publications/factbook/index.html. Provides political, geographical and infrastructural information, as well as economic indicators on individual countries.

- **Country Commercial Guides**, annual publication. US State Department. Available free at www.state.gov. The guides provide a comprehensive look at countries' commercial environments, using economic, political and market analysis.

- **Economist global technology forum** (globaltechforum.eiu.com) has a regional and country information section, which provides links to other information sources and the Economist Intelligence Unit's (www.eiu.com) Country Reports.

- **Exporters' Encyclopaedia**, annual publication with updates. Dun and Bradstreet's (D&B) website provides information on trade regulations, documentation requirements, transportation and legislation affecting commerce. (www.loc.gov/rr/business/duns/duns1.html#db1c).

- **National Trade Data Bank STAT-USA**. www.stat-usa.gov/tradtest.nsf. Over 20,000 full-text worldwide industry/country and market studies conducted by US Trade Counsellors abroad.

- **UBIFRANCE**. www.ubifrance.fr. UBIFRANCE, the French agency for international business development, is a public industrial and trade organization under the supervision of the Ministry of Economy, Industry and Employment, the Secretary of State for Foreign Trade and the Directorate General of Treasury and Economic Policy.

Some other websites with market information on individual countries and regions are listed below:

Country/region	Internet address
Austria	portal.wko.at/wk/startseite.wk
European Union	europa.eu/
Czech Republic	www.mpo.cz/
Germany	www.gtai.de
Hong Kong, China	www.hketousa.gov.hk
Ireland	www.itw.ie
Japan	www.jetro.go.jp
Netherlands	www.hollandtrade.com
Portugal	www.portugalglobal.pt
Sweden	www.chamber.se
Turkey	www.igeme.org.tr
Zimbabwe	www.zimtrade.co.zw

15. Where can I access market research on my sector?

ITC's Index to Trade Information Sources on the Internet, available from www.intracen.org, regroups various sources of sectoral market research.

- The Market Information section of the Index has a subsection with hyperlinks to full-text publications, including market studies, produced by national organizations such as chambers of commerce.

- The Special Compendiums subsection on trade promotion organizations (TPOs) has hyperlinks to import promotion offices (IPOs) based in developed countries, whose task is to facilitate trade with developing countries.

- Some of the TPOs listed in the Index may themselves sell market research reports.

- TPOnet, a virtual community of the World Conference of Trade Promotion Organizations, is an electronic forum for the exchange of information by and for TPOs. TPOnet (www.tpo-net.com) is hosted and managed by the International Trade Centre.

Many IPOs carry out and publish sectoral market research. A good example is the Netherlands' Centre for the Promotion of Imports from developing countries (CBI), www.cbi.eu. Most of CBI's market research can be downloaded free, although a few publications are only available in print. Another example is the Danish Import Promotion Programme (www.dipp.eu), whose main objective is to assist exporters in Africa, Asia and Latin America who wish to enter the Danish market. DIPP also provides market information on the Danish market to exporters and business support organizations in developing countries.

The Internet is a good source of market research material. There are many product and industry portals, which publish sectoral information, such as the portal for the pulp and paper industry at www.pulpandpaper.net. Business information portals such as InternetB2BList (www.InternetB2Blist.com) and Aaaoe.com (www.aaaoe.com) provide links to a variety of products in different industry categories.

Search engine directories such as the Google Directory (www.google.com/Top/Business) are another source of information on the Internet.

To find out more about manufacturing technologies, you may also try library sites such as the Center for Research Libraries (www.crl.edu) for technical papers.

Chambers of commerce and importers associations offer a variety of information pertaining to a market or industry segment:

- The International Chamber of Commerce, www.iccwbo.org, has information on policies, reports and guides related to transport and logistics and international commercial terms.
- Links to chambers of commerce worldwide can be found at www.worldchambers.com.
- A list of importers' associations worldwide is given on www.intracen.org/dbms/CL_Search/CL_Search.Asp

Further information on a specific market can be gathered from other websites in the same industry sector. They include:

- E-commerce sites which sell similar products;
- Business-to-business sites such as AsiaTradeHub (www.asiatradehub.com);
- Auction sites such as eBay (www.ebay.com).

For more information

- Dialog. www.dialog.com.

  The Dialog online-based information services help organizations across the globe to seek competitive advantages in such fields as business, science, engineering, finance and law. Dialog offers organizations the ability to retrieve precise data from more than 1.4 billion unique records of key information, accessible via the Internet or through delivery to enterprise intranets.

16.   How do I find buyers and where can I find them?

There are two basic ways to find buyers. The first is to look for individual companies in the geographical or industry sector in which you are interested. The second is to search for business opportunities. If you want to look for buyers using the Internet, a particularly useful tool is the ITC Index to Trade Information Sources, which can be accessed at www.intracen.org. The Index lists Company Registers and Trade and Business Opportunity Registers, organized by geographical region.

Many national business databases and trade promotion organizations tend to use the Internet as an inexpensive medium to open their company registers to a worldwide audience. Among the websites with large databases with international coverage are:

- European Business Directory, at www.europages.com. Available in 25 languages, displays over 1.5 million companies from 35 countries and is freely accessible.

- Kompass International Database, at www.kompass.com. Probably the largest source of company profiles; has detailed product classifications. Covers more than 2 million companies in 70 countries referenced by 57,000 product and service keywords, 860,000 trade names and 4.6 million executive names.

- WLW Online, at www.wlw.com. A supplier search engine that covers six European countries.

- World Trade Centers Association, at world.wtca.org. Offers a directory of importers, exporters and related businesses.

If you look through sites offering trade opportunities, bear in mind the possibility of posting your own business opportunities with them, so as to increase your chances of catching a buyer's interest.

You can also find buyers by looking in business-to-business exchange sites for your industry.

A useful back-up tool for broadening your search for buyers is online translation to assist you with language problems (refer to question 22: "How do I get my website translated accurately?"). Be warned, however, that these services are useful only for gaining an initial understanding of words and phrases. For translating and/or interpreting complete documents, rely on someone who is competent in your field, as well as in the languages concerned.

For more information

- Jocteur-Monrozier, B. A Mission for Detectives: Looking for Importers. International Trade Forum 1/2001. www.tradeforum.org.
- Varey, R.J. Relationship Marketing: Dialogue and Networks in the E-Commerce Era. Wiley. 2003.

17.   Where can I find information on technical standards, phytosanitary regulations and related aspects?

If you are planning to sell products to foreign countries, it is essential that they conform to the health and safety standards of the countries in question. You must also be sure to keep your information on standards constantly up to date.

A great deal of country-specific information is available on the Internet. Governments, national standards institutes and international organizations are starting to find it easier and cheaper to disseminate official documents via the Internet than to mail printed publications.

The best places to look for this information are on the websites of:

- Governments
  Finding government websites

    - University of Michigan Library. www.lib.umich.edu/government-documents-center/explore. This is the Government Document Centre of the University of Michigan Library.
    - AdmiNet. www.adminet.com. AdmiNet aims to be a centre for delivering general information on governmental authorities and public services.

  Government websites:

    - United Kingdom's Department for Environment, Food and Rural Affairs. www.defra.gov.uk. Defra is the British government department responsible for policy and regulations on environment, food and rural affairs. It is a good source of information on legislation, policy and regulation and provides guidance on matters related to its mission.
    - Food Standards Australia New Zealand. www.foodstandards.gov.au. This is a bi-national government agency. The site provides comprehensive information on the food standards code and requirements for foods.
    - Canadian Centre for Occupational Health and Safety. www.ccohs.ca. CCOHS resources include online and printed publications, online courses, podcasts, software, regulations and guidance.

- Chambers of commerce and importers' associations

    - World Chambers Network. www.worldchambers.com. The WCN portal provides access to 14,000 registered chambers of commerce and industry, which represent over 40 million member businesses worldwide. It lists trade shows and events.
    - Swiss Import Promotion Programme. sippo.ch/Internet/osec/en/home/import.html. The Swiss Import Promotion Programme (SIPPO) supports small and medium-sized enterprises from developing and transition countries in gaining access with their products to Switzerland and the European Union.

- Transport service providers

  In addition to providing information about their own services, many transport service providers are beginning to include general and country-specific information for shippers and online tools on their sites. Some sites are listed below:

    - UPS   www.ups.com
    - FedEx   www.fedex.com
    - DHL WorldwideExpress   www.dhl.com
    - TNT   www.tnt.com
    - Parcelforce Worldwide   www.parcelforce.com

- Embassies

- International organizations

    - EU Market Access Database.   mkaccdb.eu.int.
    - World Trade Organization.   www.wto.int.
    - International Trade Centre.   www.intracen.org

- Trade promotion organizations

  - Austrian Trade. www.advantageaustria.org. Austrian Trade is the official Austrian Foreign Trade Promotion Organization.

  - TPOnet. www.tpo-net.com. TPOnet, a virtual community of the World Conference of Trade Promotion Organizations, is an electronic forum for the exchange of information by and for TPOs. TPOnet is hosted and managed by the International Trade Centre.

Some useful sites, which also feature in ITC's "Norms and standards" database, are:

- Codex Alimentarius Commission, at www.codexalimentarius.net, gives detailed information on maximum limits for pesticides and other standards for the food industry.

- Fish INFOnetwork, at www.fao.org/fi/default.asp, provides information and hyperlinks to regional fishing industries.

- International Organization for Standardization (ISO), at www.iso.org, offers information on all national organizations linked to ISO, new tools and guidance on how companies can apply ISO standards to their products. You may have to request the organization in writing for more specific information on standards.

- Green Seal, at www.greenseal.org, issues information on environmentally friendly procedures and promotes the manufacture and sale of responsible consumer products.

- The World Standards Service Network, www.wssn.net, provides links to, and information on, ISO, the International Electrotechnical Commission (IEC), www.iec.ch, and the International Telecommunication Union (ITU), www.itu.int. WSSN also provides links to numerous national standards institutes.

Basic web presence

18. What are some of the creative ways used in developing countries to serve people online?

The websites profiled below reflect how attributes of the Internet (speed of communication, facilities for storing and displaying large quantities of information, and interaction between user and provider) have been used to enhance the provision of traditional services. The sites have been arranged thematically, but in no particular order of importance.

Government assistance to citizens: civic and political

- Prefeitura da Cidade do Rio de Janeiro Online (www.rio.rj.gov.br) is the City of Rio's official site, in Portuguese. In addition to access to information on tourist and cultural events, the site offers city dwellers a direct line to city administrators, from whom they can request social assistance, public works, legal action and includes a wide variety of online services.

Government assistance to citizens: commerce

- Trade2CN. (www.trade2cn.com). Trade2CN is a website, in both Chinese and English, sponsored by China's Ministry of Commerce. Trade2CN supports businesses involved in export and import to and from China to engage in e-commerce by providing information on exhibitions and promotions, and offering an online platform for businesses to carry transactions, as well as get access to professional consultation and financing.

- The Hong Kong Development Council uses its website (www.hktdc.com) to help businesses to succeed in international trade by providing marketing opportunities, business matching services, market intelligence and SME development programmes online. It has more than 1 million subscribers, attracts more than 5 million hits a day via personal computer, mobile phone and personal digital assistant.

International assistance for business development

- **Cambodia's Silk Road to Poverty Reduction.** The ancient Cambodian tradition of women weaving and wearing silk is enjoying a renaissance. This began with a modest contribution of $20,000 in 2002 to improve the newly formed Cambodian Silk Forum. An encouraging on-the-spot survey of market possibilities in Europe for hand-woven Cambodian silk products persuaded the International Trade Centre (ITC) in 2003 to put $100,000 in an Export-led Poverty Reduction Programme. The funding enabled 20 rural weavers in the poor village of Tanorn, to increase production and marketing of high quality silk for export.

  ITC gave advice on community building, marketing and quality management and organized training in design, modern production techniques, costing and pricing. It also created an e-commerce website, www.silkfromcambodia.com, with catalogues and brochures. The local partner organization of the Cambodian Craft Cooperation was coached on how to develop export communities of weavers and replicated the experience in four other villages. About 100 families saw their lives improve as a result. The website is aimed at international retail and wholesale customers.

Private sector initiatives for business development

- eShopAfrica.com. www.eshopafrica.com. eShopAfrica.com is a fair trade e-commerce website based in Accra, Ghana. Many traditional African artisans are living in poverty despite their strong skills. The aim of this website is to raise global orders through the Internet for such artisans. eShopAfrica.com is supplied by an ever growing community of artisans – many are from Ghana but products also come from other African countries including Ethiopia, Zimbabwe and Mali.

- TafTaf. www.taftaf.com. Women in developing countries have been much less engaged in e-commerce than men. However in Senegal, a women-led community of approximately 60 artisans sells locally produced arts and crafts through their website. TafTaf also provides cultural information about the customs from which the products emerge.

Private sector initiatives for community development and services

- The Acacia Initiative. www.idrc.ca/acacia. The Acacia Initiative is an international programme to empower sub-Saharan communities with the ability to apply information and communication technologies (ICTs) to their own social and economic development. This initiative is designed as an integrated programme of research and development and demonstration projects to address issues of applications, technology, infrastructure, policy and governance.

  Conceived and led by the International Development Research Centre (IDRC), Acacia supports Canada's contribution to the African Information Society Initiative (AISI) which was endorsed by African governments as an action framework to build Africa's information and communication infrastructure.

- The Association for Progressive Communications (APC). www.apc.org. APC is an international network of civil society organizations dedicated to supporting groups and individuals working for peace, human rights, development and protection of the environment, through the strategic use of information and communication technologies, including the Internet.

Government and international organizations

- Asia-Pacific Economic Cooperation, APEC. www.apec.org. APEC facilitates economic growth, cooperation, trade and investment in the Asia-Pacific region.

- Zunia Knowledge Exchange. www.zunia.org. Zunia is an online network for knowledge exchange among development professionals worldwide. It provides access to news, events, best practices and publications on a wide range of development topics.

More Success stories can be found on the ITC website: www.intracen.org/ec.

19. How have some small companies fared from the use of the Internet as a marketing tool?

The number of companies that have excelled by taking advantage of the endless resources of the Internet is increasing every day. The list includes many traditional companies that have expanded their market share, or entered into new markets with the help of Internet-based marketing tools. Many of these successful companies are doing business solely over the Internet. Many such "clicks only" companies, as they are referred in some literature, were small companies just a few years ago. You need only read the "About us" section on many successful websites to find examples of how small companies have fared on the Internet.

YouTube, an initially profitless website started by three 20-somethings after a late-night dinner party was launched in 2005 and purchased by Google in October 2006 for US$ 1.6 billion.

The question today is not "Should I use the Internet as a marketing tool" but rather "In what way should I use the Internet as a marketing tool and how does this fit into my overall marketing plan?"

Suppliers and customers increasingly expect you to have a presence on the Web, and it is a very cost-effective method of disseminating information about your company. Many companies start by selling products through the e-commerce channels provided by sites such as eBay, Yahoo and Amazon or work with an e-commerce partner.

Even if you do not intend to set up an e-commerce site, you can still opt to create a very simple website providing essential information about your business and your contact details. The most basic website should include the following information:

- Company name and logo.
- Contact information: visitors should be able to easily find your phone number, mailing address, and fax number and send you an e-mail.
- Information about your company: who you are and what your business offers.

Business blogs are another alternative. A blog is a web page made up of usually short, frequently updated posts that are arranged chronologically. A business blog is a corporate tool for communicating with customers or employees to share knowledge and expertise. Blogs are an excellent method to share a company's expertise, build additional web traffic, and connect with potential customers. Blogs are in the mainstream these days, and they have quickly become a very affordable marketing tool for businesses. The advantages for the small business are [1]:

- Blog software is easy to use. Online software solutions such as www.blogger.com, www.wordpress.com and www.typepad.com offer tools to get started.
- It is a low-cost alternative to having a web presence. For small business owners without the time to learn web development or the money to hire a designer/developer, it is an inexpensive way to get your company's name onto the Internet.
- Updating the blog is much quicker than contacting a web designer for changes or coding and uploading website changes yourself.

Small companies in developing countries

Success stories can be found on the ITC website: www.intracen.org/ec.

The ITC Trade Forum magazine (www.tradeforum.org) includes news and case studies from around the world.

For more information

- Lim, Z. Good Affiliate Marketing Guide – How Can Blog Helps to Grow Your Affiliate Business? Available online at: http://EzineArticles.com/?expert=Zack_Lim.
- McCue, S. Farce to Force: Building Profitable E-Commerce Strategies. South-Western Educational Pub, 2006.

REFERENCES

[1] Zahorsky, D. What a Blog Can Do for Your Small Business, available at: sbinformation.about.com/cs/ecommerce/a/bblogs.htm.

20.   What benefits do enterprises expect from launching a website?

Many enterprises open websites to enable them to:

- *Enhance their credibility by projecting a more solid, up-to-date professional image*. A website is a powerful first impression, and it is critical that this impression is positive. A website gives you the opportunity to tell potential customers what you are about and why you deserve their trust and confidence.

- *Make it easier for people to do business with you*. A well-planned and well-designed website can make it easier for your customers, members, visitors, suppliers, distributors or associates to do business with you.

- *Reach more customers and markets*. One of the great benefits of the Internet is that it can help broaden your customer base at a relatively low cost. And as more and more people get access to the Internet and become confident Internet users, the potential to expand customer bases will increase proportionately.

- *Promote their products and services*. A well-designed and well-maintained website can be an excellent promotional tool. This is not to say that promoting a business on the Web is better or more effective than traditional forms of promotion. It is simply another promotional tool that should complement other forms of promotion.

- *Advertise in more markets at less expense*. The Internet differs greatly from print advertising in that space is cheap, your advertisement is accessible for a longer period of time, the content can be changed without having to ask someone to do it for you (if you use a content management system) and you can potentially reach a wider audience.

- *Answer questions on their products or services*. Customers can make an informed buying decision. If they are deciding between you and a competitor, your website could mean the difference on who gets the business.

- *Provide online quotations*. The website provides a convenient way to post online quotations in real time. Customers can try various product options and shipment methods in order to make an educated decision.

- *Improve response time to customer queries*. One of the most important consequences of using the Internet effectively is that it can reduce the time staff spend doing administrative tasks, freeing them up to concentrate on the things that really matter – servicing clients and customers and increasing sales.

- *Obtain feedback from customers*. Having a website and using e-mail wisely helps you meet the expectations of your customers and encourages them to contact you at their convenience.

- *Improve customer service*. A website provides a way for customers to benefit after a sale. If you provide information or support through a website that makes them happier about buying from you, it strengthens your business.

- *Add value and satisfaction*. By offering convenience, a point of reference and that touch of individualized customer service, you ultimately add value to your offering and your customers experience a higher level of satisfaction. Your website can add value in other ways too; by featuring tips, advice and general interest content you can entertain your customers. This will also help them remember you better.

- *Provide same-day service or service beyond regular working hours*. Through your website, your business is open 24 hours a day, 7 days a week, and your customers never have to wait in line. A website can be visited at a time that is convenient for the visitor, and it is more engaging when designed correctly.

- *Coordinate supply and customer relations from several outlets*. Many companies still rely on purchasing and back-office systems that revolve around the fax machine, telephone, or handwritten forms. Organizations that have adopted e-business are reaping the benefits that come from replacing manual processes with automated systems. This can lead to a range of efficiencies such as getting paid faster.

- *Conduct foreign market research*. You can use features on your website such as visitor polls, online surveys and your website statistics to find out what your customers like more and how they feel about certain aspects of your business to determine how you can improve your product and the way you do business. Website statistics show you how much traffic your website receives, how the visitor got to your website and where, geographically, the visitor is from.

- *Growth opportunity*. A website serves as a great place to refer potential investors to, to show them what your company is about, what it has achieved and what it can achieve in future.

The cost of not having a credible website or using e-mail effectively can be measured in terms of lost opportunities to create more revenue and cut costs. Some of the costs of not being there (online) include:

- Loss of customers to competitors who do have a good website and e-mail contact with customers;

- Loss of potential revenue from online sales or uptake of services;

- Mounting costs associated with existing inefficient office practices that an effective e-business plan could minimize;

- Mounting costs associated with existing inefficient supply-chain management; and

- Loss of credibility as an innovative, forward-thinking business.

For more information

- Business Link. www.businesslink.gov.uk.

  The Business Link, in partnership with Business Gateway in Scotland and Invest Northern Ireland, supports new and existing SMEs by providing information, advice and tools.

  The site has a special section on IT and e-commerce:
  www.businesslink.gov.uk/bdotg/action/layer?r.s=tl&r.lc=en&topicId=1073861197.

- Australian e-business guide. www.e-businessguide.gov.au.

  The e-business guide website provides information and resources on e-business for small businesses in Australia and for those who advise them. It is an initiative of the Australian Government. It offers advice, tools, and case studies.

- European Conference on Information Systems (ECIS). is2.lse.ac.uk/asp/aspecis.

  This website provides a complete list of the papers issued by the European Conference on Information Systems (ECIS) from 1993 to 2008 as well as electronic copies of all papers.

REFERENCES

[1] E-businessguide getting started booklet. Australian e-business guide. www.e-businessguide.gov.au.

[2] Simms, J. 12 Benefits of Having a Website. Web World. 2005. www.webworldindex.com/articles/12-Benefits-Of-Having-A-Website.html.

21.   What makes a website successful?

Small businesses are finding that the Internet is a relatively low-cost tool for marketing their products and services both locally and globally. A successful commercial website is one that gives value to the business as well as its customers. Therefore, any site expenditure that does not return value to the business is over-expenditure. To obtain value from your website you must carefully define what functions you expect the site to perform, ensure that those functions are carried out efficiently, and make your site highly visible to your target markets.

Most enterprises use their websites initially as an extension of their print advertising or other marketing activities. This can offer good value if you have a heavy print advertising bill which can be reduced when you start using the Web, or if you can extend the impact of an existing print advertising campaign to new markets by reusing some of the advertising material on the Web.

These are not always possible options, however. You may find that you cannot cut your print advertising much because you have a contract with the advertising media (newspaper, directory) or because your target market makes low use of the Web. While reusing your print advertising material may give you global exposure at lower costs, it will not be of much value if your products are not suitable for international sales.

If, after considering costs and benefits, you find, as many businesses do, that you cannot be certain how great the benefit will be, it may still be reasonable and even prudent to go ahead with your website plans. You will, however, have to trim your budget for the site to an affordable level of entrepreneurial risk.

Many businesses that start with a promotional site decide to move on to offering web transactions to customers or suppliers. This is another area where the Internet offers potential value, usually because it offers added convenience to your customers and sometimes because it allows you to shift some transaction costs (such as data entry) to the customer or supplier.

Once again, it is important to think about the costs of creating a site that offers online transaction facilities, and the benefits that your company can expect to derive from these facilities. Will your customers use your site for online purchasing and payment? Or will it be sufficient to allow them to order online with payment taking place on delivery or by invoice? The latter can be just as valuable as an online payment facility and much less expensive to implement.

Whether you use the site for transactions or not, it will be of little value to you if no one knows about it. If you continue to use the print medium (and this includes your business cards, letterheads, etc.), you should use this medium to promote your website. You should also take advantage of the low-cost promotional opportunity offered by site registration with the major Internet search engines. Refer to question 36: "How do I get my products listed prominently by the major search engines?"

The most important characteristic of a good website is that it helps the user to meet a need: whether for information (e.g., about products or about your company), convenient purchasing or even entertainment.

Numerous studies have been carried out to identify the factors that make a website successful, mostly by analysing indicators such as traffic achieved, turnover increase, cost savings and new customers acquired. The findings indicate that the following features are common among most successful websites:

- The enterprise responds quickly to customer queries and problems.

- Successful companies tend to put a company decision maker in charge of the website. The most successful sites are the responsibility of the sales manager rather than of the general manager or the marketing manager.

- The more ways in which a website is promoted the more successful it is.

- The more effective sites tend to be those which have their content updated frequently and regularly.

- The nationality of the company operating on the Internet is not crucial for the overall success of a website.

The Centre for the Promotion of Imports from developing countries (CBI), www.cbi.eu, is an agency of the Netherlands Ministry of Foreign Affairs and part of its development cooperation effort. CBI has created a virtual product showroom (www.cbi.eu/showroom/consumer_products.html) for industry groups such as home decoration, office supplies, garments and home textiles. An initiative like this can be successful only by taking into account the following requirements:

- The importance of featuring new products regularly.
- The need to invite feedback and follow-up from visitors to the website.
- The need to select products that fit in with the culture of the target market.
- The importance of building an easy navigation system into the website.
- The need for an attractive and professional look.
- Being a small firm is not a disadvantage. It can actually encourage attention.
- The need to keep the website up to date.

According to a national survey conducted in the United States by Allurent in September 2006, 83% of the consumers surveyed said they would buy more online if retailers added more interactive and interesting ways to display and purchase products, allowing them to feel more comfortable with, and confident in, their online purchases. In the 2008 survey, 67% of consumers said their expectations about the quality of their online shopping experience had increased since the 2006 holiday shopping season. Major reasons cited include:

- Customers realized that technology was constantly changing and improving and expected that online shopping should also be getting better (66%).

- Customers saw that most retailers consistently advertised their websites, hence they expected to see them invest in making those sites better than they were in the previous year (46%).

- More and more customers were obtaining high-speed bandwidth and expected to see more online stores presenting products better in a way that took advantage of this faster Internet speed (41%).

- A growing number of online shoppers were familiar with interactive and visual sites like Google Maps or Facebook and expected more online stores to become as innovative as these sites (29%).

It is no surprise that young consumers' expectations are more influenced by Web 2.0 sites like Google Maps and Facebook. Nearly half (48%) of 18-24 year olds cited these interactive web experiences as the reason their expectations were rising. Retailers will need to learn how to target better this young group of consumers as their purchasing power becomes more influential [1].

Successful sites embrace technology and change. Keeping abreast of developments in online marketing as well as shifts in online culture, and understanding how to read basic web analytics are key for an e-commerce website owner.

Ipsos MORI has been conducting usability testing since 1997 and has seen Internet users become increasingly demanding and more selective about the websites they visit. As a consequence, people are less likely to persevere with sites they find confusing or frustrating. A successful website should be straightforward to locate and navigate, prioritize the information of greatest importance to visitors, and use language clearly [2].

Note that a successful website does not happen by chance. In order to create a truly effective website, everything on the website must focus on the user — in the end it is their site and their tools. In other words, you should not only examine how well the site is meeting your objectives, but also ensure that the users are satisfied in terms of the fundamental aspects of content, functionality and usability [2].

For more information

- Fisher, Julie and others. Website Information Design: What Small Business Needs to Know. 12th European Conference on Information Systems. Turku, Finland, June 2004. is2.lse.ac.uk/asp/aspecis/20040048.pdf.
- Allurent's annual National Surveys. www.allurent.com.

  Allurent's annual Online Merchandising Survey is a national survey designed to provide insight into the attitudes of United States consumers to online shopping experiences and what they would like to see retailers do to improve the customer experience. A 'Research Brief' providing detailed information on the findings is available at the Allurent website.

REFERENCES

[1] U.S. National Survey. Allurent. 30 January 2008. www.allurent.com.
[2] Top Tips for your Website. Ipsos MORI. January 2009. www.ipsos-mori.com.

22.   How do I get my website translated accurately?

The websites listed below offer language translation capabilities both through translators and through software. Be aware of the serious limitations of automatic translation: it will never provide a 100% accurate translation. The translations are made by computer programs and cannot be expected to produce idiomatic translation of sentences or phrases. Accurate selection among alternative meanings of common words in one language is beyond the capabilities of most of these programs. Although the quality of translation software has improved in recent years the results can be meaningless or hilarious in the target language.

You are much better advised to seek professional translation services if you plan to offer sections of your site in a language that you do not know well. Because some words have no equivalent in other languages, and owing to variations and nuances in language use, cultural sensitivities to certain words and other potential hazards, it may be worth your while to have important documents back translated. In other words, you should get someone who is familiar with both languages to translate the text back to the original language. Do this as often as needed until you can be sure both versions say the same thing.

The following are some of the online translation services on the Web. Note that the number of languages they can translate varies.

- Google Translate. translate.google.com. Google's research group has developed its own statistical translation system for the language pairs available on Google Translate. You can translate text, webpage content or upload a document to be translated. Google also let you add the Google website translator to your website to make it instantly available in other languages.

- Yahoo Babel Fish. babelfish.yahoo.com. Babel Fish translates a block of text (up to 150 words) or a web page.

- ConveyThis. www.conveythis.com. In addition to its online free translation service it lets you install a website translation button to your website or blog and make it accessible in 40 languages. This way your visitors can instantly translate your content with their online translator of choice (including some the services that are listed in here) using a simple, drop-down interface – without ever having to leave your website!

- Traduction.Orange. www.orange.fr. Orange is a French website that offers text and website translation services for several languages.

- WorldLingo. www.worldlingo.com/en/websites/url_translator.html. WorldLingo offers a free text, document, website, and e-mail translation service. The free translator has a 500 word limit. They offer various paid translation services.

- Kwintessential. www.kwintessential.co.uk. In addition to their paid services, Kwintessential offers a variety of free translation services. They also offer a free translation widget that can be added to any website to allow their visitors to read pages in a number of foreign languages.

The following sites list translation software and services:

- Word2Word Language Resources. www.word2word.com. Word2Word provides links to language resources including language dictionaries and translators – mostly free services

- WorldLanguage.com. www.worldlanguage.com. WorldLanguage.com is a language store that provides translation software and services – mostly paid services.

The amount and quality of free translation may vary from site to site. Some commercial sites provide free language translation as a means of trying to get your business.

Languages on the Web

Statistics compiled and updated on 30 June 2009 by Internet World Stats shows the top 10 languages on the Web were [1]:

English:	478,717,443	(28.7% of total Internet users)
Chinese:	361,364,613	(21.7%)
Spanish:	132,963,898	(8.0%)
Japanese:	94,000,000	(5.6%)
French:	76,915,917	(4.6%)
Portuguese:	73,027,400	(4.4%)
German:	65,243,673	(3.9%)
Arabic:	49,372,400	(3.0%)
Russian:	38,000,000	(2.3%)
Korean:	37,475,800	(2.2%)

REFERENCES

[1] Internet World Stats – Usage and population statistics, www.internetworldstats.com.

Technical aspects of setting up a website

23.   How do I create a website?

In spite of a multitude of do-it-yourself guides and manuals, which appear to make building a website easy, creating a good website is a skilled and time-consuming job. It is wise to think carefully about whether you have the necessary skills to do this task yourself, or whether it may not be better to outsource it to a professional firm. A professional looking site will inspire confidence in potential customers. An amateurish site will quickly put people off.

Before you do anything, it would be a good idea to spend some time surfing the Web, to get an overview of what can be done, and to determine what you would or would not like on your own site.

Planning

Identify clear goals for your site:

- Who will use it?
  Determine their interests, computer skills and languages.

- Why will they use it?
  Customers should find the information they need on the first page of the site.

- From where will they access the website?
  Investigate the available technologies, their telecommunications infrastructure, the type of network access that will be used and their speeds.

- Which information is essential or critical?

- How often will it have to be updated?

- Focus on making it easy for customers to learn what they need to know, make a purchase decision, and then buy quickly.

Plan the structure of your site

Create a site map that outlines every page on your site starting with the home page and mapping how to get from one page to the next. Use tools that quantitatively measure site activity — where customers are clicking, how often and whether they end up purchasing.

Designing

- Make your site attractive and easy to use.

- Look at other e-commerce sites and adapt the best marketing and design techniques to enhance your site.

- Make a good first impression on visitors. The first page of your site, your home page, should include:
  - Your company name and logo.
  - Contact information: make it easy to find your phone number, e-mail address, mailing address and fax number.
  - An "About the Company" page for customers to learn quickly who you are and what your business offers.
  - A site menu listing the principal subsections of your site. Keep this menu in the same place on every page throughout your site to make it easy to navigate.
  - A "What's New" section for news, announcements and product promotions. Frequently updating this area will encourage customers to return often.
  - Your privacy statement, clearly describing your policy for protecting customers' personal information.

- Make it easy for customers to navigate your site. As you build your site, try to minimize the number of clicks it takes the customer to go from your home page to the point where he or she is able to make a purchase: four to six clicks are recommended.

- Keep download times short. Test pages to make sure they're not too heavy with graphics that will slow load times — and minimize the size of your images when possible (remember: many customers may be using slow connections). Most users click away to another site or log off if a page takes more than eight seconds to load.

- Let customers know they can trust you. Customers will only provide you with private information, like credit card or phone numbers, if they're sure your site is legitimate and the information they send you is protected. Make sure your site is secure — and that your customers know it.

- Make it easy for customers to pay you. Make sure you not only offer customers a variety of convenient payment methods, but also that you can process them all reliably.

For a complete list of the essential elements of a well-designed website please refer to question 27.

Decide what to include

All sites	Always	Optional
Company name and logo	✓	
Contact information – phone number, e-mail address, mailing address and fax number	✓	
An overview of your company, its products and services, and their applications	✓	
Privacy policy	✓	
Testimonials or success stories		✓
A FAQ section that anticipates and answers common customer questions		✓
Customer registration		✓
Site management and updating functions		✓
Site in different languages		✓
Possibility to download catalogues		✓
Possibility to download order forms		✓
e-commerce sites		
Complete product descriptions for each product, including features, key benefits, pricing, product specifications and other information	✓	
Customer log in for checkout and payment	✓	
Terms and conditions	✓	
Electronic receipt of orders	✓	
Search function to allow user to locate any product easily		✓
Product categorization or classification (multiple levels)		✓
Thumbnail images and full image display of products		✓
Product promotion (e.g., product of the day, top selling, etc.)		✓
Sale price and discounted price display		✓
News		✓
Customer feedback		✓
Shopping cart/basket, view cart, delete from cart		✓
Shipping options with online shipping/postage calculation		✓
Integration with stock — product availability status display		✓
Online payment gateway	✓	
Multi-currency payment option		✓
Discount coupons		✓
Tax deductions for exports		✓
Administration functions such as sales reports		✓

Accessibility

The World Wide Web Consortium has published guidelines on how to make your website accessible to people with disabilities. See www.w3.org/TR/WAI-WEBCONTENT.

Although their primary goal is to improve accessibility, following these guidelines will also make your site easier to use for all users. The latter may be accessing your site in different ways, e.g., mobile phone or automobile-based personal computer. They may also be working in difficult environments such as noisy surroundings, under- or over-illuminated rooms or in a hands-free environment. Following these guidelines will also help people find information on the Web more quickly. The guidelines do not discourage content developers from using images, video, etc., but rather explain how to make multimedia content more accessible to a wide audience.

Building your site

Many e-commerce businesses turn to professional companies to create their websites. This approach is recommended.

Build it yourself

If your budget is very limited and you just want to produce a simple site with no e-commerce, there are self-service website building tools that make it fast and relatively easy for you to create your own site. Some web hosting companies such as Verio (www.verio.com) offer free website building tools on some of their hosting plans.

- The simplest way to create your own website is to use templates – ready-made page layouts and simple website structures – included in many web-authoring software programs. You add your own words and pictures to create your website. An alternative is to use a software package that allows you to create your own web pages from scratch, giving a more individual look.

Hire a professional

Web designers and developers have the skills and experience to build a website with a professional look and good functionality. Designers tend to focus on the look and feel of a website while developers focus on its underlying structure. Many web professionals can fill both roles, but they have different strengths.

For instance, all but the simplest websites are built around a system of databases. The more complicated these databases become, the more likely it is you'll need a developer rather than a designer to construct them. If you decide to use a designer, make sure he or she can build as well as design your website, or direct you to a developer who can.

Look for designers and developers with experience of producing websites for businesses like yours. You may be able to get recommendations on web professionals from friends or advisers. Your Internet service provider or web hosting service may also offer a website design service.

If you decide to use professionals, it is essential to provide a clear brief that tells them what you want. It is also helpful to provide them with copies of your other marketing material, such as any printed brochures.

Minimizing the risks of e-commerce

If you are setting up an e-commerce website you must hire an e-commerce security expert. Your web hosting service and Internet service provider should be able to help you secure your Internet connection and website, and your payment service provider will help you with the security of your online payments. Lack of security makes many people uncomfortable with sending credit card numbers over the Internet. Merchants must prove the security of their website and win the confidence of their customers. Using a reliable payment service provider with a good reputation goes a long way to allay the fears of potential customers.

Testing

If you have set up an e-commerce website, have objective testers walk through the entire ordering process to test its usability. Is it clear exactly what customers need to do to make a purchase? Try buying a product: is the page on which you supply payment information secure? Is the payment processed correctly through your payment gateway? Make sure you use both Macintosh and PCs for testing, and test with different browsers, various browser options such as cookies turned off and pop-ups blocked, and varying modem speeds. You should also test with your target customers' profile(s). For example: if your target customers are teenagers, get a teenager to test the site; if they are middle-aged, middle-income farmers find someone with this profile to test it; if they are in another country get someone from that country and so on.

For more information

- W3Schools. www.w3schools.com.

  On W3Schools you will find complete instructions on how to build a website. The site offers tutorials and examples from basic HTML to more dynamic content using scripts and XML.

- Please refer to the references and resources provided for the questions 26 to 30 of this section.

24. What is a domain name and why do I have to register it?

Each computer that is connected to the Internet requires a unique clearly identifiable numeric address. This address, which is referred to as the Internet Protocol address or IP address in short, comprises four sequences of digits that are separated by periods, e.g.: 74.125.67.100. But people find it much easier to remember a business name than a business number such as the IP address of an online store. Hence it was decided to associate a domain name with each numerical Internet address (for example, the domain name for ITC is intracen.org, while the IP address of the server which hosts the ITC site might be 193.239.220.170).

There is no inherent correlation between any of the numbers within an IP address and a domain name: you cannot tell for sure, for example, whether a host computer is in the .com domain or located in Nigeria simply by looking at the IP address. The link between any IP number and the domain name is simply an association that is stored in a database known as the Domain Name System (DNS).

The DNS works like a telephone number that is unique in itself. Domain names are exclusive and can be accessed globally, so everyone wanting to connect to that domain name will be able to reach it. Thus it is exclusive and reliable like any phone number. "Universal resolvability" is ensuring predictable results from any place on the Internet. This significant design feature of the DNS makes the Internet resourceful and very useful. The DNS helps you send an e-mail to the right person. Each IP address will have its own distinctive domain name.

DNS is one of the wonders of the global Internet and a good example of the remarkable private international cooperation that makes the Internet possible. It is maintained and controlled by the Internet Corporation for Assigned Names and Numbers (ICANN), a private, non-profit entity established, initially with the help of the United States Government, for this purpose.

ICANN is ultimately the organization that allocates the numerical addresses for all host computers on the Internet and sets the conditions for their use, including some conditions for the use of the domain names associated with those numbers. This is a job that is too big for one corporation to manage on its own.

In fact, ICANN is mostly concerned with setting policies and ensuring international cooperation to support the global growth and efficiency of the Internet. It delegates the job of managing the numerical addresses to the Internet Assigned Numbers Authority or IANA. This authority in turn delegates aspects of this task to a large number of registrars located in each top-level domain (TLD) on the Internet. The top-level domain is the last set of letters (or suffix) after the last dot in the domain name (examples: .com, .org)

The centre of the DNS contains 13 special computers, called root servers. ICANN coordinates them and they are distributed around the world. All 13 contain the same important information – this is to spread the workload and back each other up. The root servers have the IP addresses of all the TLD registries – the global registries such as .com, .org, etc. and the 244 country-specific registries such as .fr (France), .cn (China), etc. This is critical information. If the information is not 100% correct or if it is unclear, it might not be possible to locate a key registry on the Internet. In DNS jargon, the information must be unique and authentic.

There are many supplementary lower-level domains, where it is easier to find a name that has not been taken. Up until the late 90s domain registration was limited to one online source, Network Solutions (NSI). Controlling and selling TLD's such as .com, .org and .net NSI had monopoly over the domain registrar market for a long time. Later the registration of domain names has been opened up to ICANN accredited commercial companies competing for registration business. These changes have helped make DNS more responsive to the demands of Internet growth. Also, shopping at different registrars saves money.

Domain names should be easy to understand and related to the content of the webpage. Very few companies have been successful when they have company names that are completely unrelated to the theme of the site. If you do this, you will have to work in hard on associating your domain name to the content.

Generic domain names

The part of the domain name following the dot has a meaning, which should be respected when choosing a name. The principal ones you will find on the net are:

com	Commercial organization	net	Networking organization
edu	Educational institution	org	Non-profit organization
gov	Government	biz	Business
int	International organization	info	Information
mil	Military		

Country-specific domain names

Each country has an assigned two-letter "Country-Code Top-Level Domain" (see list below), which appears at the end of the web address. To register a domain name in a country-specific domain, contact the corresponding registry: www.iana.org.

Internationalised Domain Names

Internationalised Domain Names, or IDNs, are web addresses incorporating Latin characters other than those used in English (such as the French é or German ü), as well as character sets other than the Latin alphabet, such as Chinese or Arabic.

The RIPE NCC (www.ripe.net) is an independent, not-for-profit membership organization that supports the infrastructure of the Internet through technical coordination in its service region. The most prominent activity of the RIPE NCC is to act as the Regional Internet Registry (RIR) providing global Internet resources and related services (IPv4, IPv6 and AS Number resources) to members in the RIPE NCC service region. The membership consists mainly of Internet Service Providers (ISPs), telecommunication organizations and large corporations located in Europe, the Middle East and parts of Central Asia.

For further information on domain names please refer to question 78: "What are the intellectual property issues involved in choosing and registering domain names?", and question 79: "What should I consider when choosing a domain name?"

For more information

- The Internet Society (ISOC). www.isoc.org.

  The Internet Society (ISOC) is a non-profit organization founded in 1992 to provide leadership in Internet related standards, education and policy. With offices in Washington D.C., USA, and Geneva, Switzerland, it is dedicated to ensuring the open development, evolution and use of the Internet for the benefit of people throughout the world.

- WebHostingSearch. www.webhostingsearch.com.

  WebHostingSearch is maintained by a group of webmasters, and in addition to listing and ranking web hosts, it provides various articles on how to set up a website and how to select a web host.

REFERENCES

Walsh, D. Domain Names and Registrars. December 2008.
www.webhostingsearch.com/articles/domain-names-and-registrars.php.

25.   How do I register or buy a domain name?

You can register a domain name such as mycompany.com without being on the Internet. Registering a domain name is like registering a company name in most countries: the name must meet certain criteria (such as uniqueness) and a registration fee is usually paid. A domain name must be unique within any top-level domain (see question 24: "What is a domain name and why do I have to register it?") because duplication could lead to confusion and possible misrepresentation. Many companies register their domain names as soon as they can (some do this even before their host computers are linked to the Internet) to ensure that no one else can take their chosen name.

You can register (buy) a domain name from a ICANN accredited commercial companies such as Internic at www.internic.net, or other name specialists such as NetNames at www.netnames.com or Register.com at www.register.com. You will need to tell the group what your hosting company's address is. Alternatively, domain registration is often included in a web hosting package. When creating a website people find themselves in need of the following: a domain name and storage space. That's why most web hosts offer both. In this process the web host customer can search for available domain names directly on the web hosting site.

If you want to associate a domain name with a host computer linked to the Internet (frequently the host name of a computer that provides a World Wide Web server is simply www), you need to obtain a numerical Internet address and arrange for that address to be notified to other computers on the Internet. Again, it is usually easier to have your web host do this for you, because the notification procedure requires that at least two servers maintaining domain names on the Internet know about the link between your domain name and the numerical Internet address of your host computer.

A computer with a unique Internet domain name and number does not need to be permanently connected to the Internet. The system will not break down if a host cannot be reached because the owner is not linked via a dial-up modem, for example. However, users will become impatient and lose interest if they find a host not reachable message when they try to connect to your site.

Which top-level domain should you be in? Is it better to be in the .com domain than in a country-code domain? In principle, you can register domains in almost any of the top-level domains except .mil (reserved for the military), .gov (reserved for governments) and .int (reserved for certain international organizations).

The best domain to be in is the domain where your users are most likely to look for you. This may be the .com domain. But that top-level domain is now very crowded and it is increasingly difficult to find an appropriate domain name that has not already been registered. Also, many of your users may be accustomed to adding the country code top-level domain (such as .ar, .my, and .za for Argentina, Malaysia and South Africa respectively) to the names of the hosts they are seeking. If you do not use the country code of the country where you are located, this may make it more difficult for local users to find you. Finally, most users use search engines to find sites with specific services or subject areas. Some of the most effective search engines and directories are regional search engines: they are frequently more thorough in indexing or listing sites within a region than the global search engines.

If your primary target market is outside of the United States, it may be worth it to buy a local domain (.co.uk for the UK for example), or host your site on a server in that country. Building links from other sites that are deemed to be local to a specific region should help get your site ranked higher in those search results.

How to register your domain name

Either get your Internet service provider (ISP) or web hosting service to do this for you or register the name of the site (known as the domain name) yourself, with the appointed registrar of your chosen top-level domain, and then get your service provider to do the rest. Most country code top-level domains use the .com, .org, or .edu domains within their country. You can find out who the appropriate registrar for your chosen domain is and how to contact them by asking your ISP or by checking with the global registrar of registrars at www.iana.org.

As registering is easy and inexpensive, it is best to do it as soon as you have decided on your domain name to make sure you get the name you want. You may wish to register a number of variations, just in case you want to use them later – or to avoid the risk of competitors obtaining similar names. You may also want to register common misspellings so that customers who type your address incorrectly still find their way to your site instead of receiving an error message. Some Internet service providers and most hosting sites provide this service.

Otherwise you can register the name yourself through a site that provides this service; examples are given in the getting more information chapter.

The registrar you choose will ask you to provide various contact and technical information that makes up the registration. The registrar will then keep records of the contact information and submit the technical information to a central directory known as the "registry". This registry provides other computers on the Internet the information necessary to send you e-mail or to find your website. You will also be required to enter a registration contract with the registrar, which gives the terms under which your registration is accepted and will be maintained.

To find out if the domain name you have chosen is available

If the domain name you want is already registered, either choose another name or try to buy your first choice from the current owner. To find out if the name could be available first check for a website. If one exists, unless it looks like a temporary use of the name, there is no point in going any further. If no site exists, find out who owns the name, using one of the services listed below, and contact them.

- www.internic.net/whois.html
- www.networksolutions.com
- www.dotster.com

Organizations responsible for regional and country specific domain name registration

- Europe, the Middle East and parts of Central Asia: www.ripe.net
- Asia Pacific: www.apnic.net
- Latin America and Caribbean: www.lacnic.net
- North America, parts of the Caribbean and sub-Saharan Africa: www.arin.net
- Switzerland: www.switch.ch
- United Kingdom: www.nic.uk

For further information on domain names please refer to question 78: "What are the intellectual property issues involved in choosing and registering domain names?", and question 79: "What should I consider when choosing a domain name?"

For more information

- The Internet Society (ISOC). www.isoc.org.

  The Internet Society (ISOC) is a non-profit organization founded in 1992 to provide leadership in Internet related standards, education and policy. With offices in Washington D.C., USA, and Geneva, Switzerland, it is dedicated to ensuring the open development, evolution and use of the Internet for the benefit of people throughout the world.

- Internet Corporation for Assigned Names and Numbers. www.icann.org.
- Country Specific Domain Names. www.iana.org.

26. Where should I host my website?

Very few SMEs have the financial and technical resources to host the company's website on their own servers. Here are some of the reasons that discourage most SMEs from self-hosting:

- The high cost of a fast and reliable Internet connection.
- Costs associated with providing a reliable power supply for the server.
- The skills and resources required to provide server security by:
  - Updating virus definitions, operating system patches.
  - Developing and enforcing security policies throughout the company.
  - Limiting access and enforcing the required physical security of the server.
- Server maintenance cost, including regular backups.

The alternative is to use the services of third party host providers. Web hosting providers offer their clients hosting arrangements that include shared hosting, dedicated hosting and co-location. The plans differ in terms of cost (normally monthly fees), level of support, options and bandwidth.

Shared web hosting

Shared hosting, which is one of the most popular web hosting plans, means the client's website is on a server that may host other websites simultaneously. This server is located at the service provider's location. In this type of service the system administration, backup, regular maintenance and security are provided by the hosting company. The main benefit of this plan is its lower cost, since many of the overhead expenses are divided among the clients who share the same server. Shared web hosting allows a user to have its own domain name. The disadvantage is a relatively slower performance, as the server resources and its bandwidth are shared by more than one website. Most shared hosting services offer programming features such as ASP, PHP, MySQL, and multiple e-mail addresses for each website.

Dedicated web hosting

With dedicated hosting, the web hosting provider makes a web server available to you. Dedicated hosting is a good option for someone who wants more storage and bandwidth and control over the server. The advantages of having dedicated hosting are: unlimited databases and e-mail addresses as well as unlimited bandwidth. In both shared hosting and dedicated hosting the hosting company owns the server hardware. Dedicated web hosting allows a user to have its own domain name. There are two types of dedicated web hosting plans: managed and unmanaged. In managed hosting, the system administration, backup, regular maintenance, and security are provided by the hosting company. In unmanaged dedicated web hosting, the client controls system administration, backup, maintenance and updates. Clearly, unmanaged hosting is complicated and takes more time than a managed hosting solution.

Co-located web hosting

In a co-location service, the hosting company rents a physical space to the client to install its own server hardware. The client will install its own software and maintain the server. The service provider is only responsible for providing a reliable power supply and Internet connection. Similar to the unmanaged dedicated hosting, system administration, backup, maintenance and updates are the client's responsibility. Co-located web hosting allows a user to have its own domain name.

E-Commerce web hosting

Most hosting companies offer e-commerce packages. In addition to the basic hosting features, an e-commerce package usually includes basic commerce software such as shopping cart, catalogue and tools for quickly creating a storefront. An e-commerce hosting plan may be shared or dedicated. According to HostIndex (www.hostindex.com), the dominant software solutions used by hosting companies include Mercantec SoftCart and Icentral ShopSite. Another service offered by most e-commerce web hosting providers is transaction processing. This includes ensuring that online transactions are made securely through SSL (Secure Sockets Layer) encryption. If you also plan to accept credit card transactions online, you'll need payment processing services, from a reliable company. Most hosting companies have the ability to set up complete payment processing systems, including the actual merchant account (which you will need to bill customer's credit cards) [1].

Free web hosting

Some companies offer free web hosting services. Banner ads are common on this type of website hosting (for example, Angelfire.com). Banner ads can be cumbersome and annoying for visitors. Most free hosting plans do not provide users with MySQL databases, multiple e-mail accounts or the ability to run any scripting language. The type of domain one receives in free web hosting is typically a sub-domain (yoursite.webhost.com) or a directory (www.webhost.com/~yoursite). Unless necessary, it is recommended that businesses avoid these kinds of web host services [2].

Getting the right host will definitely reduce your problems. A good host should inform you of scheduled downtime via e-mail before it happens. Of course, there is no way of predicting any unscheduled downtime, but many hosts will offer an uptime guarantee which will compensate you in some way. The hosts that guarantee good service will generally offer better terms in case things go wrong. Potential loss of revenue is just one of the reasons for wanting to choose a good host.

Always ask the host about upgrade options so you can have an upgrade plan in place for when it is needed.

For more information

- WebHostingSearch. www.webhostingsearch.com.

  WebHostingSearch is maintained by a group of webmasters, and in addition to listing and ranking web hosts, it provides various articles on how to set up a website, and how to select a web host.

- HostIndex.com. www.hostindex.com.

  HostIndex is a hosting directory. It also provides various articles on hosting in general and e-commerce hosting in particular.

- 36 Questions to Ask Your Web Host Before You Buy. March 2009. www.articlesbase.com/web-hosting-articles/36-questions-to-ask-your-web-host-before-you-buy-795178.html.

REFERENCES

[1] Considering E-Commerce Hosting Plans?. HosIndex.com. www.hostindex.com/ecommerceoutlook.shtm.

[2] WebHostingSearch. www.webhostingsearch.com.

27.   What are the essential elements of a well-designed website?

Small firms in developing countries have been discovering that the Internet can be used as an effective tool in their global marketing strategy. However, before investing in a website, it is important to determine whether the returns you expect from it will justify your expenditure.

If you decide that you should have a website to market your products and services internationally, you should:

Think about the key words searchers would use to find sites similar to yours and include these words in key areas of your site (title, etc.). Search engines determine a site's relevance and therefore its ranking with them primarily on the basis of the location and frequency of key words.

Keep the site fast by using a minimal number of graphics and photographs. It is best to keep images under 12 kilobytes so that all users can download them quickly. Keep animations to a minimum, unless showing movement is important to demonstrating your product. Keep colours simple, unless a particular shade is important to your message.

The information provided should correspond closely to what visitors to your site will want to know. Surveys show that only a very small percentage of visitors to a site are likely to buy on the first visit, so provide information of sufficient interest to attract visitors back to your site several times. You also need to provide other information, preferably in your area of expertise, that is current and changes regularly.

Make navigating your site easy for the user. Design the site so users can switch easily from one location on your site to another, and know where they are on the site at all times.

Provide information on your firm. Articulate the firm's strategic goals. Provide information on your staff (including number of employees) and display photographs of key staff to personalize the customer relationships managed by your website. Describe the firm's production capacities, manufacturing processes, quality control systems, previous export experience, history and financial standing. Post employment opportunities.

Give a complete list of your sales products; indicate delivery schedules, warranties and technical assistance offered; describe how your products are packaged and how they are delivered; and specify prices and terms of payment. Provide detailed product information.

Provide a customer service section. Place telephone and fax numbers, e-mail and mailing addresses on each page of your website. Indicate the times when a real person can be reached by telephone. Make it clear what is the best way to contact you if they have a technical question, a sales question or they want to return an item. Respond to e-mail within 1 to 76 hours of receiving it. Carry a section with answers to frequently asked questions. Include a user's manual, state your after-sales service policy and list your repair centres. List your retailers.

Have a media section with news releases, photographs and biographies of top executives. Develop an online newsletter.

Provide links to kindred organizations. List your products on websites that advertise foreign buyers and contacts.

Graphic design

Web pages should look appealing and be easy to use. Guidelines include [1]:

- Simple layout
- Centred orientation
- 3D effects, used sparingly
- Soft, neutral background colours
- Strong colour, used sparingly
- Icons, used sparingly
- Plenty of whitespace
- Nice big text

Do not forget to make your site accessible for people with disabilities. Online shopping is becoming very popular with older people and people with reduced mobility.

Here are some other common mistakes that e-commerce sites make, according to a recent article on Smashing Magazine [2]:

- Hiding Contact Information: If your site does not provide any contact information, or hides it so the consumer cannot find it easily, they are less likely to trust your site, and therefore less likely to do business with you.

- A Long or Confusing Checkout Process: The more steps you put between them placing an item in their cart and actually paying for it, the more opportunities you give them to leave your site without completing their purchase.

- Requiring an Account to Order: If you require a customer to sign up for an account before they can place an order, it is another obstacle you have placed in their path.

- An Inadequate Site Search Engine: if a customer knows exactly what they are looking for, many will opt to use a search engine instead of sifting through categories and filters.

- A Poor Shopping Cart Design: your shopping cart is an extremely important part of your e-commerce website. It needs to allow users to add multiple products, to revise quantities or other options about those products, and it needs to remain transparent at the same time.

- Lack of Payment Options: you need to provide as many payment solutions as is practical to optimize the number of orders you get.

- Not Including Store Policies: Before a customer buys from you, they will likely want to know what your shipping policies, return policies and other store rules are.

For more information

- World Wide Web Consortium. www.w3.org.

  The World Wide Web Consortium (W3C) is an international consortium where member organizations, a full-time staff, and the public work together to develop web standards, interoperable technologies (specifications, guidelines, software, and tools), and Guidelines. W3C is a forum for information, commerce, communication and collective understanding.

- Xemion Design Directory. www.xemion.com.

  Xemion was launched in 2005 by a web design company. In addition to a list of web design companies, the website offers articles, tips and techniques on web design and how to select and hire a web design company.

- Design Melt Down, www.designmeltdown.com. This site includes a collection of design elements, trends, and problems in web design.

REFERENCES

[1] Current style in graphic design for the Web. Web Design from Scratch. www.webdesignfromscratch.com.

[2] Chapman, C. 15 Common Mistakes in E-Commerce Design. Smashing Magazine. October 2009. www.smashingmagazine.com/2009/10/08/15-common-mistakes-in-e-commerce-design-and-how-to-avoid-them.

28.   What is the secret of successful website designing for e-commerce?

Understand your market

Find out as much as you can about your potential market. Is it ready for online systems?

Make sure you can support your site

Before building your website, create the right processes and procedures to support it and make sure you have sufficient resources to deal with orders, i.e., deliver products, collect payments, make it easy for customers to contact you, keep the information up to date. Customers will be put off by out-of-date or incorrect information, difficult site navigation and purchasing process, poor order fulfilment and late delivery, lack of customer support and lack of business information.

Comply with legal requirements and standards

If you sell or promote your products online, there are a number of special requirements that you must comply with:

- Provide customers and potential customers with the full name and contact details of your business, including an e-mail address and street address.

- List any trade associations, professional bodies the business belongs to.

- Indicate prices clearly (if applicable), together with details of any associated taxes and delivery costs.

- Clarify the steps involved in concluding a sales contract with your business.

- Give customers the chance to check their order and correct any errors before confirming it.

- Acknowledge receipt of an order electronically without undue delay.

- Make sure customers can store and reproduce any terms and conditions you supply — for example, put them in a format which can be saved on a computer and then printed.

- Tell customers how they can access online codes of conduct relevant to their order.

- Businesses selling over the Internet must also comply with rules on distance selling.

- Your website will store customer information electronically so you will also need to ensure your information systems comply with data protection regulations.

Choose a web address (domain name or URL)

Addresses should be easy to remember, short and descriptive. If you are an established business, keep your own name if possible. The part of the domain name following the dot has a meaning, which should be respected when choosing a name. Find out if the name that you have chosen is available and register it with a domain name registration service.

Choose a payment service provider

If your site is going to process online payments choose a payment service provider. You should do this before starting to build your website as there is no guarantee that you will find a payment service provider who will accept your business or you may find that its charges are beyond your budget.

Choose a freight handling service

If you start accepting orders online, you will need to deliver your products to your customers. Negotiate conditions with a freight handling service, as you will need to quote prices for delivery at the order stage of the transaction. You may wish to integrate your website with that of the freight handling service in order to benefit from the online services it provides.

Choose a website hosting option

For a monthly fee, service providers will provide your site with space on a server, as well as web server software, access to their high-speed Internet connection, tools for managing, maintaining and securing your site, customer support and e-commerce features. There are many web hosting options to choose from.

Choose a web designer and developer

Web designers and developers have the skills and experience to build a website with a professional look and good functionality. Designers tend to focus on the look and feel of a website while developers focus on its underlying structure. Many web professionals can fill both roles, but they have different strengths.

Look for designers and developers with experience of producing websites for businesses like yours. If you decide to use a professional, it is essential to provide a clear brief that tells them what you want. It is also helpful to provide them with copies of your other marketing material, such as any printed brochures.

Build a user-friendly site

Plan your site carefully. First, identify clear goals for your site: what do you want your customers to be able to do? What business benefits do you expect? Second, plan the structure of your site, focusing on making it easy for customers to learn what they need to know, make a purchase decision and complete their purchase. Make your site easy to navigate and user-friendly. Ensure that photographic images on your site are accurate and show products in their best light. Make ordering procedures straightforward and quick. Provide a way for customers to track the progress and availability of their order.

Security

Many people are uncomfortable about providing credit card details over the Internet. Do everything you can to minimize the risks of e-commerce, reassure the client that your website is secure and win their confidence.

Test your site thoroughly

Take time to review and test your site thoroughly before going live. Broken links, incorrect phone numbers, and grammatical or spelling errors diminish the professional effect. Have objective testers walk through the entire ordering process to test its usability. Is it clear exactly what customers must do to complete a purchase? Test buying a product: is the payment page secure? Is the payment processed correctly through your payment gateway? Make sure you use both Macintosh and PCs for testing, and test with different browsers, diverse browser options, such as cookies turned off and pop-ups blocked, and varying modem speeds. Also test with your target customers' profile(s). For example: if your target customers are teenagers get a teenager to test the site; if they are middle-aged, middle-income farmers, find someone with this profile to test it; if they are in another country get someone from that country and so on.

Promote your site

Once your site is up and running, you will need to tell people about it. Put your domain name everywhere: letterhead, brochures, advertisements, business cards and promotional gifts such as hats, jackets, and t-shirts to promote your site and establish your online corporate identity. Don't forget to include your domain name in press releases, too. The following are additional ways of promoting your site:

- Notify search engines.

- Publicize your site through websites likely to interest your target market segment; a lot of Internet traffic comes through links, advertisements or mentions on other sites.

- Negotiate tie-ins with other sites.

- Use word of mouth.

- Advertise in traditional media.

- Add your website address to all e-mails, company stationery and brochures.

- Send your customers a newsletter by e-mail or post.

- List your company with local online business directories, such as those produced by local chambers of commerce.

- Include an "e-mail this page to a friend" option on your site.

Examples of well-designed sites

Each year WebAward (www.webaward.org) selects the best website designs in 96 industry categories. You can check out top sites in your industry here. Sites are always changing so any list will quickly become out of date. Look at popular sites on the Internet. For a list of most visited websites you may refer to sites such as:

- Alexa. www.alexa.com/topsites. Alexa offers a variety of processed information about the Web, including traffic details, related links.

- Web100.com. www.web100.com. Web100.com ranks and reviews websites.

For more information

- Waters, J. The Real Business of Web Design. Allworth Press, 2003.
- Current style in graphic design for the Web. Web Design from Scratch. www.webdesignfromscratch.com.
- Xemion Design Directory. www.xemion.com.

  Xemion was launched in 2005 by a web design company. In addition to a list of web design companies, the website offers articles and tips on, and techniques for, web design and how to select and hire a web design company.

29. How do I know whether I have developed a good website and whether I am ready for e-commerce?

Have I developed a good website?

You can congratulate yourself on having developed a good website and on being ready for e-commerce if you can say yes to the points listed below.*

Key points	Yes	No
1. Your website is running.		
2. It is updated at least weekly.		
3. It is linked to related sites.		
4. It features your company address, telephone and facsimile numbers and e-mail address prominently.		
5. It provides the names of key staff.		
6. It provides biographical data on, and photographs of, key employees.		
7. It asks every visitor to take some action.		
8. It requires no more than three clicks to take a visitor to the desired information.		
9. It uses CRM (customer relationship management) software to track visitors' preferences and interests.		
10. It makes your privacy policy clear.		
11. It specifically asks permission to share client names and other information.		
12. It provides links to the websites of members of any group to which your site belongs.		
13. It has taken into account your survey findings on your clientele's preferences.		
14. It offers other products, services or activities in response to client needs.		
15. It acknowledges all orders, and it promotes sales or special incentives once a month.		
16. It allows clients to share information on message boards or in chat rooms.		
17. It has shopping carts for online purchasing.		
18. It offers messaging or immediate telephone call-back from a real person.		
19. You answer all e-mail within 24 hours.		
20. You send e-mail newsletters once a month to clients and customers.		
21. Your company can handle a large increase in volume.		
22. You conduct an annual online survey to assess developing needs.		
23. The web designer continues to attend meetings to keep up to date with your overall corporate strategy.		

*With thanks to Carol Conway of the Corporation for Enterprise Development in Chapel Hill, North Carolina for providing the template. Some questions have been altered to suit the needs of developing countries.

Is my company ready for e-commerce?

There are various online tools to help you assess your company's readiness for e-commerce.

- The ITC E-commerce Fitness Checker is a self-assessment tool designed to check on an enterprise's electronic commerce readiness and identify possible gaps in planning. This checklist is also of use to enterprises already engaged in e-commerce. The online tool is available at www.intracen.org/ec.

- The consulting group of the Business Development Bank of Canada (BDC) has also developed various assessment and diagnostic tools. The two free diagnostic tools: "E-Business relevancy diagnostic" and "E-Business readiness diagnostic" will provide you with helpful information on your firm's readiness for e-commerce planning and implementation. The E-Business diagnostic tools are available at: www.bdc.ca/en/business_tools/diagnostic_tools/default.htm.

30. What questions should I ask of an Internet service provider, web hosting company and web designer?

Given the explosion in the number of Internet service providers (ISPs), web hosting services and web designers around the world, it is important to select them carefully.

Questions to ask your Internet service provider

- Do you offer a flat-fee service?
- How many hours of access can I get per month within the basic fee structure?
- How many users can I add per modem line without additional charges?
- Is a free website included in the basic subscription fee?
- Do you offer 24-hour technical support?
- How long is the average wait to speak to a real person?
- When I travel, will I be able to have local dial-in access?
- How fast is your e-mail delivery?

Questions to ask about your web hosting company

- **Is it well established?** How long has it been in business? Who are its customers? Do you know other people who use its services? Ask for references and contact them.

- **Is it conveniently located?** Select locally if possible, so you can see its installation and contact it easily if there is a problem. If a local supplier is not available or local access to the Internet is not viable, select your preferred alternative location.

- **What is the speed (bandwidth) of the Internet connection being offered?** How does this speed compare with that of other service providers?

- **Is shared hosting available?** Shared hosting is the most cost-effective solution for smaller sites. It means that your site will be housed on the same server as several other websites.

- **Are dedicated servers available?** Paying the host for your own dedicated server, a solution used by larger and busier sites, provides faster access.

- **How much disk storage space is being offered?** Smaller sites may need only 300-500 MB (megabytes) of website storage space, while busier e-commerce sites may need at least 9 GB (gigabytes) or their own dedicated web servers.

- **What is the hosting company's upgrade policy?** As your site grows, your hosting service should be able to accommodate you with a range of options.

- **How available will your e-commerce site be?** An e-commerce site must be accessible to customers 24 hours a day.

- **Does the hosting company offer domain name registration?** If you have not already registered your domain name the hosting company may do it for you.

- **Are e-mail accounts available?** E-mail accounts that match your domain name are often available. Are they included in your monthly access and hosting fee?

- **What are the tools offered?** You may need access to such things as web design tools and shopping carts. Check this with your website designer.

- **What other services are offered?** Does the hosting company offer other services such as access and traffic logs?

- **What security services are offered?** Security on the Internet is a major concern. What services are offered in this regard? Examples are alerts if changes are made to your website, SSL (secure sockets layer) encryption.

- **Does your host offer customer services 24 hours a day, 7 days a week?** A major advantage of using a web hosting service is that you do not have to worry about keeping the web server running.

- **What are the costs of using the hosting company?** Fees vary with the configuration you choose. Normally there will be a monthly hosting fee. There may also be an annual fee for domain name registration. Taking optional tools and services will usually mean additional charges.

Questions to ask your web designer

Web designers and developers have the skills and experience to build a website with a professional look and good functionality. Designers tend to focus on the look and feel of a website while developers focus on its underlying structure. Many web professionals can fill both roles, but they have different strengths.

For instance, all but the simplest websites are built around a system of databases. The more complicated these databases become, the more likely it is that you'll need a developer rather than a designer to construct them. If you decide to use designers, make sure they can build as well as design your website, or direct you to a developer who can.

Look for designers and developers with experience of producing websites for businesses like yours. You may be able to get recommendations on web professionals from friends or advisers. If you decide to use professionals, it is essential to provide a clear brief that tells them what you want. It is also helpful to provide them with copies of your other marketing material, such as any printed brochures. Your requirements can be summarized in a technical specifications document that clearly defines the following:

- Technical solutions — e.g. authoring language, database solution, maintenance solution, web server and hosting requirements, security

- Scope and nature of the content

- Functionality and interactivity on the site

- Graphic and information design, and navigation parameters and rules (but not the actual design itself)

- Documentation and training deliverables

- Costs of all aspects of construction and delivery of the website

- Development and payment schedule for the project.

Questions to ask:

- **Are the web designers well-established?** How long have they been in business? Who are their customers? Do you know other people who use the web designers' services? Ask for references and contact them.

- **What experience do they have?** Have they worked for businesses like yours? Have they produced other sites using the type of features you want? How many websites have they developed for a fee?

- **Designer or developer.** Will they design your site, build your site, or both?

- **Examples of work.** See examples of sites they have produced. Assess these sites. Do you like the styles and layouts? Is it easy to navigate your way around the sites and find key information? Do the sites load quickly? Do they have the quality you want in a website? Don't be put off if the designers' or developers' previous work seems too sophisticated. They might also be good at simple stuff.

- **Your site.** Ask the designers specific questions about your project that you are concerned about.

- **Services.** What services can they provide? Can they host your site for you? Will they help publicize your site and register it with (regional, global, specialized) search engines? Can they maintain the site in the future or train you to manage it yourself?

- **Ownership.** Make sure that the website design will be your intellectual property. Are they prepared to sign an agreement assigning copyright to you?

- **Cost.** Find out how much they charge. Will they charge a flat fee or a daily rate? A flat fee may be better if you think there will be changes during development. Will they accept payment on completion or expect interim payments? How will they charge for maintaining your site or providing other services?

- **Project management.** Do they propose a sound, workable project management methodology?

- **Contract.** Everything should always be put down in writing.

Note that good website design companies combine graphic, technical, marketing and consultative skills. To find a professional web designer in your local area, you may start at directories of designers such as the Xemion's design directory (www.xemion.com).

It is useful to develop a scoresheet for use when evaluating responses by Internet service providers, web hosts, and web developers.

At the final stage of the development process, the web developer should hand the site over to your organization. You should ask for the following services at this stage:

- Conducting training in using the maintenance software.

- Installing any third-party software or templates that your staff will use to maintain the site.

- Providing the site documentation — e.g., navigation maps, indexes of files and the files themselves.

- Returning hard copy and soft copy materials used during the development of the website.

For more information

- Australian e-business guide. www.e-businessguide.gov.au.

  The e-businessguide website provides information on, and resources for, e-business for small businesses in Australia and for those who advise them. It is an initiative of the Australian Government. The site offers advice, tools and case studies.

31. How are fees set for website development and updating?

Fees for developing and maintaining a website vary considerably. Generally, they are based on an hourly fee for the type of expertise needed, multiplied by the number of hours the project will take. Fees are determined by several considerations, including the following:

- The experience of the web design company: as a rule, the greater the experience, the higher the fee.

- The size of the company: large companies, with larger overhead costs, may charge higher fees.

- The eagerness of the company to obtain your business: fees may be reduced, or extra services included, if the company is "hungry" for your project.

- The size of the project to be undertaken: the larger the number of services, pages and features, the higher the fee.

- How quickly you want to have your website up and operating.

You can reduce the costs of setting up and maintaining your site by thorough preparation prior to meeting your developer and by cooperating with the developer once work has begun.

Before choosing and meeting the developer, you should:

- Learn as much as you can about the possibilities and opportunities for your company, i.e. prepare your e-commerce plan.

- Prepare to articulate your goals for your site to the developer: what are the results you want from being on the Web?

- Determine what you want to have included in your site and draft the site map.

- Draft the text for the Web.

- Gather any visuals and documents you want to include.

- Establish a process for obtaining internal approvals for the various stages of the developer's work.

- While working with the developer:
  - Consider the developer's suggestions for improvements: they may save you money in the development and make your site more effective.
  - Make the fewest possible changes once the process has begun: the better you communicate to begin with, the fewer the changes. The fewer the changes, the lesser the costs and delays.
  - Obtain internal approvals as quickly as possible.

For more information on the questions you should ask from your Wed developer please refer to question 30: "What questions should I ask of an Internet service provider, web hosting company and web designer?"

Many businesses make the mistake of only considering the cost of developing a new website and forget the annual costs associated with site operation, maintenance, and future improvements. The annual cost depends on the type of business, the number and type of transactions carried out by the website. For some businesses the maintenance costs are not high, for others they can far exceed the development cost. If these costs are not identified and estimated accurately, and the required money allocated for it, it may significantly affect the website's chances to succeed and to achieve the company's long term goals.

For more information

- Australian e-business guide. www.e-businessguide.gov.au.

  The e-business guide website provides information and resources about e-business for small businesses in Australia and for those who advise them. It is an initiative of the Australian Government. It includes advice, tool, and case studies.

32.   What hardware is required for engaging in e-commerce?

SMEs generally opt to use the services of an ISP or web hosting company to host their website. For a monthly fee, these service providers will provide your site with space on a server, as well as web server software, access to its high-speed Internet connection, tools for managing and maintaining your site, customer support, e-commerce features and more. This eliminates the need to purchase special hardware for e-commerce.

There are many ISP and web hosting options to choose from:

- WebHostingSearch. www.webhostingsearch.com. WebHostingSearch is maintained by a group of webmasters, and in addition to listing and ranking web hosts, it provides various articles on how to set up a website, and how to select a web host.

- HostIndex. www.hostindex.com. HostIndex is a hosting directory. In addition, it provides various articles on hosting in general and e-commerce hosting in particular.

- FindMyHosting.com . www.findmyhosting.com. FindMyHosting.com provides a free review guide of the best web hosting providers online. Each web host is hand picked, tested and given an in-depth review insuring the webmaster the best overall hosting experience.

- Yahoo Small Business. smallbusiness.yahoo.com. Yahoo Small Business offers various hosting plans, including e-commerce plans, for small businesses.

- WebHostDirectory. www.webhostdir.com. WebHostDirectory offers a variety of information on hosting such as web hosting listings, web hosting guides, web host search and hosting news.

Please refer to question 26: "Where should I host my website?" for more information on how to choose a web host.

Even though your website is hosted elsewhere, you will still need one computer for each person who needs to access the Internet, send and receive e-mails or communicate with customers. You will need a computer that is fast, very reliable, can be upgraded, and can not only connect to the Internet but also run standard business software such as word processors and spreadsheets.

You will also need an Internet connection – modem, ADSL or other, depending on what is available, and affordable for your business. The choice of dial-up or broadband connection also depends on your business plan and the role you want the Internet to play in it.

Small businesses, which need technology primarily for word processing and low-impact Internet access should seek recommendations on a reliable hardware supplier, and then ask this supplier to configure a machine to their budget. Use the Internet to check prices on sites of hardware vendors and retail outlets.

Service and support is critical for an SME, hence when searching for a hardware provider take that into utmost consideration.

Online marketing techniques to increase online visibility

33. How can I improve communication and customer service through e-mail and websites?

The long-term success of any business or organization is built on relationships. E-mail lists, surveys, newsletters, blogs, moderated discussion groups and conferences can help build such relationships. To obtain more mileage from these activities, you could carry out what is called customer profiling, i.e. building a data file on every client, interacting with clients on a one-to-one basis or within groups of like-minded individuals. You could also supply clients with information on a need-to-know basis.

Tips on how to enhance your customer orientation:

- Appoint someone to manage client relations through communication, customer services and information dissemination.

- Add clients' e-mails to your database and create a segmented e-mailing list.

- Differentiate between your clients on the basis of their needs.

- Get clients to talk to you by using online surveys, listservs, and moderated discussion groups. For more information, please refer to question 38: "What are news groups, listservs, direct marketing and industry websites and how can I use them?"

- Improve your communication with customers by sharing your knowledge and expertise through your business Blog.

- Create a weekly or monthly e-mail newsletter.

- Have direct links to every customer's website.

- Conduct regular electronic surveys and send your customers the results.

- Use video-conferencing as a low-cost way of interacting with your clients.

- Archive reports online (with related topical links).

How can e-mail improve customer relations and service?

E-mail is a widely used but little understood communication tool that can provide instant, free, targeted messages to existing and potential customers, your employees, managers and suppliers, your colleagues in the industry and industry professionals. Some ways of targeting communications to these different groups are set out below.

- **Existing customers**. Send regular e-mail updates to customers, letting them know of sales, new products, or company developments.

- **Servicing customers**. Only 1% - 2% of those who visit a website buy anything, while 90% of those who enter a physical store buy something. Much of the disparity in the buy rate has to do with customer service. E-commerce companies need to address the problem of providing customer service online. A good customer service ensures contact with a real person who will solve problems, respond quickly and well to all inquiries, and follow up after a purchase. Automated responses to customer inquiries are strongly discouraged.

- **Potential customers**. Direct potential customers to your website, which should show photographs or illustrations of your products, a company profile and history, a price list and delivery schedule, to name just a few features.

- **Employees.** Circulate among your employees updated information on your company's overall sales performance, its new customers, employee contributions, new ideas; distribute minutes of senior staff meetings, employee manuals, etc.

- **Management.** Most e-mail messages to senior staff members (e.g. those concerned with finance) could also be sent to others (in the marketing, production departments, etc.) so that all key management staffs are kept up-to-date on company matters. These persons should also copy each other in their internal e-mails.

- **Suppliers.** Suppliers should be given regular updates on shipping and delivery requirements, production and supply schedules.

- **Colleagues and professionals in kindred professions**. Establishing a moderated listserv (you can do this on your computer by entering e-mail addresses into a database or an address book) gives professionals within a particular industry the opportunity to share views, industry developments and concerns.

Keep in mind that anything written, typed, faxed, photocopied or stored can be distributed at essentially no charge via e-mail. This includes brochures, memoranda, employee manuals, employee lists, applications for employment and guides.

Spam

Spam, also known as unsolicited commercial e-mail or bulk mail, once a mere nuisance, has become a serious problem for individuals and businesses alike. According to Symantec (www.symantec.com) during the month of September 2009, spam averaged slightly over 86% of all e-mail messages [1].

Spam undermines user trust online, reduces firm productivity, and increases costs for Internet service providers. A variety of measures and initiatives have been undertaken to address spam by OECD countries, but it is recognized that no single approach will likely succeed without close international coordination. The OECD Task Force on Spam has developed an anti-spam toolkit (www.oecd-antispam.org), a collection of guidelines and recommendations to help governments, regulators and industry players orient their policies relating to spam solutions.

A number of companies now offer software that organizations can run on their e-mail server computers to limit the amount of spam that gets through to their employees.

You should avoid sending unsolicited e-mail to your clients regardless of its content. By spamming, even once, you risk losing your customer's trust and putting your company's reputation on the line.

For more information

- Small Business Bible, www.smallbusinessbible.org.

  Small Business Bible is a site intended to guide budding and experienced entrepreneurs who plan to start a new home based business or a small business firm. It helps small business owners to understand the intricacies of how to handle business online and in person.

- Krotz, J.L. E-marketing: How to engender trust and avoid spam filters. Microsoft Office Live Small Business. office.microsoft.com/en-us/officelive/fx102556521033.aspx.

- LivePerson. www.liveperson.com. LivePerson's real-time chat platform helps businesses to communicate and build relationships with their customers on the Web.

REFERENCES

[1] State of spam; A monthly report. Symantec. Report no. 34, October 2009. www.symantec.com.

34.   What sort of information should I obtain on the use of my website?

In order to ascertain whether your website is useful and what your viewers find interesting, as well as to obtain an indication of the return on your investment, you can ask the company hosting your site for certain type information. The information that can be given to you will depend on the nature of the website logs maintained by your service provider and its log analysis software. Some types of analyses require heavy log processing. Most providers will offer some, but few will offer all types of analyses. Ask your service provider whether it can provide the following information on your website:

- The most and least frequently clicked pages.
- The pages through which readers enter and exit your website.
- The pages through which readers enter and exit without viewing other pages.
- Files most frequently downloaded.
- The host computer name, domain name and country of the visitor.
- Number of hits and clicks by day, week or hour.
- Total hits, failed hits, cached hits.
- The bandwidth used.
- The most accessed directories.
- In some cases, the source of the hit, including whether the hit was from a search engine referral.
- Top key words entered in search tools to find your website.
- Most commonly entered search terms once viewers enter your site.

There are several free, open source or proprietary tools that can process your host log file and generate advanced statistics, graphically. These log analyzers work as a Common Gateway Interface (CGI is a standard protocol for interfacing external applications with a web server, usually used to process online forms), or from command line and show you all possible information that your log contains, in few graphical web pages. Here some examples of web log analysers:

- AWStats: awstats.sourceforge.net
- Analog: www.analog.cx
- Webalizer: www.mrunix.net/webalizer
- Sawmill Analytics: www.sawmill.co.uk

In addition to the W3C standard for web server log file [1], there few other proprietary formats.

For more information

- Buchanan , R.W. and Lukaszewski, C. Measuring the Impact of Your Website. John Wiley & Sons, 1997.

  In-depth advice and guidelines on benchmarking, measuring and managing a productive website. Extensive case studies from over 50 pioneer companies, including Chrysler, Federal Express and 3M, illustrate how this valuable methodology works in real corporate settings.

- Does your web host provide good statistics?. Good Web Hosting Info (GWHI) Newsletter No. 2, June 2005. www.goodwebhosting.info/article.py/44.

- Doyle, W. 10 Most Important Questions to Ask Your Web Host NOW!. www.amazines.com/Internet__Marketing/article_detail.cfm/1101422?articleid=1101422.

=============== **REFERENCES** ===============

[1] Extended Log File Format. W3C Working Draft WD-logfile-960323. www.w3.org/TR/WD-logfile.

35.   How do I drive traffic to my site?

Promoting products or services on the Internet can be considered a form of targeted or niche marketing. It will tend to drive prospective buyers with a specific interest in your products to your website. Web advertising can therefore be more effective than mass advertising on television and the print media or mass mailings.

Here are some ways of ensuring that traffic is directed to your site:

- Register with multiple search engines. Refer to question 36: "How do I get my products listed prominently by the major search engines?".

- Improve your ranking in major search engines. Refer to question 27: "What are the essential elements of a well-designed website?".

- E-mail customers the address of your new website, allowing them to click to your site instantly.

- Send media releases announcing the website and its address.

- Establish links to websites that are compatible with yours, i.e. those that reach the same target market and are not in competition with you.

- Write articles describing websites of interest to your industry.

- Print your web and e-mail addresses on your stationery and business card.

- Advertise in the local media.

- Include your web address in the yellow pages.

- Notify sales representatives about the website.

- Offer discounts to those who order online.

- Send humorous postcards about the website.

As the above list suggests, you should cross-promote your site through offline promotion in other media, and through online promotion using reciprocal links. If users find the information on your website useful, they will bookmark your site and visit it again.

For more information

- Zeff. R. and Aronson, B. Advertising on the Internet; 2nd edition. John Wiley & Sons. 1999.

- Brown, B.C. How to Use the Internet to Advertise, Promote and Market Your Business or Website with Little or No Money. Atlantic Publishing Company. January 2006.

- O'Keefe, S. Complete Guide to Internet Publicity: Creating and Launching Successful Online Campaigns. John Wiley & Sons. January 2002.

36.   How do I get my products listed prominently by the major search engines?

Many reports indicate that as many as 85% of Internet users find sites through search engines. It is important for any enterprise selling or marketing its products on the Internet to make sure that these products are listed with the search engines that its prospective customers are likely to use.

However, due to the huge number of websites now online it is increasingly difficult and time consuming to find information using a search engine. According to a survey by Netcraft, there were over 182 million websites worldwide in October 2008 [1]. For a business to ensure appropriate visibility among its customers, they have to make sure that their site is listed on the first page of relevant searches.

An increasing number of search engine sites offer companies a paid placement which is the option of purchasing a top listing on results pages for a particular set of search terms. The rates charged vary tremendously depending on the search terms. In other words, businesses can pay to have their site featured prominently on the first pages.

How a search engine works

A typical search engine looks for matches to words and phrases in a large index that it compiles from web pages found on the public Internet. The search engine uses software known as a spider, a crawler, or a robot (or simply bot), because it is configured to follow the links in the Web from one page to another, usually one site at a time, much like a spider following the threads in its web.

Web pages are indexed by search engine software in a variety of ways but, in general, the index reflects the text content of at least the key pages on a website. Because the Web has an enormous text content, search engines are often selective about the depth to which they will index a site and the amount of text on any page that they will attempt to index. In addition to words that appear on the web page, web designers can specify additional key words, using HTML tags. These key words, referred to as meta tags, are hidden from the website viewer, but visible to spiders. Hence the spiders look for meta tags on a page, the page title or the words in the first few hundred characters of a page. Not all of these items are important to every search engine; some ignore meta tags and some engines use other factors to determine what to index on a page. For more information and latest developments look up search engine on Wikipedia (en.wikipedia.org/wiki/List_of_search_engines).

No matter how they index a web page, all search engines respond to a user query in similar ways. They draw from their index database a ranked listing of pages whose entry in the index matches the search terms entered by the user. The rank of any site in this list of search results reflects the exactness of the match, according to criteria established by the search engine programmers.

This is why it pays to think carefully about the terms that your users are likely to enter into a search query when looking for your products (or your competitors' products). You must ensure that your pages give prominence to those terms in the areas (page title, meta tags, top text content) that the spider robots are most likely to select for indexing. The more closely your content reflects the most popular queries, the more likely it is that your web page if it has been indexed by the search engine will be listed near the top of the results found by the users query. You should be aware, however, that intentionally and unnecessarily repeating content such as meta tags on a web page to increase your chances of getting a hit has a negative effect on a sites ranking with most search engines.

How can you ensure that a particular search engine will index your page?

Most indexing search engines allow you to register a URL that will be added to the 'to do' list of the search spider. Look for a link such as Add a URL somewhere on the search engine page. Follow the link and carefully follow the instructions given. Most engines require you to enter a URL and an e-mail address. You do not need to enter a separate address for all the pages on your site. In most cases, the spider will follow links on your site from one page to the next although sometimes only to a predetermined depth. Also, some spiders are not very good at handling links through a frameset or for dynamic websites where the content is stored in a database.

Search engine optimization

The combined art and science of having a particular URL listed near the top of search engine results is called search engine optimization, search engine positioning, or search engine placement. Based on what was described above any search engine optimization starts with the proper site design.

Hints, tips, news, many articles on search engine optimization can be found on many websites, such as SearchEngineWatch.com (www.searchenginewatch.com). You should also use advice given by the search engines themselves, as with Google: www.google.com/support/webmasters/bin/answer.py?hl=en&answer=35291.

Many websites such as: www.searchenginecolossus.com, www.submit-wizard.co.uk, and www.trafficseeker.com, offer various site submission and search engine optimization services to online businesses. You should compare these sites for price quotes and for a list of the other services offered.

Search advertising networks

Many search engines do not sell inclusion and placement rights on their pages directly to advertisers. They use search engine placement brokers, which are companies that aggregate inclusion and placement rights on multiple search engines and then sell those combination packages to advertisers. Mirago (www.mirago.com), and LookSmart (www.looksmart.com) are two examples of such brokers.

Search engines

According to a report by Nielsen Online (www. nielsen.com), Microsoft's Bing search engine was the fastest growing major search provider among users in the United States, as of August 2009 [2]. At that time, the market leader Google, dominated the search engine market with nearly 65% of searches. Yahoo held second place in terms of overall share with 16%. The top ten search engine providers of August 2009, ranked by searches in the United States are presented in the following table [2].

Search Provider	Searches ('000)	Share of searches (%)
Total	10,812,734	100
Google	6,986,580	64.6
Yahoo	1,726,060	16
MSN/WindowsLive/Bing	1,156,415	10.7
AOL	333,231	3.1
Ask.com	186,270	1.7
My Web	128,432	1.2
Comcast	50,328	0.5
Yellow Pages	37,923	0.4
NexTag	31,830	0.3
Local.com	16,314	0.2
Source: Nielsen MegaView Search		

Directories

Some companies, including the search engine sites, provide classified hierarchical lists of categories into which they have organized commonly searched URLs. The sites are called Internet directory, or web directory. A web directory is likely to be more selective than search engines. You should check how much it costs to be registered with, and listed on, directories. You need to apply to a directory to have your site listed. Here are some web directories:

- Google Directory.   directory.google.com.
- Yahoo! Directory.   dir.yahoo.com.
- The Open Directory Project (ODP).   www.dmoz.org.
- The World Wide Web Virtual Library.   vlib.org.

For more information

- SearchEngineWatch.com. www.searchenginewatch.com.

  SearchEngineWatch provides tips and information about searching the Web, analysis of the search engine industry and help to site owners trying to improve their ability to be found in search engines.

- Google's Search Engine Optimization Starter Guide. Google. 13 November 2008. www.google.com/webmasters/docs/search-engine-optimization-starter-guide.pdf.

- Barney, L. SEO tools to increase your SEO optimization efforts. Promotion World. 23 October 2009. www.promotionworld.com.

REFERENCES

[1] October 2008 Web Server Survey. Netcraft. October 2008. www.netcraft.com.

   Netcraft is an Internet services company based in Bath, England. Netcraft provides research data and analysis on many aspects of the Internet. Netcraft has explored the Internet since 1995 and is a respected authority on the market share of web servers, operating systems, hosting providers, ISPs, encrypted transactions, electronic commerce, scripting languages and content technologies on the Internet.

[2] Marshal, J. Top Search Providers for August 2009. ClickZ, 15 September 2009.

37.   How do I write effective e-mails, and what are appropriate ways of communicating through the Internet?

The greatest advantage of e-mail and online communication is their cost-saving element. Once your online service is established, you either pay very little, or nothing at all, for each e-mail, telephone call or fax sent or received over the Internet, unlike telephone calls, faxes or telexes from fixed or mobile phones.

Many businesses now use e-mail for most of their communications, to send memoranda, notices, reports and newsletters, and to post offers to buy and sell. Almost any data created using common desktop software may now be sent via e-mail. E-mail can be used to transmit text, data, graphics, sound and video.

Because e-mail can be relatively easily intercepted, business-critical, confidential or financial information should not be sent by e-mail unless it is encrypted, and this type of information should never be sent to or from unsecured locations such as Internet cafés.

E-mail for marketing has to be used very carefully. The message must be clear and the language has to be appropriate. Make sure marketing e-mails are clearly identifiable as commercial communications and clearly identify on whose behalf it has been sent. Unsolicited marketing e-mails and mass marketing by e-mail (SPAM) is generally considered to be anti-social behaviour on the Internet. In some countries it is illegal or subject to regulations. Many web hosting services and Internet Service Providers (ISP's) forbid it in their terms and conditions and increasingly software to block this type of e-mail is being put into place. Make sure recipients can identify unsolicited marketing e-mails immediately – perhaps by putting the words "unsolicited advertisement" or "unsolicited commercial communication" in the header.

The points that follow on the components of an e-mail message are intended to help you improve and manage your use of e-mail as a form of communication.

*   In the **Subject**: line, be brief, use active verbs and provide key details of your message. Many readers decide whether to read a message on the basis of the subject line alone. If your messages are mislabelled, you not only waste your reader's time, but you also take the chance of failing to communicate your point or having your message deleted unread as junk mail or 'spam'. If you can put the most important point of your message in just a few words on the subject line no more than four or five words your e-mail will be more effective.

    Also, be careful to review those automatic Reply subjects (e.g. lines that begin Re: Re: Re: Staff meeting). By the time the message has bounced back and forth a few times, the subject of the exchange is usually quite different from the original message. Always change the subject line to convey the current message.

*   The **CC**: or carbon copy line allows you to send a copy of your message to other persons.

*   **BCC**: stands for blind carbon copy. This feature allows you to send a copy of your message to another person without letting the addressee in the To: line know that you have done so. For mass mailings, use the BCC feature to address each recipient so that all the e-mail addresses are not shown to the recipients.

*   **When sending e-mail, send copies only to those who need to see your message**. Your business associates may get many more messages than you do, so consider carefully whether you need to send them a copy of your message. Others may regard what you may consider an effort to communicate as of no interest or value. Worse still the copy may be considered offensive or wasteful of your reader's time.

*   **Give your name, title, address, telephone and fax numbers** (with your country code) and e-mail address in all correspondence. You may want to create an automatic signature for insertion at the end of each message so that you do not have to type this information each time you send a message.

*   **It is important to ensure that your message is clear.** Remove ambiguous or confusing language that may be misinterpreted, spell out acronyms, and check for spelling and grammar. It is important to be on your guard against too much informality or frankness in e-mail messages. Although e-mail is a quick-and-easy, casual medium like conversation, most people find it much harder to convey their meaning as accurately in writing as they can in person. If your reader cannot see the smile on your face, she may take your joke seriously or be offended. Your peevish remarks, too, will probably hit home more sharply in writing than in person and seem more like genuine anger or wounding sarcasm. It is a good rule to be consciously mellow in e-mail. Once you have pressed the send button, it is difficult to take back your words or soften them in an afterthought.

- **If you need your reader to act on something mentioned in the e-mail, state it in the beginning.** If you are communicating with more than one person, address each paragraph to a particular person. For example, you may want to instruct Mr Ahuja to handle a particular task in one paragraph, and Ms Aruba to handle another task in the next paragraph.

- **Reply promptly to messages, usually within 24 hours.** Use the Automatic Response feature when you are away so that a sender knows when to expect you back or whom to contact during your absence.

- **Do not type out words in CAPITAL LETTERS, as this is the equivalent of shouting.**

- **Try to avoid sending attachments or complex graphics,** as they can take time to download. If you must send attachments, be sure that the recipient has the same software needed to be able to view them. The best format to use for documents is PDF, and rich text format (RTF). The best format for graphics is JPEG or GIF.

- **Open attachments sent to you with great care.** Software viruses that can cause serious harm to your computer system are generally spread by attachments. To protect your system, be sure to:

    – Install a virus shield.
    – Set up the virus shield so that it will automatically and regularly scan your hard drive.
    – When you receive e-mail with attachments, do not open it in your e-mail system, but save it to your hard drive. When you open the file, your anti-virus program will have searched for a virus, and if it had found one, will have eliminated it.

Advertising standards

Review advertising standards for guidelines on e-mail marketing.

- Australia   www.advertisingstandardsbureau.com.au
- Canada   www.adstandards.com
- Europe   www.easa-alliance.org
- Ireland   www.asai.ie
- United Kingdom   www.asa.org.uk

Other ways of communicating over the Internet

In addition to e-mail, many businesses are using real-time methods of communicating over the Internet. Use of Internet relay chat (IRC) and Voice over Internet Protocol (VOIP) applications allow businesses to interact with customers instantly, and with minimum cost.

Voice over Internet Protocol (VOIP)

VOIP uses the Internet as a transmission medium for telephone calls. Many service providers offer these applications free of charge.

- www.voip-info.org
- www.skype.com
- www.voipbuster.com

Instant messaging

This is a form of real-time Internet chat. It is mainly designed for group (many-to-many) communication in discussion forums called channels devoted to specific subjects.

Video conferencing and live demos

The Internet can also be used for online meetings and live product demonstrations, some examples are: Glance (www.glance.net), Livemeeting (www.microsoft.com), and Cisco Webex (www.webex.com). There is also the free and open-source alternative DimDim (www.dimdim.com).

Video conferencing options are also available from:

- www.skype.com

Collaborative working

Google Docs (docs.google.com) has created an online platform to create, edit and share documents, spreadsheets, and presentations, calendars and chat all from a web-based interface.

Huddle (www.huddle.net) is another free online collaboration platform where you can share files, collaborate, manage projects and organize virtual meetings.

For more information

- NetManners.com. www.netmanners.com. A good source of information on e-mail etiquette.
- Core Rules of Netiquette. www.albion.com/netiquette/corerules.html. Extracts of guidelines for correct/accepted Internet behaviour.
- Sign Me Up!: A marketer's guide to creating e-mail newsletters that build relationships and boost sales. *By* Blumberg, M. *and others*. Return Path Books, 2005.

38. What are news groups, listservs, direct marketing and industry websites and how can I use them?

Internet technology makes it easy to send bulk mail. However, before deciding to use any of the communication methods described below, you should be aware of the dangers of spamming (i.e. sending bulk unsolicited e-mails or news group postings). Bulk unsolicited e-mail is not only annoying to potential customers, it is also illegal in an increasing number of countries, some of which impose significant penalties. All bulk e-mails must give the recipient an opt-out mechanism (such as the possibility for replying with Remove in the Subject line). Sending bulk e-mail is like cold-calling customers (making unsolicited calls), and should be treated with the same caution.

News groups

Enterprises can build up their credibility as experts by hosting news groups dedicated to the discussion of a particular subject. These are generally open to all and can be run at low cost using widely available, often free, software from an Internet server. The major drawback of Internet news groups is that they require the user to have access to newsreader software. However, this software is often built into most popular web browsers. Users must have a valid account with the Internet news server hosting the group.

Usenet news groups are public international news groups, which allow participants to discuss issues related to a particular product, service, issue or interest.

Private news groups managed on your own server or hosted by one of the many low-cost hosting services can be an effective way of building up your enterprise as a source of expert information. Many online merchants use private news groups as a forum for users of their products to exchange information, helping to cut after-sales service costs in some cases.

Google Groups (groups.google.com) has created a searchable archive of more than 700 million Usenet postings from a period of more than 20 years. You can also create your own group on Google Groups.

Listservs or electronic mailing lists

A listserv is a low-cost or no-cost means for providing instant information and updates, via e-mail, to a group of individuals who seek information on a particular product, service, issue or interest. Listservs are simply electronic lists of individuals stored in an e-mail system, who receive group or mass communication via e-mail on a regular basis. Listservs may or may not be moderated (screened for content). They may distribute digests (summaries of messages compiled according to themes) rather than individual e-mails.

The word "listserv" is now often used as a generic term for any e-mail-based mailing list application of that kind. L-Soft international, Inc. has a registered trademark for the term, and argues that it is not legal to use the term commercially except in reference to the L-Soft product; using the word in the generic sense is not a trademark infringement, but does contribute to "trademark genericide". The standard generic terms are electronic mailing list or e-mail list.

Direct marketing

E-mail address lists can be used to promote your services, advertise coming events or solicit new customers. Mailing lists can be an inexpensive way of reaching large numbers of target customers, especially for a mass market approach.

Unfortunately, many online merchants have overused this method, creating a strongly adverse user reaction to e-mail spamming. Some e-mail lists currently being sold for direct marketing purposes are random collections of mail addresses that are poorly maintained. They contain addresses, which if genuine, are frequently those of persons who have not asked to be added to the list and who do not welcome the large number of irrelevant offers, unwelcome opinions and even offensive material that they receive from the users of the list. Be very cautious about associating your company with such a list.

If you plan to use an existing e-mail list, purchase one prepared by a reputable marketing company. Here are some tips on using e-mailing lists for direct marketing:

- Ascertain whether the list contains genuine e-mail addresses, preferably of individuals who have explicitly agreed to be added to the list (opted in): many so-called opt-in lists are, in reality, lists from which the addressees have simply not opted out often because they are unable to do so. Subscribers to the list should closely fit your target group.

- Lurk to monitor the behaviour and the standards of a mailing list before posting a message.

- Test any bulk e-mail on a friendly audience before sending the mail to your target list.

- Carefully compose the subject line to encourage readers to open your message.

- Have a call to action line in your message to encourage readers to respond or visit the site; have a process in place to track any responses received.

By far the best e-mail list for direct marketing is one that you have created yourself. This need not involve much expense. You can generate your own mailing list by selecting e-mail addresses from your contact database, registrations on your website, subscriptions to your electronic newsletter, etc. If you do create your own mailing list, increase the response rate by guaranteeing that all replies will be confidential and that you will not distribute the respondents e-mail addresses.

You can draw up a simple e-mail list by following these steps:

- Create an e-mail address. If you host your own mail server it will be easy to create this address. You can also ask your Internet service provider to do this for you. Or, you could create the address at a free e-mail service such as Yahoo or Hotmail, but this will not have the same marketing impact as an address in your own domain name.

- Use a descriptive word for the new e-mail address, e.g. newsletter in the address newsletter@ourdomain.com or customer-service in the address customer-service@ourdomain.com.

- Now, place a simple MAILTO link on your company web page using an HTML tag such as HREF=MAILTO:NEWSLETTER@OURDOMAIN.COMCLICK TO SUBSCRIBE

- Add some instructions for the user in the body of your web page: To receive a free e-mail copy of our Newsletter, click on the link and enter Subscribe on the subject line of your message. There is no need for any other information. Thank you.

- [Optional] Configure your e-mail system, e.g. Outlook, to store all messages with Subscribe in the subject line to a special folder. This will keep all of your newsletter subscribers in one place, from which it will be easier to collect their addresses for future reference.

- Add the From: address in each e-mail you receive to your list of subscribers. Most e-mail software will allow you to create a group of addresses from the addresses of the mail you receive.

Remember that your customers have trusted you with their contact details. If you send them unsolicited e-mail, always offer to stop sending e-mails if they request you to do so. Honour this pledge: harassing a customer is a sure way of losing business.

Many companies offer e-mail marketing tools. Here are some examples:

- Email Marketing Director. www.arialsoftware.com.
- Group Mail. www.group-mail.com.
- Handymailer. www.handymailer.com.
- e-Campaign. www.lmhsoft.com.
- Atomic Mail Sender. www.amailsender.com.
- Topica. www.topica.com.

Industry websites

Many industry associations and government trade agencies are developing online directories highlighting their member firms' capabilities. Many of these directories have links to member firms, and these firms in turn have links to the directories and the host agencies. Some industry associations allow their affiliated firms to set up sites within the association's main site, thus enabling the firms to have their own site at lower costs.

For more information

- EmailUniverse.com. www.emailuniverse.com.

  EmailUniverse.com aims to deliver resources, directories, community, tools, tips, tricks, suggestions, ideas, and strategies to help entrepreneurs and enterprise-level people who are responsible for e-mail newsletter marketing.

- OpenSource software. www.sourceforge.net, look under the communication/e-mail section.

39. How do I organize an effective, well-attended discussion forum or virtual conference?

To use the Internet as an interactive tool, many organizations utilize discussion forums (moderated or un-moderated) and virtual conferences. There is still confusion about the various formats and their effectiveness. The best starting point is to compare an interactive Internet event with a similar live event from the point of view of objectives and resources required. For both virtual and live events, success will depend on one's objectives, resources, planning and execution. The organization of any interactive event should focus on the four aspects discussed below.

Content development and strategic orientation: Determine what kind of content you wish to develop as a result of a virtual conference and how it will be used once the event is over.

Promotion: Use real events (such as conferences), flyers, magazine articles, e-mail announcements, links to related websites, telephone calls, faxes, visits to organizations, luncheon meetings and the creation of advisory boards to encourage participation. The more high-profile the event, and the higher the expectations in terms of strategic results, the greater the investment required on promotion.

Technical support: Take into account the participants' technological know-how and the available hardware, software and national telecommunications infrastructure. Consider the organizers' ability to provide preparatory technical support before the event and help-desk support for participants during the event as well as their capabilities for monitoring participation during the event (number of hits, national origin of participants, for example).

Overall management and logistical organization: Consider the financial and human resources required for content development, promotion and the provision of technical support. Plan for the organizational resources required before, during and after the event. Do not forget post-event analysis (e.g. reports on the event) and promotion of results.

The sections that follow highlight the organizational points for various events, starting with those that require the least resources.

Un-moderated discussion forums

In an un-moderated discussion forum, messages are posted without being subjected to any screening. A user's ability to post is controlled only by the user's access permissions on the site.

Real-life parallels: Person-to-person or conference telephone calls; group meetings.

Investment required: Low.

Duration: Open.

Most appropriate use: A means of communication between live events, such as annual conferences or monthly meetings.

Contents and etiquette: Best determined by a group that meets live. Sometimes members ask the virtual forum a question to which various members reply to the whole group. Others use the virtual forum to post invitations, announcements and news of interest to all, or for the joint development of an agenda for a live meeting. Each submission may vary from two lines to a page, and attachments may be included.

Most appropriate technology: An electronic mailing list that automates mailing lists on the Internet or on any large network; also used for an automated e-mail discussion list. One organization usually offers to host the listserv, which means providing space on a computer server, creating a group e-mail address, and inputting all new addresses. Technical maintenance consists of adding or deleting relevant addresses, once or twice yearly. Social networks have also emerged over the last few years as powerful tools to manage communities and make them interact. Social networking sites such as Facebook (www.facebook.com), MySpace (www.myspace.com), or more business oriented sites such as LinkedIn (www.linkedin.com) are some examples.

Organizers should not expect to chat or to hold extensive and sustained discussions in this format. Chat groups may be interesting, as they are in real life in one's free time, but do not expect professionals on a group e-mail list to contribute significantly to an unstructured format during their working hours.

Moderated discussion forums

A moderated forum is an online forum in which all posts are pre-approved by a moderator before being posted for the group.

Real-life parallels: Seminars, workshops.

Investment required: Low to moderate financial investment; moderate human resources.

Duration: Limited, generally between one day and one month.

Most appropriate uses: To document and share experiences on a particular topic; to facilitate business-related networking; to explore client concerns and needs.

Most appropriate technology: A moderated electronic mailing list (organizers approve, reject or modify comments before putting them online); Internet forum software; collaborative platforms such as wikis or blogs (the choice depends on the technological capacities of organizers and participants)

Securing effective participation. First, choose an effective moderator. He or she must be familiar with the topic; comfortable with stimulating interaction electronically; able to provide a concise introduction, midway summary, and a conclusion reflecting the forum's discussion, and not just his or her expertise. Then, line up comments before the event starts. It is necessary to prime the pump by soliciting advance comments from various participants, or the discussion is likely to fall flat. Finally, enlist a large number of participants. In a classroom, a few individuals speak, most listen and a few do not even do that. This is also true for discussion forums. A rule of thumb is that only one in five will participate in a well-moderated forum.

Virtual conferences

The biggest advantage of virtual conferences is that they enable people from around the world to participate with no, or minimal, travel costs. Such conferences help develop common positions, lead to an understanding of client needs, stimulate networking and encourage the participation of individuals who may not dare to speak at a live conference. Because they are resource-intensive (though far less so than a live event), full-fledged virtual conferences are not held too often. People frequently assume that Internet events require little resources other than technical support platforms. As the points below indicate, conference management, promotion, contents and strategic development are required for virtual conferences as much as for live ones. In addition, organizers need to work with participants to create the appropriate conference tone and etiquette, and to ensure that suitable technical support is available.

Real-life parallel: Live conference events.

Investment: Moderate to high. This is offset by the fact that there are few or no travel costs and participation can be broader than at live conferences.

Most appropriate uses: Developing and promoting joint strategies; disseminating best practices; fostering bilateral networking; providing a collective venue for product or project announcements.

Most appropriate technology: Depends on the technology available to participants, online meeting or video conferencing software.

Securing effective participation: Put together a strategy that develops awareness among potential participants, creates interest in the event, and encourages them to participate in it. Pay attention to logistical arrangements to make the event attractive and easy for participants to follow.

Some ways of ensuring effective participation are listed below.

Develop a strong, attractive programme: Line up high-profile keynote speakers; create an advisory board, the members of which should contribute presenters, moderators and/or discussants on behalf of their organizations; identify the events (live or virtual) which have recently taken place on the same theme and ask their organizers to make a presentation in your forum on the recommendations or best practices that emerged from those events; carefully plan the sequence of presentations from speakers, so that the forum can move smoothly towards conference conclusions.

Do not leave conference interaction to chance: Before the event starts, line up a moderator, conference speakers, and individuals who will provide comments from the audience. As with moderated discussion forums, strong moderators, strong commentators and a wide base of participants are essential.

Create a sense of expectation: Develop and post a conference agenda, so that participants can anticipate contributions of special interest to them. Conduct an official opening and closing of the conference.

Promote the conference creatively: Write an announcement and request related websites to post it; ask these websites to create a link to your conference website (if available); send out very short e-mail announcements to hundreds of targeted participants; line up luncheons, office visits, telephone calls or electronic advance meetings with key speakers and moderators; encourage advisory board members to send the conference announcement to their staff, websites or magazines.

Establish conference etiquette: Train participants to make concise and readable presentations, so that the information given can be easily assimilated by busy professionals. Ensure that keynote speakers limit their contributions to 1 – 3 pages. Comments on discussions should not exceed one page. Discourage laudatory comments, and encourage substantive ones. Encourage participants to send bilateral comments to the person concerned, and not to the entire forum. Put contact information at the beginning or end of each contribution (whether from a speaker, discussant or moderator), including the name of the person concerned, his or her organization and e-mail address, to encourage the type of networking that occurs in live conferences. People may be interested in announcements on new projects or products, but this information must be inserted properly or participants will feel they are being made a target for advertisements. Keep a record of the presentations and discussions in archives on a website, for use by researchers and organizers after the event.

Free discussion forums

- Google Groups. groups.google.com. Google Groups is a service from Google that provides a platform to create discussion groups.

- Yahoo Groups. groups.yahoo.com. Yahoo Groups offers free moderated and un-moderated mailing lists.

Free virtual meetings

In addition to paid services such a Cisco WebEx (www.webex.com), GotoMeeting (www.gotomeeting.com), and Nefsis (www.nefsis.com), there are a few free alternatives such as DimDim (www.dimdim.com), and Yugma (www.yugma.com). You should note that some free service providers may not provide the same quality and stability of the well-known paid services.

Part II

USE THE INTERNET TO SELL YOUR GOODS AND SERVICES

Online procurement

40. What procurement operations can be replaced or supported by electronic means?

Standard Internet applications replace meetings with suppliers and facilitate the exchange of information. E-mail, Internet telephony (VoIP), video-conferencing and online discussion forums are easy to use and less expensive than the telephone, fax and regular mail. E-commerce applications have substantially improved purchasing and supply chain operations. Many companies say that by doing business electronically they have been able to cut procurement staff, the costs of materials, and the time it takes to select suppliers. Among the reasons for this are:

- The appearance of sector-specific market exchange and auction sites where one can identify new suppliers, purchase at attractive prices and obtain information on supply markets.

- Development of electronic purchasing platforms (also referred to as operating resources management) by multinationals. Boeing has led a group of companies in the aerospace industry to create Exostar (www.exostar.com) as solution to support the complex supply chain and security requirements of the global aerospace and defence industry.

In the wholesale and retail trade sector, the Internet can take supply chain management to a higher level, as it enables real time, remote procurement, inventory management and logistics applications [1]. For instance, the transportation and logistics sector uses the Internet to exchange information between remote locations, but also increasingly for fleet control and monitoring [1]. In European manufacturing, the Internet has become essential to remote supply chain management [2].

Some procurement operations that can be replaced by electronic means are listed below.

Procurement operation	Electronic applications	Advantages	Disadvantages	Example
Analyse markets; get latest industry insights	Sector-specific websites	Quick and easy access, free		National Agri-Marketing Association (NAMA) (www.agribusiness.com) for the agricultural sector
Identify and appraise suppliers	General and industry directories	Allow access to various suppliers		Infobel .com (www.infobel.com/teldir) for identifying and accessing firms worldwide
Operations linked to the ordering process	Internet catalogues or sell-side systems	Specific information on product and prices; free	Difficult to make comparisons between suppliers	Digi-Key (www.digikey.com) sells electronic parts
Finding suppliers	Electronic marketplace	Easy to compare suppliers		W.W.Grainger (www.grainger.com) Provides maintenance and operating products for businesses
Sourcing and purchasing items from specified suppliers and at agreed prices	Intranet catalogue or buy-side system	Simple, fast, automation possible; allows performance monitoring	Expensive to implement and maintain; demanding for suppliers	Ariba (www.ariba.com) and Perfect Commerce (www.perfect.com) are intranet catalogue software sellers
Sourcing and the ordering process	Online trading communities or portals, sell-side auctions	Good pricing; no specific system needed; strengthens commercial relationships	Not common; subjective selection of suppliers; difficult to monitor purchasing performances	McMaster-Carr (www.mcmaster.com) Supplier to industrial and commercial facilities

Procurement operation	Electronic applications	Advantages	Disadvantages	Example
Preparing the negotiation process	Electronic requests for proposal (RFP) or buy-side auctions	Competition helps to cut prices	Requires preparation; proprietary system; initial investments and fees	State of California e-procurement site (www.eprocure.dgs.ca.gov)
Managing the supply contract	Electronic networks or extranet (combined with enterprise resource planning, or ERP) Web-based ERP (combined with extranet or other services)	Single standard; can absorb many applications such as electronic data interchange (EDI); easy to use Good process integration; efficient supply chain management	Membership often restricted to larger firms; high connection costs include fees for services Initial large investment; suppliers are forced to implement a system still in evolutionary development	Cisco (www.cisco.com) runs a large supplier extranet. Openbravo (www.openbravo.com) Has an open source ERP system
Managing inventory	Web-EDI (through an extranet)	Efficient for large amounts of data; can use existing EDI connections in extranet; no maintenance; supports process streamlining	Web-EDI requires a large initial investment; not very useful for small and one-time purchases; continuous communication costs	Truecommerce (www.truecommerce.com) specializes in Web-EDI for SMEs
Managing logistics	Web-based logistic services	Cuts costs; reduces stocks; permits supply tracking	Need transporters cooperation; additional costs	DHL (www.dhl.com) like most courier services offers a tracking service
Measuring and comparing performance	Electronic surveying of suppliers and electronic benchmarking	Fast, reliable and cheap	Supplier may withhold information from buyer; the precise data needed are difficult to obtain	C3 Statitical Solutions (www.c3stats.com) for electronic surveying

There are a number of buying operations of SMEs that can be carried out over the Web. These include: obtaining technical information on parts and items; keeping up-to-date on technology trends; searching for parts; obtaining quotes from several suppliers; checking and comparing prices; checking supplier stock availability; obtaining financial information on suppliers; placing and following the progress of orders. These web operations are now being made available for an increasing number of sectors, which should be of interest to purchasers in developing countries.

For more information

- Information Economy Reports. UNCTAD. www.unctad.org.

  The Information Economy Report focuses on trends in information and communications technologies (ICT), such as e-commerce and e-business, and on national and international policy and strategy options for improving the development impact of these technologies in developing countries. It replaces the E-commerce and Development Report published by UNCTAD from 2001 to 2004.

- eMarket Services. www.emarketservices.com.

  eMarket Services is a non-profit project funded by the trade promotion organizations of Canada, Ireland, Norway, Spain and the Netherlands. Its mission is to make it easier for companies to use e-marketplaces to find new customers and suppliers for their international business. It offers a directory of e-marketplaces around the world, case studies, and industry reports.

REFERENCES

[1] ICT and e-business impact in the transport and logistics services industry. e-Business Watch, May 2008. www.ebusiness-watch.org/studies/sectors/transport_services/documents/Study_04-2008_Transport.pdf.

[2] Information Economy Report 2009: Trends and outlook in turbulent times. UNCTAD. www.unctad.org.

41. What benefits can an SME derive from using e-commerce in its supply chain?

Many companies are using the Internet and e-commerce technologies to manage their supply chain, and as a result improve its efficiency by increasing process speed, reducing costs, and increasing manufacturing flexibility. Better supply chain management enables SMEs to respond to changes in the quantity and nature of ultimate consumer demand. Here are some of the benefits that SMEs can derive from incorporating e-commerce in their supply chain:

- Small businesses often find it difficult to administer their trading and other operations. The latter can be automated to a large extent through the Internet, reducing documentation and facilitating the tracking of transactions.

- Customer-query response time and annual audit costs can be cut as transactions become easier to trace and less time is needed to update records. This will allow a small firm to concentrate on its core processes.

- E-commerce can be used to generate better and more detailed customer and supplier data. This will help with production planning and lead to improved products and services.

- Most small firms cannot afford the high costs of hiring research or consulting firms to carry out customer surveys; e-commerce will enable them to conduct their own electronic surveys.

- An e-commerce-enabled firm increases its visibility and exposure, both domestically and internationally. This will allow it to enlarge both its supply base and its customer base beyond domestic boundaries.

- Many multinationals using Internet technology in their supply chains are now requiring prospective suppliers to be Internet-enabled to be included in their lists of suppliers.

- E-commerce will enable small firms to join purchasing consortia, which provide advice on efficient purchasing and bundle purchases for their members, giving them the benefit of economies of scale, i.e. lower costs resulting from large-scale buying. Purchasing consortia are informal agreements among SMEs and they have been particularly effective in countries where there is a strong SME sector, such as Germany.

- A small firm connected to a few electronic marketplaces or auctions can be just as effective as a larger firm. The smaller firm has an advantage in that neither suppliers nor customers expect it to build complex proprietary e-commerce applications.

Dell Computer (www.dell.com) has become famous over the years for its use of the Web to sell custom configured computers. Dell has extended its e-commerce expertise to supply chain management to give customers exactly what they want. By increasing the amount of information it has about its customers, Dell has been able to reduce dramatically the amount of inventory it must hold. Dell has also shared this information with members of its supply chain. Dell's top suppliers have access to a secure website that shows them Dell's latest sales forecasts, along with other information about planned product changes, defect rates and warranty claims. In addition, the website tells suppliers who Dell's customers are and what they are buying. All of this information helps these suppliers plan their production much better than they could otherwise. The information sharing goes in both directions in Dell's supply chain: suppliers are required to provide Dell with current information on their defect rates and production problems. As a result, all members of the supply chain work together to reduce inventories, increase quality, and provide high value to the ultimate consumer [1].

For more information

- Institute for Supply Management (ISM). www.ism.ws.

  ISM's website offers a variety of educational materials, web seminars, online courses, articles, and best practices on supply chain management (SCM) and procurement, and the use of Internet technology in SCM.

REFERENCES

[1] Schneider, Gary P. Electronic Commerce. Seventh Edition. Course Technology, a division of Thomson Learning, Inc., 2007.

42.   How do I start e-purchasing operations? How much will the various options cost?

It is possible to reap the benefits of e-purchasing without an enterprise resource planning (ERP) system and without setting up an internal catalogue. Information can be obtained and transactions carried out with no major investment in technology.

Basic uses of the Internet and e-commerce for purchasing

Once you have access to the Internet, explore the different categories of sites that are available for business-to-business purchasing. You may find that the type of goods you are looking for feature on general or sector-specific independent auction sites, such GoIndustry Dovbid (www.go-dove.com) or AsiaTradeHub.com (www.asiatradehub.com), or industry-specific sales sites, such as ChemConnect (www.chemconnect.com). Any software (if at all) required to use such sites can normally be downloaded free of charge. If you purchase goods from these Internet sites, pay attention to verification requirements, and assess the offer as carefully as you would any distance purchase. Investigate whether or not you can comply with the buyer credit and reference requirements. Inspection and banking services and even transportation services can be identified through similar websites.

Non-financial considerations

Consider how your internal systems can cope with controlling purchases over the Internet and with making payments. If your suppliers are SMEs located in other countries, you could explore the possibility of using electronic fund transfers to escrow bank accounts as a means of avoiding the high costs of letters of credit.

Investing in a buying system

The alternative to searching the Web for a supplier selling the goods you require is to set up on your site a list of all the goods that you wish to purchase, a sort of open invitation to tender. Before you let potential suppliers view your list, you may want to ask them to register their company details and references. Their offer can then be collected either through a formatted table on your web page or by e-mail through an address given next to the item concerned.

Off-the-shelf buying systems can be relatively inexpensive and are generally low-maintenance, requiring little use of valuable human and financial resources. It may be possible to share the investment with other buyers and gain a more significant web presence. Some of the funds that each buyer would have used for equipment could then be devoted to advertising the site in potential supplier markets. According to a 2009 report by Forrester, the e-purchasing software market will experience a continued growth in 2009 despite the global downturn economic downturn [1]. This is a strong evidence of the tangible value of these solutions across the board.

Teaming up with suppliers

You may find that some of your suppliers have already invested in information systems and possess an Internet-based extranet. Extranets permit multiple forms of data exchange, integration of existing electronic data interchange (EDI) systems, and make possible additional functions like online auctions. Generally, an extranet link will cost very little. If the potential advantages of using the Internet to buy supplies and monitor your supply pipeline are good, but your suppliers are not yet Internet-enabled, you may find it worthwhile to help them on that path.

For more information

- Supply Chain Digest. www.scdigest.com.

  Supply Chain Digest is a weekly, online newsletter with information, news and commentary that summarizes and synthesizes important information for busy supply chain and logistics professionals.

REFERENCES

[1] TechRadar™ For Sourcing & Vendor Management Professionals: ePurchasing, Q3 2009, Forrester, 22 July 2009. www.forrester.com/Research/Document/Excerpt/0,7211,48199,00.html.

43. How can I use e-commerce to generate value in my supply chain?

E-strategies for generating value

According to a September 2009 survey by Computer Sciences Corporation (CSC), 33% of 176 survey respondents reported that they leveraged their supply chains to reduce costs by 1% to 5% in the last three years, while another 27% reported cost reductions of 6% to 10% [1].

There are many Internet stories of successful B2B applications. B2B buying consortia, industry-specific sales consortia and independent Internet trading exchanges are generating impressive benefits for their members. These include significant savings on transaction costs and reductions in inventories as a result of improved service levels and reliability. The cost savings recorded by multinational corporate buying consortia on the Internet have led many other multinationals to ask prospective suppliers to be Internet-enabled as a pre-qualification.

The most cited examples of successful implementers of supply chain Internet technology are Ford, British Telecom, General Electric and Xerox Corporations. There are many more similar operations in industries as diverse as chemicals, wood and wood pulp, electronics, health equipment, freight and logistics.

Every firm, regardless of their size, considering whether to use e-commerce in its supply chain should be aware of the following:

- Prospective suppliers need to be informed early enough to enable them to adapt their systems, inform their banks and train their personnel in regard to the new purchasing operation.

- Implementation should start with, and be limited to, a targeted segment of non-critical or long-term suppliers until the system is completely debugged.

- It is important to use a reliable Internet service provider for managing the technology; this will reduce initial investment requirements.

How can Internet technology benefit my supply chain?

The largest benefits come from reducing transaction costs and increasing the speed of information flow. Improvements to the speed of the passage and quality of information along the supply pipeline can shorten lead times, reduce inventories and work in progress. They will also enable enterprises to understand and respond better to their customers' service requirements. A common impact is the transformation of transportation services from a cost centre to a profit centre. Even companies that do not have a large transport fleet can benefit from higher load factors and fewer empty journeys.

Internet freight exchanges are now operating throughout the world, for example in the Central Asian republics, Latin America, Indonesia, the Russian Federation and the United Republic of Tanzania.

Examples of the use of e-commerce to generate value in the supply chain

- **More efficient transport operations**. Transport and freight exchanges on the Internet allow firms to maximize the use of a transportation fleet by reducing empty journeys and finding lower-cost alternatives for deliveries outside a geographic area. Container exchanges and packaging auctions also cut costs. Labels can be produced centrally and distributed electronically to remote printers. In many countries, the operations of ports, customs, shipping agents, and airline, rail and freight forwarders are coordinated across the Internet. This reduces waiting times, facilitates clearance, cuts transport fuel costs and improves delivery dependability. New enterprises have sprung up to meet demand for fast, overnight or guaranteed same-day delivery of small packets for the B2C e-commerce markets. Airline, marine and rail schedules can be viewed and reservations made via the Internet.

- **Improved transparency in supply pipeline information along the supply chain**. Quicker notice of changes in demand and the reason for those changes can prevent wasted production runs and result in higher service levels. If firms can rely on the receipt of such information, they can reduce the capital that would otherwise be tied up in safety stocks, buffer stocks and work in progress.

- **A cut in lead times**. Once e-commerce is established in a supply chain, suppliers to the firm become more responsive to the needs of the ultimate buyer. Information captured at point of sale can be collated automatically and made available for review. This reduces lead times and helps to improve product quality and design. This advantage is particularly desirable for fast-moving consumer goods and supermarket operations.

- **Reduction in transaction times and costs**. Personnel formerly engaged in time-consuming but essential contract administration can be freed to work on other value-adding activities such as customer service. Automating electronic payments and tax reporting can reduce costs for both suppliers and customers. In fact, some multinationals which have achieved dramatic savings in transaction costs through the Internet are now insisting that any new supplier should be Internet-enabled.

Case study

A British bicycle assembler imports bicycle parts for its assembly line in the United Kingdom from manufacturers in Vietnam. Parts in each category used to be shipped by the respective Vietnamese manufacturer as they came off the production line, 10 to a box, covered with cutting fluid, greased paper and straw. Each box was labelled with the British bicycle assembler's address and the producer's part number.

At the assembly plant in the United Kingdom, three persons were employed to unpack, clean, grease, label and then repack the parts on trays according to each bicycle model's bill of materials before they were taken out to the assembly line. The assembly plant used 200 to 250 trays a day.

Now, design drawings, delivery box quantities, bar code labels and pipeline information are transferred across the Internet through a link established by the British buyer. The largest of the Vietnamese manufacturers collects the parts from the other local manufacturers, and greases and pre-assembles them before packing them for shipment on single trays in boxes of up to 250 parts according to the British assembly-line requirements. The trays are labelled with the British assembler's bicycle model number and bar-codes (transmitted over the Internet), and the boxes are delivered straight to the assembly line in the United Kingdom without further handling.

In this example, the buyer and suppliers all benefit. The suppliers obtain a much higher price for their parts and attract more international customers; an expensive logistics problem in the United Kingdom has been solved; lead time has been cut; out-of-quality returns have fallen to almost zero; and assembly-line disruptions owing to part mix-ups are a thing of the past.

The benefits of Internet technology principally result from better use of information and low-cost communication.

Source: International Trade Centre, Cybermarketing (Geneva, 2000).

For more information

- Supply Chain Management Review. www.scmr.com.

  Supply Chain Management Review addresses a broad spectrum of supply chain activities, and the technology that integrates these activities to drive competitive advantage.

- Supply Chain Strategies for the Internet Era. The Boston Consulting Group. 2001. www.bcg.com/documents/file13689.pdf.

REFERENCES

[1] The seventh annual global survey of supply chain progress, Computer Science Corporation (CSC), 2009. www.csc.com.

44. Do I need to reconfigure or reorganize my supply chain to obtain optimum benefits from e-commerce?

Case studies show that engaging in e-commerce often demands a restructuring of one's supply chain.

- E-commerce renders some functions and intermediaries (such as export intermediaries and warehouses) unnecessary. For example, farmers in India now have access to information on farm prices in the large cities through the Internet terminals that are available in many villages. They have discarded the traditional traders who bought their goods at low prices and sold at large margins. The farmers now make their own arrangements for transporting their goods to, and selling them in, the cities offering the best prices.

- E-commerce enables supply chains to track goods as they go down the chain and to take advantage of cross-docking.

- E-commerce challenges the utility of long and complex supply chains. Many firms have in the past set up complex supply chains, which are unlikely to work well with new technologies. Most supply chains are built around storage capacity and physical goods. With the extra information that becomes available through electronic communication, the storage of goods may become unnecessary. If a firm masters the information flow, it can take advantage of another form of cross-docking to move goods from the production line direct to a delivery truck, or to move them to their destinations in small batches instead of in bulk. The new supply chains are constructed around the flow of information.

- An e-commerce-enabled firm is able to find better sources of supply over the Internet and can therefore modify its supply base in accordance with evolving requirements.

- E-commerce enables firms to react faster to opportunities and to become demand-driven.

Reorganizing a supply chain

A firm that is willing to reorganize its supply chain has to answer three questions. What is its strategy? Which technologies should it select? What organizational changes are required to consolidate and reinforce those technologies?

- The choice of technology follows from the choice of strategy. Every firm should use the technology that best fits the strategy (i.e. the logic of the supply chain). The table below gives examples of best and worse fits between various supply chain models and electronic solutions. If a firm's strategic objective is to bargain over prices, its buyers need to look for appropriate electronic auctions. If the firm plans to work with a single supplier over a long period, it would probably be in their best interests to invest in a joint electronic network.

Supply chain strategies and electronic solutions

Electronic supply chain	Electronic auctions and online marketplaces	Electronic network with suppliers	Internet catalogue	Intranet catalogue
Scale contract	(medium shade)	(medium shade)	(dark shade)	(black)
Cooperative	(light shade)	(black)	(white)	(medium shade)
Price-based	(black)	(white)	(medium shade)	(white)
Supplier search process	(medium shade)	(medium shade)	(black)	(dark shade)

The darker the shade the better the fit.

Source: Koppius et al. [1]

> Novartis (www.novartis.com), a Swiss pharmaceutical company, invested in an Intranet catalogue to handle 98% of its purchases of MRO (materials, repair and operations) goods and services. The catalogue has lowered purchasing costs and reduced ordering time from two days to 15 minutes. In addition to these tangible benefits, the catalogue obliges employees to buy from pre-selected suppliers, thus making purchasing cost-effective and removing the temptation to choose suppliers on the basis of personal motives.

Once the strategic options are defined and the corresponding technology is selected, the organizational changes required to reinforce these technologies need to be considered. The distribution organization should be appropriate for the technology. If a business distributes its products to retailers direct from its manufacturing sites, it may well benefit from moving to a cross-docking distribution topology, e.g. where nothing arrives at the distribution centre until it has been scheduled for departure to a customer. Cross-docking operations require tight scheduling of incoming and outgoing vehicles, information on their loads, and information on customer orders. This information is usually provided by suppliers and customers, through advance shipment notices and advance order notices, over the Internet. The advantages offered by such a demand-driven service include more focused truck fleets, fewer journeys, fewer and smaller warehouses, shorter distribution times, shorter pipelines leading to shorter working capital cycles and lower bank-loan charges.

Case study

Li & Fung (www.lifung.com) is an export trading company in Hong Kong, China, which acts as intermediary for large United States and European retailers. Li & Fung does not own physical factories, but knows what every factory in its network can produce. It saw the possibilities offered by the Internet and applied them to its network of producers of clothing and consumer goods by reorganizing its supply chain around information. When retailers order, Li & Fung develops a manufacturing schedule that it communicates to producers with spare capacity. The goods produced are then aggregated in one container for direct delivery to the retailer, eliminating the need for a warehouse. Victor Fung says: "As far as I am concerned, inventory is the root of all evil." Using advanced information technology, in particular e-commerce, Li & Fung has removed that evil.

Generally, e-commerce enables suppliers to communicate more effectively with buyers, even if they are located in separate countries with different time zones and languages. Engaging in business-to-business e-commerce should provide a supplier with opportunities for reorganizing its business to adapt to new requirements. But this has its own price. Once a buyer and supplier decide to engage in business-to-business e-commerce, they may decide to make joint investments in their Internet infrastructure to coordinate their transactions better. This requires a certain financial capacity.

For more information

- Institute for Supply Management (ISM). www.ism.ws.

  ISM's website offers a variety of educational materials, web seminars, online courses, articles, and best practices on supply chain management (SCM) and procurement, and the use Internet technology in SCM.

- The Supply Chain Council (SCC). www.supply-chain.org.

  The Supply Chain Council (SCC) is a global non-profit consortium whose methodology, diagnostic and benchmarking tools help nearly a thousand organizations make dramatic and rapid improvements in supply chain processes.

REFERENCES

[1] Electronic Sourcing Strategy. O.R. Koppius, M.J. Mol, E. van Heck and R.J.M. van Tulder. 1999. This paper presents three case studies on the relation between Internet-based technology and supply chain strategy.

45. Do generic supply chain management systems exist? What are the issues associated with their integration?

According to Wikipedia, supply chain management (SCM) is the management of a network of interconnected businesses involved in the ultimate provision of product and service packages required by end customers [1]. There have been many success stories where companies such as Dell (www.dell.com) and Cisco Systems (www.cisco.com) have been able to successfully operate solid collaborative supply networks. Several agencies of the United States Department of Agriculture have joined forces, since fall 2006, to implement a modern Web based supply chain management system using commercial off-the-shelf technology [2].

According to a research published in 2004, the five critical success factors of web-based SCM systems are [3]:

- Communication: The Internet is an effective communication tool for information sharing throughout the supply chain.

- Top management commitment: In addition to financial support, the management can also provide the psychological and behavioural support for the smooth implementation of SCM.

- Data security: SCM establishes a flow of valuable confidential trade information throughout the supply chain. Providing confidentiality and security is critical for firms to engage in SCM.

- Training and education: Adequate training of end users as well as the employees is important in allowing them to realize fully the benefits of web-based SCM.

- Hardware and software: A reliable SCM system in terms of hardware and software is essential for encouraging its use. Reliability of the SCM system affects the performance of the system, as well.

Most enterprise resource planning (ERP) products can perform most of the required tasks for SCM. ERP is a company-wide information system with different modules addressing human resource management, purchasing, inventory, production planning and other operations. SAP (www.sap.com), and Oracle (www.oracle.com) are the two main leaders of ERP solutions, with specific SCM products; SAP SCM (www.sap.com/solutions/business-suite/scm/index.epx), and Oracle SCM (www.oracle.com/us/products/applications/ebusiness/scm/index.htm).

Supply chain management systems were developed after ERP systems, and so tend to have better Internet capabilities. An SCM system is a bespoke information system that not only works across the company, but also uses links to customers and suppliers. In addition to the large ERP providers, SCM solutions are also offered by companies such as JDA/Manugistics (www.jda.com/manugistics), and i2, (www.i2.com). There are also a few open source ERP solutions available, such as Openbravo (www.openbravo.com).

SCM systems deal with five business functions: planning, buying, making, moving and selling. They are built around or on top of existing ERP systems and are therefore fully compatible with the latter systems. However, this means that users have to redesign their ERP systems to obtain the advantages of SCM.

Compatibility

Different ERP systems are generally not compatible with each other. This has proved a major problem for many enterprises. An Oracle's JD Edwards EnterpriseOne user and a SAP user cannot simply exchange files; they need a translation layer. This can be a purpose-built dedicated translation interface program between two fixed users or, more usefully, an interface to an Internet transmittable format that allows wider and more flexible access. An integration program with the Internet will translate ERP user files into Internet protocols, which follow a standard format. As long as both parties to a transaction use an integration program, the compatibility issue is restricted to the recognition of the digital vocabulary used by each party.

Developing the right translation layer is usually costly. At any rate, introducing an Internet-compatible ERP system requires not only Internet access but also well-developed computer knowledge and the assistance of external consultants, both for development and for continuous maintenance and upgrading.

For more information

- Council of supply chain management professionals (CSCMP). www.cscmp.org.

  CSCMP is developing, advancing, and disseminating supply chain knowledge and research. The website provides access to the Supply Chain Quarterly, and to several other publications, case studies, standards, and benchmarking tools.

- SearchManufacturingERP.com. searchmanufacturingerp.techtarget.com.

  SearchManufacturingERP.com provides manufacturing IT and business professionals with information on enterprise resource planning (ERP) technology and ERP best practices in the manufacturing industry.

- Panorama consulting group. www.panorama-consulting.com.

  Panorama consulting group publishes annual reports where it compares leading ERP solutions in terms of market share, implementation duration and cost, satisfaction and benefits realization.

REFERENCES

[1] Supply chain management. Wikipedia. http://en.wikipedia.org/wiki/Supply_chain_management.

[2] Web-based Supply Chain Management (WBSCM). United States Department of Agriculture. www.fns.usda.gov/FDD/WBSCM/default.htm.

[3] Ngai, E. W. T., Cheng, T. C. E. and Ho, S. S. M. Critical Success Factors of Web-based Supply Chain Management System Using Exploratory Factor Analysis, Production, Planning & Control. Vol. 5, No. 6, pages 622-630, 2004.

46. How do I access opportunities for procurement contracts with international organizations?

You should contact the local public procurement organization for advice. Your local chambers of commerce, importers associations, trading associations may also be able to advise you on how to enter the public procurement market. Another possible source is the ministry of finance, which if it handles public procurement may work through a central tender board or its equivalent. If these centralized sources of information on bidding opportunities do not exist, contact the individual ministries for information on their procurement processes. The ministries responsible for public works, education and health normally have the largest contracting requirements. See question 14: "Where can I obtain information on foreign markets?" for links to government websites.

Information on procurement at international organizations

Up to 90% of bidding opportunities in many developing countries are associated with procurement for international agency projects. The World Bank and regional banks such as the African Development Bank, European Bank for Reconstruction and Development, the Asian Development Bank and the Inter-American Development Bank provide most of the money spent in these projects through loans or grants.

The United Nations publishes the fortnightly Development Business, (www.devbusiness.com), which is available on subscription. Development Business carries information on business opportunities generated through the World Bank, regional development banks, and other development agencies. Development Business provides the following information:

- Monthly Operational Summary (MOS). This is a monthly listing all the projects being considered for financing by the World Bank and the Inter-American Development Bank; it also carries a quarterly listing of projects under consideration by the African Development Bank. MOS tracks projects from identification to loan or credit signing. Nearly 900 projects are listed, providing enough information for companies to begin marketing their services among the borrowers.

- Project approvals. This section describes projects as they are approved by the World Bank. It details the project's scope, financing arrangement, and consultancy requirements; gives the names and addresses of the implementing agencies; and provides procurement schedules for the items to be procured under the projects.

- General procurement notices (GPNs). These are issued by the borrower for projects that have international competitive bidding components, generally around the time of project appraisal, and at least eight weeks before bidding documents are available. GPNs describe the type of procurement expected to take place during project implementation. This is the earliest public notice of procurement, and signals companies to contact the borrower if they are interested in supplying the goods or services listed in the notice. Publication of GPNs in Development Business is mandatory.

- Specific procurement notices (SPNs). These are invitations to bid for specific items or works. SPNs describe the item(s) being procured and give details of purchasing bid documents, deadlines for submitting bids, and other requirements. Publication of SPNs in Development Business is mandatory for large contracts. SPNs are also published in the local press of the borrowing country.

- Contract awards. These list the successful bidders for major contracts. This information is useful in identifying firms for possible collaboration on future contract competitions.

The World Bank Procurement Group also maintains a page on the World Bank's website (www.worldbank.org/html/opr/procure/contents.html). This contains subscription information for Development Business, full texts of the Bank's procurement guidelines, general information on procurement, a list of available Standard Bidding Documents, and schedules for the Business Briefings in Washington and Paris.

Information on business opportunities is also available from the regional banks, the European Union and some countries at the following websites:

- African Development Bank: www.afdb.org
- European Bank for Reconstruction and Development: www.ebrd.org
- Asian Development Bank: www.adb.org
- Inter-American Development Bank: www.iadb.org
- Islamic Development Bank: www.isdb.org
- European Union, Tenders Electronic Daily (TED):   ted.europa.eu
- Canada, MERX: www.merx.com

47. What sources of information does the Internet provide to help buyers?

The Internet offers small and medium-sized enterprises immediate access to a vast pool of supply information. This information, when regularly collected and analyzed, will help buyers to understand their supply market, its pricing and other mechanisms. Understanding and applying market information can determine success in purchasing negotiations. Some websites offering information on specific supply markets are listed below.

Sector-specific information on market trends, suppliers and pricing

URL	Sector, owner, country, language	Information and services offered
www.agribusiness.com	Agriculture; National Agri-Marketing Association (NAMA); United States; English	Industry news and insights, electronic newsletter with latest NAMA events and other happenings.
www.manufacturing.net	Manufacturing; Advantage Business; United States; Media; English	Manufacturing information – regulations, industrial trends, plant openings and closings, supply chain updates, distribution and trade issues, prices, employment, finance, economic forecasts and world events
www.textilenews.com	Textile industry; Mullen Publications; United States; English	Textile news and news that affects the industry, including trade matters; technical developments, mill news and industry trade shows worldwide.
www.isteelasia.com	Steel; iSteel Asia; Global; English and Chinese	A secure, neutral trading platform created by and for steel industry professionals.
www.plasticsnews.com	Plastics; Crain Communications; United States; English	Commercial, financial, legislative and market-related developments worldwide that affect North American plastic product manufacturers and their suppliers and customers.
www.asiapapermarkets.com	Pulp, and paper; Vital Solutions; Global; English	Online marketplace for the pulp and paper industry focusing on Asia, Australia, Africa and the Middle East.

Trade and transportation news and services

URL	Sector, owner, country, language	Information and services offered
www.joc.com	Transportation; United Business Media; United States; English	Breaking news, analysis, sailing schedules, logistics tools, market data, blogs and links.
www.ups-scs.com/index.html	Transportation; UPS; United States; English	Services and industry solutions available from UPS Supply Chain Solutions.

It is probable that most sector-specific websites will lead buyers to discover new potential suppliers. Where no Internet sites exist for a specific supply market, where sites do not identify possible suppliers, or where additional supplier information is required, it is always possible to use country-specific electronic yellow pages or specialized directories that provide contacts, commercial and financial information on the selected supplier.

Identifying and contacting companies in any sector worldwide

URL	Sector, owner, country, language	Information and facilities offered
www.europages.com	Various sectors; Euredit; various countries and languages	European business directory.
www.kompass.com	Various sectors; Reed Elsevier; various countries and languages	Identifies companies by name or by product and provides access to the companies' contact, financial and organizational details
www.infobel.com/teldir	Various sectors; Kapitol; various countries and languages	Links to online telephone directories worldwide.

Having identified potential suppliers, buyers may also purchase over the Internet, if an electronic solution exists for their sector and for the country they wish to buy from.

Electronic marketplaces, trading communities and specialized portals: buying in specific regions of the world or from specific sectors

URL	Sector, owner, country, language	Description
www.alibaba.com	Various; Alibaba Group; worldwide; English	A global trade marketplace connecting millions of buyers and suppliers worldwide. The parent company has Chinese marketplace (www.alibaba.com.cn) for domestic trade in China, and a Japanese marketplace (www.alibaba.co.jp) facilitating trade to and from Japan.
www.mbendi.co.za	Oil, gas, chemicals, IT, mining; Mbendi Info Services; South Africa; English and French	Database of African companies, products and services and the business opportunities they offer. Provides information and links to African stock exchanges, major events and news.
www.globalcoal.com	Coal; globalCOAL; United Kingdom; English	Buying and selling coal, market information and news on the coal market.
www.chemconnect.com	Chemicals and plastics; ChemConnect; United States; English	Open market for manufacturers, buyers, and intermediaries in the chemicals and plastic products industries.
www.made-in-china.com	Various; Focus Technology; Global; English and Chinese	Connecting buyers with Chinese suppliers

Another way of purchasing cost effectively is through electronic auctions, although this is time consuming. Auctions can be sell-side auctions (where sellers advertise what they are willing to offer) or buy-side auctions (where buyers post their requirements and wait for suppliers to make commercial proposals).

Sell-side auctions

URL	Sector, owner, country, language	Description
www.farms.com	Agricultural; Farms.com; United States; English	Portal for the agricultural industry offering market information and auctions for cattle, poultry, swine, biotechnology, chemicals, feed commodities and grain.

Well-known electronic buy-side auctions

These include general auction sites (with no specific sector focus) such as Sorcity (www.sorcity.com) or AuctionBiz (www.auctionbiz.com) and specialized buy-side auctions.

More information is available on sites such as the AuctionGuide (www.auctionguide.com), the guide to auctions and auctioneers.

For more information

- Supply chain management – Modular Learning System. International Trade Centre. www.ipscm-learningnet.net/index.php.

  ITC's Modular Learning System in Supply Chain Management (MLS-SCM) programme consists of a series of training packs on supply chain management and professional certification programme available in English, Spanish and Chinese. Module 15 covers e-procurement.

Developing an e-commerce strategy

48.   What do I need to do before my company sets out to develop an e-commerce strategy?

Developing an e-commerce strategy requires careful planning and total commitment. E-commerce must be regarded as a long-term operation rather than a short-term profit-grabbing opportunity. Drawing up an e-commerce strategy will confirm whether an Internet presence is desirable for your company and when, and will enable you to make effective use of this powerful business tool.

An e-commerce strategy does not differ fundamentally from any other business plan, and before you draw one up, you must ensure that your company:

- Understands the characteristics of the online marketplace, such as the global nature of the competition, the technical and regulatory requirements for online sales, and the role that information plays in electronic trade.

- Understands its customers and their buying habits, and gauges the e-readiness of countries they reside in. These are factors that must be monitored on an ongoing basis, as they are likely to change over time.

- Has the human resources and financial and physical assets available to implement and maintain e-commerce systems

- Has the technical and supply capacity for selling products and services in a global online market.

- Has production and sales processes in place that will enable it to handle a significant increase in business.

- You must determine whether the decision to go into e-commerce is supported by all levels of management, clarify the steps in the entire process of electronic buying and selection, and identify the staff likely to be involved. It may be useful to create awareness among the staff of the potential presented by e-commerce and to train them in specific aspects of e-commerce before the strategy is drawn up. This will give you and your company a clearer idea of what e-commerce involves.

For more information

- Australian e-business guide. www.e-businessguide.gov.au.

  The e-business guide website provides information and resources about e-business for small businesses in Australia and for those who advise them. It is an initiative of the Australian Government. It includes advice, tools, and case studies.

- Business Link. www.businesslink.gov.uk.

  The Business Link, in partnership with Business Gateway in Scotland and Invest Northern Ireland, supports new and existing SMEs by providing information, advice, and tools.

- SME Toolkit. www.smetoolkit.org.

  The SME Toolkit is a programme of the International Finance Corporation (IFC), a member of the World Bank Group, and is available in multiple languages through local partners around the world. Through its website, SMEs can access business resources, training, information, and links to various free online training, and website builder software.

- Industry Canada. www.ic.gc.ca.

  The Industry Canada website provides various business tools and resources for e-commerce. In addition it contains information on companies, statistics, financing, innovation, research, regulations and standards, sustainability and environment, as well as trade and investment.

49.   What are the essential elements of the e-commerce strategy of an enterprise?

A well-prepared strategy should include an assessment of the online sales potential of the product or products concerned, an estimate of the investments required to establish and develop the business, a plan for running the business and for measuring its progress, and an indication of the expected return on investment. It should facilitate an application for financing. In your e-commerce strategy you should evaluate the online sales potential of your product to other businesses (B2B), and retail online sales (B2C), separately.

The core elements of a business strategy for e-commerce are the following:

- *Executive summary*: You should write this important part after the rest of the plan has been completed. Your prospective investors will probably only read this part in your first contacts with them. It is the place for a brief, straightforward and factual presentation of your plan. If the summary attracts the interest of investors, there will be plenty of opportunity later to demonstrate your enthusiasm for your project. State what makes your firm successful, and then list its advantages over competitors that already have a presence on the Internet.

- *Objectives:* Define your long-term goals and determine how e-commerce will help you to attain those goals.

- *Orientation:* State how you want to use the Internet.

- *Present situation:* Identify the products that will sell well over the Internet and give the reasons why.

- *Set the criteria for an evaluation of your web operations*. These could include the number of hits per month, number of pages viewed, number of non-repeat visitors, number of actual contacts, number of transactions, and number of orders.

- *Promotion:* Describe how you intend to promote your website.

- *Market analysis:* Describe the opportunities in the e-commerce market for your firm.

- *Existing competition*: Present the findings of your analysis of the existing competition and of your firm's competitiveness within the industry. List the websites of all major and minor competitors. What is the estimated market share of each competitor? What are the expected trends in your industry for e-commerce?

- *Target customers:* Present the demographic and socio-economic profile of the customers you expect to target online. Why do you believe they will purchase from you over the Internet?

- *Research on a focus group:* Present the findings of your research on a small focus group of potential customers from the target market. This research should have enabled you to gain a feedback on your product's sales potential in an online environment.

- *Calculated risk:* Present your projections for the performance of your industry and your firm over the next three to five years, both online and offline.

- *Marketing strategy:* Show how you intend to attract online customers, importers, agents, wholesalers to do business with you, and how their interest is to be sustained.

- *Content:* Set out the elements you intend to include on your site.

- *Advertising:* Present your advertising plans. These should take account of foreign labelling and packaging requirements, translation issues, customer relations, culturally sensitive advertising and semantic barriers.

- *Public relations:* Set out your plan for a regular and consistent product/service update programme. This could provide for an electronic newsletter, writing for technical magazines, press releases, organizing customer get-togethers, and hosting online discussion groups.

- *Sales strategy:* Details to present include:
  - **Pricing/profitability**: Work out an international pricing strategy for selling, distributing and buying online.
  - **Order and payment processing**: How will orders be taken, by telephone, fax, mail, online? How will payment be made, by mail, online, bank-to-bank transfers?

- **Methods of distribution**: Determine where and how to deliver abroad. How will confirmation of orders and shipment be sent?
- **Sales promotion tactics**: Will the product or service be promoted only online or also with the aid of traditional tools, e.g. direct mailing, e-mail, cold calling, print, radio and television advertising?

- *Service:* Would you provide service, if required, to your customer after the sale is completed?

- *Business relationship:* Draw up a plan for this, and determine the type of relationship to be established (e.g. agent/distributor) for developing international business relationships, including aspects such as cross-cultural training.

- *Integration:* Outline how your systems will integrate with the systems used by your bank, customers, suppliers and distributors.

- *Manufacturing plan:* Indicate initial volume, expansion requirements, source of materials, manufacturing sites.

- *Financial projections:* Be realistic and conservative.

- *Twelve-month budget:* Anticipate costs for the first year of your plan.

- *Cash-flow projection:* Calculate cash receipts and cash disbursements.

- *Five-year plan:* Provide a five-year profit-and-loss forecast.

- *Balance sheet:* Show the firm's liquidity and cash position.

- *Break-even analysis:* Calculate number of units that need to be sold to break even.

- *Source and use of funds:* State where financing is to be obtained to start or expand the export operation.

- *Use of proceeds:* Show how profits and loans will be used.

- *Conclusions:* Restate basic e-commerce goals, total capital required, profit expected, business schedule, and general comments.

- *Appendix:* Include the curriculum vitae of key individuals involved in the plan; list key accounts, potential customers; provide market survey data, drawings, agreements and financial projections for the plan.

For more information

- The e-commerce fitness checker. International Trade Centre – Enterprise Competitiveness. www.intracen.org/ec/.

  This ITC self-assessment tool is designed to check on an enterprise's electronic commerce readiness and identify possible gaps in planning. This checklist is also of use to enterprises already engaged in e-commerce.

- Chaffey, D. E-business & E-commerce Management: Strategy, Implementation & Practice. FT Press, August 2009.

- Jelassi, T. Strategies for E-Business: concepts and cases (2nd Edition). Prentice Hall, August 2008.

  This book utilises extensive research, strategic frameworks, a methodological toolset and original real-world case studies to link e-business to overall corporate strategy.

- Australia e-business guide, tools. www.e-businessguide.gov.au/resources/tools.

  This website contains many tools for use by businesses and e-business advisers. There are template documents, sample spreadsheets and checklists throughout the website. This page is a collection of some key tools for quick access.

50.   What traps should I avoid when developing an e-commerce strategy?

Not seeking advice: Firms that are new to e-commerce or seeking to expand into an unfamiliar foreign market often fail to obtain expert advice before developing their e-commerce plans.

Not obtaining management commitment: You should ensure that your top management is firmly committed to the development of the plan. All the company's functional divisions – management, administration, finance, marketing, production, and training – should be involved in its formulation, though one person should be assigned the overall responsibility for this. Such an overall view will facilitate this person's subsequent task of obtaining the approval of, and financial support from, your financial partners for the implementation of the plan.

Not conducting solid market research: Online market research has made it easier than ever before to study any country's demographic, political and socio-economic conditions; to pinpoint trade leads, import/export opportunities by industry, country and product; to identify foreign importers of specific products; and locate sources of information on markets and e-commerce marketing techniques. Use traditional sources as well, particularly if you have not previously sold your product in other countries. You may want to conduct research in small focus groups of target customers to elicit comments on the desired characteristics of your product, as well as to ascertain their interest in, and experiences with, purchasing on the Internet. If you are not already exporting, you may want to send samples of your products, or have your representative take samples to your prospective markets and ask for customer evaluations. You may also want to study the unique preferences of groups of potential foreign customers.

Not analysing market research findings: E-commerce strategies should be based on sound market research and analysis. The analysis should confirm whether or not your product is suitable for sale on the Internet and whether or not it will sell in certain markets; whether your product design, size, colour or colour combinations and other characteristics will be attractive to specific markets; or whether it will meet the unique preferences of groups of potential foreign customers.

Question 55 What factors should I assess to help me in my choice of markets?") outlines a market factor assessment (MFA) tool for use in the development of an e-commerce strategy. The MFA is a diagnostic of demographic, political, economic, social, consumer and competitive factors. It enables a firm to rate each potential market on a market-condition scale. While country-by-country strategies are essential in the context of a general export development strategy, it is also important to consider individual firms when you are dealing with e-commerce. No matter how highly a country may rate in the MFA, a particular firm can be unsuitable, and conversely, you may find a good customer who can overcome many of the problems of a lower-ranked country.

Not determining export and import flows (industry analysis): Many firms find it difficult to obtain information on countries exporting and importing particular products. For exporters to target their e-marketing message and to succeed in a particular market, it is essential to determine whether their product will be competitive. There are many sources of information on competitive opportunities in a market. The best, but most expensive, is to talk to customers, or to agents, wholesalers and retailers in the marketplace – especially if you will be selling or delivering products through them. E-mail, a low-cost communication tool, may be of some help here, but you will need to find the right person to reach by e-mail, and to compose a message that is likely to get the sort of answer you need. If you are lucky, finding the right e-mail contact can be as simple as looking through the contact points on the websites of agents, customers, wholesalers and retailers. More often, however, you will need to make several attempts to reach the right person. Other sources of information are: the International Trade Centre (www.intracen.org), which maintains extensive databases of trade information and directories of sources of information at the country, industry and product level; government agencies (such as ministries of trade); and industry associations (chambers of commerce) in your country and in the importing country.

Not determining the optimum export price: Product pricing is important to your financial projections. Many first-time or infrequent exporters do not consider the various non-domestic costs that can contribute to the unit price. Each element of the e-commerce plan should be addressed in your financial projections and in your three-year budget. Among the elements to consider in your pricing strategy for international e-commerce are the following:

- Web design
- Website updating
- Website monitoring for messages
- Web order processing

- Inland freight charges
- Unloading at terminals
- Insurance
- Translation

- Electronic marketing
- Percentage mark-up
- Sales commissions
- Freight forwarding fees
- Financing costs
- Letter-of-credit processing fee
- Export packing charges

- Credit terms
- Payment schedules
- Payment currencies
- Commission rates
- Warehousing costs
- After-sales servicing
- Cost of replacing damaged goods.

Not acknowledging how buyers make decisions: It is important to address how buyers make purchasing decisions on the Internet. The most important factor in a buyer's decision to purchase, online or offline, is whether or not he or she trusts the seller; every effort should therefore be made to ensure that your site projects your trustworthiness.

Overall marketing communications: Many first-time e-commerce businesses are passive rather than active, selling only because someone from another country contacts them. Firms often fail to sell online because they do not know about the low-cost, or no-cost, marketing opportunities available to them. In addition to the usual online marketing techniques, the best marketing opportunities are provided by: catalogues listing indigenous products; international buyer programmes; agent/distributor services; catalogue exhibitions; and trade associations.

Not checking the buyer's creditworthiness: Before agreeing to any deal, it is essential to verify the creditworthiness of a potential buyer, distributor or partner. A chamber of commerce or similar source in the buyer's country will supply a business reference, but this is not a credit reference. A small business should not extend traditional trade credit for online sales to unknown firms. If possible, use an escrow service or insist on the use of major credit cards (VISA, Master Card, American Express, etc.)

Choosing methods of distribution: Many firms use direct e-commerce as their only means of conducting international business. A website will give the small enterprise maximum control over marketing, financing and market growth. However, other methods of advertising, marketing and distribution exist. These include appointing a commissioned e-commerce sales agent, letting an e-commerce management company handle sales, appointing an online sales representative, negotiating a distribution agreement, a licensing joint venture, and offshore production. In addition to helping exporters to implement successful e-commerce strategies, these methods will enable them to benefit from the know-how and contacts of a partner experienced in e-commerce.

The world of ecommerce is changing so rapidly that if your original idea or strategy is not working you have to be ready to abandon that concept and develop a new one to succeed. Fortunately, the fast pace of ecommerce also enables you to put a new plan into effect very quickly [1].

For more information

- How to start a business. eBusiness-Resource.com. www.ebusiness-resource.com. 2009.

  eBusiness-Resource.com is a free website where you can find answers on how to start a successful online business. It covers topics such as business model, business strategy, business plan, and implementation.

- Entrepreneur. www.entrepreneur.com.

  The Entrepreneur website and the Entrepreneur Magazine provide business advice and cover the latest trends in management, sales, marketing, technology and money – highlighting products, services and strategies that will help readers to run better businesses. Resources on business strategy may be found under the "Starting a Business", and "Starting an Online Business" options from the main menu.

REFERENCES

[1] Pierce, K. How to Avoid 7 Fatal Ecommerce Mistakes. Volusion e-Commerce Blog, February 2009. onlinebusiness.volusion.com/articles/avoid-ecommerce-mistakes.

51.   What are some e-commerce lessons, challenges and solutions for developing countries?

Many aspects of the Internet are still evolving rapidly, but businesses in developing countries should not wait to introduce this revolutionary tool. Instead, they should take advantage of the lessons learned by those who have already begun to use the Internet.

Lessons

- Link the use of the Internet to your organization's main business goals. Senior management should drive electronic business, rather than relegate the task to IT technicians.

- Ensure that you have the resources for marketing and maintenance and not just for the design and installation of your site. Some experts suggest that a third of the resources should be dedicated to start-up costs, another third to promotion, and the final third to updating and maintenance.

- According to a 2008 consumer report by Nielsen, books are still the most popular purchases online, followed by clothing/accessories/shoes, videos / DVDs / games, airline tickets and electronic equipment [1]. Products such as computers, cars and electronic appliances are now also being sold through the Internet. Some products are even suitable for sales and delivery via the Internet only. Digital music (as opposed to CDs), e-books (as opposed to printed ones), downloadable software, travel services and financial services are at the forefront of e-commerce

- The Internet can be used to reduce communication costs, foster closer links between organizations in different locations, store and utilize business and contact information, and streamline purchasing and supply management.

Challenges

- Gaps in the telecommunications infrastructure.

- The need to develop sites with local content, services and information in order to respond to customer needs in specific local markets.

- Translation difficulties.

- Adapting existing laws to this new medium.

- Costs of installation and access.

- Limited supply of computers in developing countries.

- Limited Internet access owing to little or no availability of local Internet service providers (ISPs).

- Increased marketing costs to obtain qualified traffic.

A frequently cited constraint to engaging in e-commerce is inadequate infrastructure. According to a recent ITU report, only a little more than a quarter of the world's population are using the Internet, and have access to a computer at home[2]. Furthermore, according to UNCTAD's Information Economy Report 2009, mobile access has become the most equitably distributed information and communications technology (ICT) [3]. This report indicates that while the distribution of fixed telephone lines has not become much more equitable since 2005, Internet access has. This implies that the users in developing countries, especially those countries where the fixed telephone line infrastructure is less developed, have turned to alternatives such as mobile and wireless for Internet access. It is hoped that wireless technologies, and particularly WiMAX, which promises to provide high-speed connectivity over a range of up to 50 km, will help fill infrastructure gaps in rural and poorly served areas.

The price of ICT services is another constraint. Unfortunately, the relative price for ICT services is highest in Africa, the region with the lowest income levels. The price for fixed broadband access remains prohibitively high in most developing countries, effectively limiting access.

There is still a dramatic broadband divide, with very few fixed and mobile broadband subscriptions in Africa [2]. There are substantial differences within regions as well. The US accounts for 82.6% of mobile broadband in the Americas. In Asia and the Pacific, Japan and the Republic of Korea account for 70%.

Finally, traditional export and distance-selling problems also apply when selling via the Internet. These cover such areas as labelling, shipping, return of goods, warehousing or stock management, payment collection and legal action, and export-related paperwork.

Solutions

For more information on how to address common challenges of establishing e-commerce please refer to the following questions:

- Question 15: "Where can I access market research on my sector?"

- Question 19: "How have some small companies fared from the use of the Internet as a marketing tool?"

- Question 22: "How do I get my website translated accurately?"

- Question 55: "What factors should I assess to help me in my choice of markets?"

- Question 56: "If my country's telecommunications infrastructure is inadequate, what are my e-commerce options?"

- Question 60: "What financial costs, both hidden and unhidden, of e-commerce should I be aware of?"

- Question 68: "Are there international or national legal frameworks for e-commerce?"

For more information

- Information Economy Reports. UNCTAD. www.unctad.org.

  The Information Economy Report focuses on trends in information and communications technologies, such as e-commerce and e-business, and on national and international policy and strategy options for improving the development impact of these technologies in developing countries. It replaces the E-commerce and Development Report published by UNCTAD from 2001 to 2004.

- OECD Information Technology Outlooks. Organisation for Economic Co-operation and Development (OECD). www.oecd.org/document/20/0,3343,en_2649_33757_41892820_1_1_1_1,00.html.

  OECD Information technology outlook reports analyse the recent developments in the IT industry and its impact on the economy.

REFERENCES

[1] Trends in online shopping – A global Nielsen consumer report. Nielsen, February 2008. th.nielsen.com/site/documents/GlobalOnlineShoppingReportFeb08.pdf.

[2] The World in 2009: ICT Facts and Figures. International Telecommunication Union, 2009. www.itu.int/ITU-D/ict/.

[3] Information Economy Report 2009: Trends and outlook in turbulent times. UNCTAD. www.unctad.org.

52.   What products will consumers seek to purchase online?

Consumers are now purchasing a wide variety of products online and, as mentioned in earlier chapters, even when not purchasing online many Internet users search for products and compare prices. Many customers in a wide range of business fields expect the products or services they are interested in to be available online, including consumer goods, financial services, tickets for download or supplies they need for their business [1].

Regarding the most frequently purchased items, according to e-Business W@tch for 2005 similar types of products are being purchased in various European countries [2].

More than 85% of the world's Internet users surveyed have purchased something online, according to The Nielsen Online "Global Online Survey on Internet Shopping Habits," conducted in October and November 2007. The report indicates that more than half of Internet users had made at least one purchase online within the past month [3].

- The number of Internet users who have purchased something online, by region, in October-November 2007 (as percentage of respondents) [3]:
- Western Europe: 93%
- North America: 92%
- Asia-Pacific: 84%
- Latin America: 79%
- Eastern Europe, Middle East and Africa: 67%
- Worldwide: 86%

More than 4 out of 10 online buyers worldwide (41%) had purchased books from a web merchant within the last quarter of 2007. Clothing (36%) was the next most popular online purchasing category. Travel was the fourth most popular online purchasing category (airline tickets/reservations 24%) [4].

Travel is often one of the first retail categories to succeed in developing e-commerce economies, according to eMarketer. Positive consumer experiences booking travel online creates confidence that can lead to purchases in other more complex e-commerce categories [4].

Few other categories in consumer online purchase are:

- Computer-related products
- Music and films
- Consumer electronics
- Tickets for sporting and entertainment events
- Subscriptions to online publications

Research has shown that product-specific success factors include having a strong brand, selling a unique product and offering competitive prices online.

Products that buyers prefer to touch, smell, or examine closely can be difficult to sell using electronic commerce. For example, customers might be reluctant to buy items such as high-fashion clothing or antique jewellery if they cannot closely examine the products before agreeing to purchase them.

An interesting issue is the extent to which it is possible to change the purchasing behaviour of consumers and businesses. Perhaps it is easier for businesses to change to reduce costs, improve delivery time, communicate with suppliers, and to attain efficiencies in ordering, shipment and delivery. Furthermore, perhaps the incidence of business-to-business purchasing is higher because it is so distinctly unlike a traditional personal shopping experience. It is important to question whether consumers want to wander around big bazaars, shops in local town centres, malls and grocery stores, or whether they would prefer to shop online so they can spend more time on leisure or with the family.

For more information

- ClickZ Network. www.clickz.com.

  The ClickZ Network is the largest resource of interactive marketing news, information, commentary, advice, opinion, research, and reference in the world, online or off. From search to e-mail, technology to trends, coverage is expert, exclusive, and in-depth.

REFERENCES

[1] The European e-Business Report 2008. 6th Synthesis Report of the Sectoral e-Business Watch. www.ebusiness-watch.org.

[2] Overview of International e-Business Developments, The European e-Business Market Watch. July 2005. www.ebusiness-watch.org.

[3] Global Online Survey on Internet Shopping Habits. The Nielsen Company, 28 January 2008. www.nielsen.com.

[4] World's Web Users Are Shopping Online. eMarketer. 1 February 2008. www.emarketer.com/ Article.aspx?R=1005884.

53.   What services sell well on the Internet and why?

The services that are being sold successfully on the Internet include the following:

- Accounting
- Advertising
- Auction services
- Commercial education and training
- Computer services and software
- Customs brokering
- Financial services
- Health (telehealth)
- Insurance
- Market research
- Personnel search
- News and broadcasting
- Travel and tourism
- Translation
- Website design and maintenance
- Management consulting
- Education
- Print and graphic design services
- Writing services of all kinds (freelance journalism, technical writing, editing, etc.)

A quick search using a major search engine such as Yahoo or Google will reveal many more categories of services being supplied across the Web.

The success of a services business on the Internet depends on some of the same elements that make any business successful, such as the degree to which the products of the business meet a market need. However, services businesses are particularly suited to the Internet because their products tend to be produced or delivered with digital information processes. Most service businesses involve the collection, storage, manipulation and dissemination of information.

Digital information can be collected and disseminated at lower cost using the Internet than by any other means. Telecommunications services are among the most successful users of the Internet. Voice over IP services using the Internet Protocol to transmit voice telephony over data channels is one area of rapid growth, including in remote parts of the globe.

The low cost of Internet communications is also one of the reasons why Internet personnel-search processes have been so successful: they offer much lower costs to the advertiser and a wider distribution than is possible with a print-advertising campaign. They also offer much lower search costs to people seeking jobs: they are able to pinpoint a larger selection of potential employers than is usually available in the print media. These savings on both sides of an information search and dissemination exchange tend to grow rapidly as the information exchange network grows.

Internet processes can also add a dimension of customer service that no other information medium offers, such as direct access to value-added information without going through an intermediary. This partly explains the success of online travel booking services. By eliminating the intermediary, the travel service reseller is able to cut final prices to the consumer.

Suppliers of services need to bear in mind, however, that where a service (including most of the services listed above) has personal components, such as the requirement to adapt a product to personal preferences, or the need for detailed consulting advice, these components are unlikely to be delivered exclusively through the Internet.

The practice of some Internet merchants of making a real person available to offer consumer assistance or to respond to consumer questions at the time of sale is a reminder that many business services (retail services in this case) have a strong consulting and interpersonal component. The Internet as a medium can certainly help with the delivery of this component, but is only slightly more suited for this purpose than, say, the telephone.

As expected the total advertising spending has plunged with the financial downturn. But the Internet has withstood recessionary pressures far better than other media, especially in mature markets such as France and Germany in Western Europe [1]. Because of the recession, however, online ad spending in the United States dropped 5.3% to $10.9 billion during the first half of 2009. A report by Interactive Advertising Bureau and PricewaterhouseCoopers in October 2009 shows that spending in the second quarter fell 5.4% to $5.4 billion from the year-earlier period, and was roughly flat with the $5.5 billion total for the first quarter of 2009 [2].

For more information

- European Travel Commission. New Media Trend Watch. www.newmediatrendwatch.com.

  New Media Trend Watch is a source for e-commerce statistics and buying trends.

- Export.gov. www.export.gov.

  Export.gov brings together resources from across the U.S. Government to assist businesses in planning their international sales strategies and succeed in the global marketplace.

- World Advertising Research Centre. www.warc.com.

  WARC gives access to thousands of case studies, articles and best practice guides, market intelligence, ad forecasts, brand profiles, conference reports.

REFERENCES

[1] von Abrams, K. Online Ad Spending in Western Europe. eMarketer. October 2009. www.emarketer.com/Report.aspx?code=emarketer_2000609.

[2] Internet Ad Revenues at $10.9 Billion for First Half of '09. Interactive Advertising Bureau. October 2009. www.iab.net.

54.   What factors determine which products or services will sell well on the Internet?

A survey conducted by Nielsen in October and November 2007, indicates that more than 85% of the world's Internet users surveyed have purchased something online. The report also found that more than half of Internet users had made at least one purchase online within the past month [1].

During the same period, manufacturers and merchant wholesalers relied far more heavily on e-commerce than retailers or selected service businesses. For instance Business-to-business (B2B) activity in the United States alone accounted for 93% of e-commerce transactions, in 2007 [2].

For success in online sales, both B2B and B2C, the following points should be taken into consideration:

Use of unique terms to describe the product or service. If your product or service can be characterized or described in unique terms, it will fare better on the Internet because it will be easier to find with the aid of search engines. It is also important to refer to your product or service with the combination of terms that searchers are likely to use when looking for your type of product, and to ensure that these terms appear with sufficient frequency on the web pages that you have asked your search engines to index.

Competitive pricing. Where the Internet helps customers to compare prices for identical goods, the goods priced lowest will sell the most. Also, for all products, online prices may have to be lower than in-store prices to create an incentive to overcome the consumers' lack of trust in online retailers, due in part to the absence of a personal exchange in the transaction, and to compensate for the customers' inability to take the product with them.

The touch factor. Consumers continue to want to touch, see, smell or try a product as well as talk to someone about it before they buy. Sellers will need to make many of their products available at retail outlets or other physical settings where consumers can see and touch them before they return to the Internet to make the purchase.

Uniformity of product. Manufactured and mass-produced goods are easier to sell online than handmade or custom-produced items. Manufactured goods are more consistent in their characteristics, have predictable production costs and are generally better known to consumers.

Non-immediate needs. Consumers are more likely to order non-urgent consumables online, rather than goods they need immediately. Manufacturers that are able to work to pre-set production, shipping and delivery schedules are also more likely to use the Internet for their procurement purposes.

Consumer understanding of the product. It is believed that B2B commerce on the Internet will increase faster than consumer purchases from e-commerce firms (with the exception of the largest of these firms, such as Amazon). The reason for this is that, unlike many consumers, businesses are familiar with the specifications of the products they need and are therefore more comfortable with ordering on the Internet.

Regularly purchased products. Standardized products purchased on a regular basis (groceries, children's clothing, office supplies, books, etc.) are familiar to consumers and therefore easier to purchase over the Internet. Such purchasing will save them time and relieve them of some of the boredom of repetitive shopping.

For more information

- ClickZ Network. www.clickz.com.

  The ClickZ Network is the largest resource of interactive marketing news, information, commentary, advice, opinion, research, and reference in the world, online or off-line.

- World Advertising Research Centre, www.warc.com.

  WARC gives access to thousands of case studies, articles and best practice guides, market intelligence, ad forecasts, brand profiles and conference reports.

REFERENCES

[1] Global Online Survey on Internet Shopping Habits, The Nielsen Company, 28 January 2008. www.nielsen.com.
[2] The 2007 E-commerce multi-sector "E-Stats" report, U.S. Census Bureau, 28 May 2009. www.census.gov/econ/estats/.

55.   What factors should I assess to help me in my choice of markets?

Market research will help you to determine which foreign markets have the best potential for your products. You should select a few target markets on the basis of such factors as their demographic, physical, political, economic, social and cultural environments; market accessibility; and the opportunities they offer for your products. Assessing these and other relevant market factors, referred to as market factor assessment, will help you to estimate demand for your products or services and to assess how well your firm will perform in specific markets. In order to arrive at a final selection of two or three foreign markets, it is important for you to assess up to 10 countries that appear to offer import opportunities for your product. To carry out a market factor assessment, you should ask the following questions:

- What is the overall population of the country and its growth and density trends?
- Is the population of targeted age groups adequate (e.g. 1-10, 11-24, 25-40, 41-60, etc.)?
- How is the population distributed between the urban, suburban, and rural areas?
- Are there climatic and weather variations that may affect your product or service?
- What is the shipping distance from your point of export to the country?
- What is the average age and quality of the country's transportation and telecommunications infrastructures?
- Are there adequate shipping, packaging, unloading and other local distribution networks?
- Is the system of government conducive to conducting business?
- To what degree is the government involved in private business transactions?
- What is the government's attitude to importing?
- Is the political system stable or do governing coalitions change frequently?
- Does the government seek to dismantle quotas, tariffs and other trade barriers?
- Is the country committed to fostering higher levels of foreign trade?
- Is the market closed to foreigners, despite a free and open appearance?
- What are the country's GNP and balance of payments?
- What is the percentage share of imports and exports in the overall economy?
- What is the country's import-to-export ratio?
- What is the country's inflation rate and what are its currency or exchange regulations?
- What is its per capita income? Are income levels increasing?
- What percentage of the population is literate? What is the average educational level achieved?
- What percentage of the population is identified as middle class?
- Will the product or service need translation or adaptation?
- What legal aspects affect distribution agreements in the country?
- What are the documentary requirements and import regulations affecting your product?
- What intellectual property protection laws will apply to your product?
- Does the judicial system offer a fair and unbiased review of commercial disputes?
- Are tax laws fair to foreign investors? What is the rate of tax on repatriated profits?
- Is there an identified need for your product in the country?
- What percentage of the product is produced in the country and what percentage is imported?
- Is the product or service understood and accepted by country?
- How many foreign competitors are in the country now? From which regions?

After carrying out research on several countries to obtain answers to the questions listed above, rate each country according to a market condition scale of 1 (poor) to 5 (excellent), and enter the points in a table similar to the one below. Sum up the points. The higher the score, the greater the likelihood that the country concerned will offer a suitable market for your products.

MARKET FACTOR ASSESSMENT TABLE

Market factor	Country 1	Country 2	Country 3	Country 4
Demographic/physical environment				
Population: size, growth, density				
Age distribution				
Urban and rural distribution				
Climate and weather variations				
Shipping distance and frequency				
Air freight facilities				
Physical distribution and communication network				
Regional and local transportation facilities				
Political environment				
System of government				
Government involvement in business				
Attitudes to foreign trade				
Political stability and continuity				
Fair/free trade mindset				
National trade development priorities				
Economic environment				
Overall level of development				
Economic growth: GNP, balance of payments				
Percentage share of imports/exports in overall economy				
Inflation rate				
Currency and foreign exchange regulations				
Per capita income: current status, distribution and potential for growth				
Disposable incomes				
Expenditure patterns				
Social and cultural environment				
Literacy rate, educational level				
Existence of middle class				
Similarities/differences relative to home market				
Language barriers				
Market access				
Adequate distribution network				
Documentation requirements and import regulations				
Local standards, practices and non-tariff barriers				
Patents, trademarks, copyright protection				
Adequate dispute resolution mechanisms				
Tax laws, rates				
Product potential				
Customer needs and desires				
Domestic production, imports, consumption				
Exposure to, and acceptance of, product				
Attitude to products of foreign origin				
Competition				

(Adapted from The Basics of Exporting [1])

For more information

- Beall, Anne. Strategic Market Research: A Guide to Conducting Research that Drives Businesses. IUniverse, November 2008.

- Market Research World. www.marketresearchworld.net.

  Market Research World, previously Market Research Portal, offers a host of online resources and research-related articles relevant to market research buyers, researchers, newcomers to the industry, students and individuals with an interest in the market research industry.

- B2B International. *www.b2binternational.com*.

  B2B International is a market research consultancy specializing in business-to-business research. The website offers various valuable resources such as interactive tools, industry links, articles, white papers, podcasts, e-book, and case studies.

 **REFERENCES**

[1] The Basics of Exporting. Southern United States Trade Association. www.susta.org.

56. If my country's telecommunications infrastructure is inadequate, what are my e-commerce options?

Even if the telecommunications infrastructure in your country is not well developed there are still many ways that you can benefit from the potentials of the Internet, and e-commerce.

Many non-governmental and non-profit organizations provide artisans and service providers in developing countries access to global markets. They pay cash for the products concerned and take responsibility for promotion and shipping. With a focus on art and handicrafts, a group such as Novica (www.novica.com), is a good example.

Some import promotion programmes offer a section on their website for companies to place their product details. One good example is the Danish Import Promotion programme (www.dipp.eu), which aims to assist exporters in Africa, Asia and Latin America who wish to enter the Danish market. DIPP also provides market information concerning the Danish market to exporters and business support organizations in developing countries.

When the infrastructure in your country is not ready yet, you may be able to host your e-commerce site in another country, either with a web hosting service in that country or using a service provided by another company. Yahoo Small Business (smallbusiness.yahoo.com) is one example that offers various hosting plans, including e-commerce plans, for small businesses.

In many developing countries where Internet access is not commonly available, or is too expensive to be used by SMEs, especially in rural areas, the problem has been addressed by building sites offering collective access points. These are known as multipurpose community telecentres. Many such telecentres have been built in remote locations around the world by entities such as:

- The United Nations Development Programmes (UNDP) Sustainable Development Networking Programme: www3.undp.org. This programme is now closed and the site is available for information purposes only.

- The United Nations Educational Scientific and Cultural Organization (UNESCO): www.unesco.org.

- The International Institute for Communication and Development: www.iicd.org.

- The International Development Research Centre of Canada – PAN Asia Networking programme: www.idrc.ca/pan.

The United Nations Asia Pacific Training Centre for Information and Communication Technology for Development (APCICT) page contains resources on all aspects related to telecentres, for telecentre operators, telecentre project managers, trainers, policymakers and researchers: www.unapcict.org/ecohub/resources/browse-resources/telecentres.

Some consultancies, such as Telecommons, www.telecommons.com, specialize in establishing connections in remote areas at minimal costs.

Merchants seeking international e-commerce without having well-developed local telecommunications facilities may be able to use satellite communications to link to international networks. The World Bank has funded a number of trials of this technology, including in certain African countries. Some commercial vendors are also making the technology available in rural areas in both developed and developing countries. Several vendors of private satellite services are actively pursuing this market. If appropriate satellite signal coverage is available, the investment required (in a modem, satellite dish and signal processing equipment) is not too large. Furthermore, advanced technical skills will not be essential to maintain the site. A list of available satellite communications services may be found on the Satellite Signal website (www.satsig.net).

In many developing countries, entrepreneurs are finding various ways to cope with the technical shortcomings of telephone infrastructure. These include the use of satellite, microwave and GSM cell phone networks, and establishing themselves as Internet service providers.

Infrastructure is not the only potential barrier. Political and legal issues related to the mandates and obligations of telecommunications regulatory structures and institutions can also be hurdles to the development of national networks and can affect access to global networks.

E-commerce relies on telecommunications. If the infrastructure is poor or unreliable or limited to urban areas, then e-commerce becomes much less attractive to the small and medium-sized business. If e-commerce is possible at all, it may be too restricted in coverage to provide sales benefits, or too expensive relative to other forms of business communications and marketing.

E-commerce is attractive mainly because it offers cheaper ways of serving customers better and of cutting the costs of communications, and inventory and supply management. If e-commerce is more expensive or less effective than other forms of communications with your customers or suppliers, then e-commerce may not provide an adequate return on your investment.

However, the rate of change is exciting: what seems impossible or expensive today will be commonplace and cheap tomorrow. New technologies are allowing areas with poor infrastructures to leapfrog the stages of development in telecommunications and install the best technology at the lowest costs.

The following sites provide case studies and success stories on connections in remote areas:

- International Telecommunication Union: www.itu.int
- International Institute for Communications and Development: www.iicd.org
- International Development Research Centre of Canada- PAN Asia Networking programme: www.idrc.ca/pan
- Bytes For All, a forum dedicated to rural and remote networking: www.bytesforall.org

You should note that even if you are not ready for e-commerce, you may still benefit from some of the free services that the Internet has to offer. Businesses linked to the Internet have access to free e-mail services such as Gmail (mail.google.com), and Yahoo Mail (mail.yahoo.com). You may also send free faxes using sites such as FaxZero (www.faxzero.com), or MyFax (www.myfax.com/free) to many countries around the world. Some companies offer free web hosting in addition to their paid plans, such as Heart Internet (www.heartinternet.co.uk).

For more information

- Network Startup Resource Center (NSRC). www.nsrc.org.

  NSRC is a non-profit organization that has worked since the late 1980s to help develop and deploy networking technology in various projects throughout a number of regions and countries.

- The Internet SOCiety (ISOC). www.isoc.org.

  The Internet Society (ISOC) is a non-profit organization founded in 1992 to provide leadership in Internet related standards, education, and policy. ISOC is a professional membership society with more than 80 organizational and more than 28,000 individual members in over 80 chapters around the world. It is the organization home for the groups responsible for Internet infrastructure standards, including the Internet Engineering Task Force (IETF) and the Internet Architecture Board (IAB)."

- ITU's E-Strategies. www.itu.int/ITU-D/cyb/estrat/index.html.

  Given the need to establish and support the development of national e-strategies in developing and least-developed countries as well as emerging economies, the ITU-D ICT Applications and Cybersecurity Division aims to assist these countries.

Financial aspects of running an e-commerce site

57.   What are the different methods of payment that can be used with e-commerce?

According to a 2009 report by Forrester, European online buyers use a mix of online and offline payment methods when purchasing on the Internet [1]. Even in Europe no two countries show exactly the same patterns when it comes to online payment [2]. Hence, you should not only tailor your payment method to appeal to your own customers, but also provide as many payment solutions as is practical.

The major international online payment method is credit cards, and these also dominate national transaction in many markets. The Pago retail report 2008 estimated that credit cards were used in over 81% of all e-commerce transactions [3]. In some countries debit cards and payments via online banking are widely used alternatives to credit cards. There are also other payment means, such as mediating services, mobile payment systems and electronic currency, which may be appropriate for different transactions. However, except for the mediating service PayPal, the majority of alternative online payment means have not yet gained a wide user base among merchants and consumers.

There are significant barriers to the introduction of new payment systems, including high initial investment costs and market conditions that favour established incumbents with a wide user base.

Providers have addressed earlier perceived transaction security problems regarding the use of credit cards and online banking. Other systems (notably mediating services and mobile telephony systems) have the potential to address specific markets, such as person-to-person transactions and micropayments. The development of mobile payments may also allow greater payment convenience. Micropayments are increasingly important but cost-effective international payment systems for very small payments are still to be developed.

The most common methods of payment available for Internet-based commerce are described below. All these methods are safe. Particularly for business-to-consumer (B2C) trade, some are faster than others, and Internet users usually regard speed of transaction the next most important consideration after price when deciding who to buy from.

Payment service providers

Here are several well-known payment service providers:

- PayPal. www.paypal.com. PayPal allows members to send money without sharing financial information, with the flexibility to pay using their account balances, bank accounts, credit cards or promotional financing. PayPal has more than 78 million active accounts in 190 markets and 19 currencies around the world. It is an eBay company and is made up of three leading online payment services: the PayPal global payments platform, the Payflow Gateway and Bill Me Later.

- RBS WorldPay. www.rbsworldpay.com. RBS WorldPay, part of the Royal Bank of Scotland Group, provides a globally connected, locally coordinated payment processing service for all sorts of businesses, big and small.

- Google Checkout. checkout.google.com. Google Checkout allows customers to buy quickly and easily with a single login.

- eBillme. www.ebillme.com. eBillme is an alternative payment option that allows consumers to pay cash securely when they are shopping online. It integrates online banking bill pay with existing e-commerce infrastructures.

- AmazonPayments. payments.amazon.com. Amazon offers several business solutions for online payment:

- Checkout by Amazon, which allows customers to use shipping addresses and payment methods stored in their Amazon.com accounts when checking out. It has options to check out with Amazon's 1-Click and Amazon PayPhrase. It includes tools for businesses to manage shipping charges, sales tax, promotions, and post-sale activities including refunds, cancellations, and chargebacks.

- Amazon SimplePay allows customers to use payment information from their Amazon.com account to pay for digital goods, services, donations, subscriptions and marketplace transactions.

- Flexible Payment Service (Amazon FPS) is built on top of Amazon's payments infrastructure and allows Amazon customers to pay elsewhere using the same login credentials, shipping address and payment information they already have on file with Amazon.

- Paymate. www.paymate.com. Paymate provides secure Internet-based payment services to buyers in 57 countries around the world and sellers in Australia, New Zealand and the USA. Paymate can be used to receive online payments via credit card. You do not need to have a merchant facility with a bank, a secure website or gateway processor service.

Most payment service providers charge a fee on a per-transaction basis. The fee depends on the payment method, and may be lower than credit card fees.

Payment methods used in B2C trade

Credit cards: Payment by credit card has the advantage of being simple and fast, and of enabling sellers to receive confirmation of payment before the goods are shipped or the services provided. To offer this facility, you need to become a credit card merchant. All the major credit card companies provide detailed information on how to do this through banks and on their websites (which are listed in the answer to question 61: "How do I set up payment arrangements with credit card companies?").

The ease with which merchants can be certified and the use of encryption protocols have given consumers more confidence in the security of their credit card data.

Alternative Internet payment options such as pre-paid cards: If your potential customers do not have credit cards or are reluctant to give credit card information over the Internet, they may use alternative Internet options such as pre-paid cards to purchase online. Some examples are:

- Paysafecard. www.paysafecard.com. Paysafecard is a secure and easy-to-use online payment system in Austria and Germany. Paysafecard enables online purchasing without the need to divulge any personal data, whilst using a prepaid PIN code to validate transactions.

  Paysafecard is funded by eTEN, the European Union programme providing funds to help make e-services available throughout the EU.

- SNAP. www.snapcard.com. SNAP provides the consumer with a comprehensive payment card for all sorts of electronic transactions, including Internet shopping, money transfer and mobile payments.

- Splash. www.splashplastic.com. Splash is a payment card which you can load with money – by automatic top up from a bank account, wage transfers, with cash or with a credit/debit card. Splash can be used in shops, online and across the world.

- Paynova. www.paynova.com. Paynova offers an international payment service via the Internet. With Paynova as the single source of transactions, e-retailers can get 21 payment options in 12 languages and 12 currencies in a security-certified interface (PCI). Consumers can also open a Paynova account to make purchases and carry out transfers between family members, friends and acquaintances.

Payment on delivery: Payment for the goods is collected at the point of delivery by the deliverer. This is a method that has been popular for small goods sent through the postal services. This method allows for shipping as soon as the order is confirmed. However, with this means, it is more difficult to ensure that the purchaser is genuine, and there can be a significant delay between payment (to the deliverer) and payment to the vendor.

Payment methods for business-to-business (B2B) trade

Most B2B transactions today use traditional billing systems, such as the ones described below. However, this may be changing.

Advance payment: The buyer pays for the goods before shipment takes place. Although this method of payment is ideal for sellers, it is difficult to find buyers who will agree to it, other than in some specialist B2B transactions. A variation on advance payment, the use of Internet escrow services, appears to be gaining in popularity. These services notify suppliers to ship a product only after they have verified a payment into their trust account from the buyer. Once the buyer has received and signalled acceptance of the goods, the escrow agent releases the funds to the seller.

Letters of credit: These are popular for export trading. By presenting a letter of credit guaranteed by the bank of a foreign buyer, exporters can obtain an advance on the amount due under the sales contract, including pre-shipment financing. Exporters must verify with the local bank involved with the transaction (the paying bank) what the documentary requirements are for payment on the letter of credit, as they will not receive payment if they are unable to present conforming documentation. Exporters can protect themselves against the risk of default by insisting on a confirmed letter of credit (a letter of credit confirmed by another bank).

Invoice payments: Probably the majority of business-to-business transactions are made between companies that deal with each other regularly. In these cases, B2B electronic sites may issue invoices that are identical to the invoices used in non-electronic commerce. Some businesses offer their clients discounts for electronic orders because electronic transactions are less costly to the supplier.

Factors you should to consider when selecting a payment method

While various alternative payment methods are available for merchants, it is important they understand the relevance of each method to their business. Each merchant should evaluate the alternatives. Here are some questions to ask the payment service provider or payment processor [4]:

- How many days does it take for me to be funded for the transactions?
- Can I delay capture until I fulfill the product or service?
- Is payment guaranteed for properly authorized transactions?
- What is the typical percentage of fraudulent transactions? Who bears the financial responsibility for fraud loss?
- How are disputes and charge-backs handled?
- Can I finance my customer's purchase?
- What are the typical interchange fees?
- How long does it take to integrate the payment method? Can I go direct to the provider or do I have to integrate through a processor?

For more information

- 3rd Payment Habits seminar. Helsinki, 27 August 2009.
  www.bof.fi/en/rahoitusmarkkinat/kehityshankkeet/payment_habits_2010/seminar2009.htm.

  Hosted by the Bank of Finland hosted, the focus of this seminar was on the factors which affect consumer choice, the impact of payment regulation, evolving e- and m-payment systems and the statistical developments of payment instrument usage. Papers presented at the seminar, such as a study on the perception and behaviour of consumers, or a review on the safety of payment instruments, can help to understand the impact of various payment methods.

- Janakiraman, B. Alternative payments: More ways to close the sale, e-Commerce Times, 26 January 2009.
  www.crmbuyer.com/story/65954.html?wlc=1257434333.

  This article analyses drivers of payment innovation, presents various available options to choose from, and related questions for e-commerce merchants to ask.

- Online Payments: What's Next? Australian Payments Clearing Association (APCA), July 2009.
  www.apca.com.au.

  This document was prepared for the Reserve Bank of Australia by APCA. It analyzes the competitive dynamics of the existing online payments market in Australia, reviewed overseas comparisons and sought to identify service gaps for future consideration by industry participants.

REFERENCES

[1] European consumers need multiple online payment methods, Campus L. *and others,* Forrester, 15 July 2009. www.forrester.com.

[2] How Europeans pay for goods and services, Hesse, A. *and others,* Forrester, 11 December 2008. www.forrester.com.

[3] Pago Retail Report 2008 – Purchase and Payment Behaviour in Online Retail, Deutsche Card Services. www.deutsche-card-services.com/en/ecommerce-report0/pago-retail-report-2008.html.

58.   Will e-commerce payment procedures be standardized?

Payment systems are an essential part of the infrastructure for e-business and e-commerce, and there is considerable policy focus on ensuring that payment systems and electronic payment and settlements function appropriately.

One of the few international policies on electronic payment systems is the European Union's E-Money Directive introduced in October 2000 to offer protective regulation that would not inhibit market competition (Directive 2000/46/EU). The E-Money Directive offers a common regulatory approach to e-money providers for European countries. However it is an exception, and there is little uniformity in payments across countries. For example, in the United States legislation differs across states, and in other countries, there is not yet a system to regulate online payments. Japan previously adopted stored-value card legislation, but it is not clear how this would deal with electronic money providers such as PayPal. In other countries legislation is under consideration.

According to the OECD Information Technology Outlook 2008, policies regarding e-payment have been historically less common, although the number of countries attributing high priority to such policies had increased from the previous survey of 2006 [1]. The report has also identified few countries that had decreased the aforementioned priority, partly due to the effectiveness of policies enacted earlier. According to this report, OECD countries have adopted no single e-payment standard, and not all payment methods are equally adopted across countries.

Industry coordination and standards issues cover a range of interrelated topics. Agreements on standards establish common technical rules for payment information exchange and interoperability conditions to allow for the reciprocal use of payment instruments.

There have been a number of industry initiatives to promote the development of payment systems, for example in the area of mobile payments. For instance, in 2008 the GSM Association (GSMA) and the European Payments Council (EPC) started working together to accelerate the deployment of services to enable customers to pay using their mobile phones.

The number of policies to promote e-invoicing by business, as another element of an electronic payment system, has increased among OECD countries since 2006 [1]. Denmark and Sweden have shifted towards full electronic invoicing among public authorities. The European Union is developing a European e-invoicing framework.

The initiatives described below are based on existing e-commerce infrastructures:

Bolero: Founded in 1998, with significant backing from the bank community and from the global logistics industry, Bolero was created as a neutral, trusted third party to develop a comprehensive set of standards that would remove the barriers to global, cross-enterprise business. Bolero implements and enforces these standards in an open platform to enable paperless trading between buyers, sellers, logistics, banks, agencies and customs anywhere in the world, delivering transaction visibility, predictability, speed, accuracy and security.

The Bolero Association, www.boleroassociation.org, represents its members and participants in dealing with the Bolero System operating company (Bolero International Limited) www.bolero.net. Its aim is to create a common e-commerce platform for world trade. It enjoys a close working relationship with Bolero International, but the two companies are separate legal entities. Bolero International is jointly owned by SWIFT (Society for Worldwide Interbank Financial Telecommunication), Through Transport Mutual Insurance Association Ltd. (TT Club), APAX Partners, Baring Private Equity Partners and Palio Portfolio Ltd. It is responsible for the operation of the Bolero System.

Payment service providers: A number of companies are now offering payment facilities similar to credit card companies. While they are specifically intended for Internet-based commerce, they extend access to a larger audience. PayPal (www.paypal.com) and RBS WorldPay (www.rbsworldpay.com) are two examples.

For more information on payment service providers please refer to question 57: "What are the different methods of payment that can be used with e-commerce?"

For more information

- Payment Services. European Commission; Internal Market.
  ec.europa.eu/internal_market/payments/index_en.htm.

  This site provides legislation and consultation papers on e-money, e-invoicing, fraud and cross-border payments in Euros.

REFERENCES

[1] OECD Information Technology Outlook 2008. Organisation for Economic Co-operation and Development (OECD). 2008. www.oecd.org/document/20/0,3343,en_2649_33757_41892820_1_1_1_1,00.html.

59.   How do I check whether the financial systems are technically ready to handle e-commerce transactions?

There is no simple way of determining the status of the financial systems in your country or in other countries. However, you could approach the following for relevant information:

- Banks
- Internet payment service providers
- Financial institutions
- Trade associations or chambers of commerce
- Contact point in your or the other country's national or regional e-commerce task force, if this exists
- Contact point in your or the other country's trade or telecommunications ministries

Financial systems vary considerably from country to country and even within countries. In addition, in some countries the infrastructure for handling e-commerce may not be available outside large cities. Information on e-commerce structures should also be available from the sources listed above.

If the telecommunications services in your country do not allow websites to be linked to secure payment facilities and in particular to those offered by credit card companies, it may be possible for your website to be hosted by a foreign service provider capable of offering the necessary links. If even this is not feasible (for legal, fiscal or other reasons), the only option open to you is to wait for your local situation to change before engaging in e-commerce involving online payments.

For information on web hosting services please refer to question 26: "Where should I host my website?"

For more information

- Economist global technology forum. globaltechforum.eiu.com.

   The Economist global technology forum has a regional and country information section, which provides links to other information sources and the Economist Intelligence Unit's (www.eiu.com) Country Reports. Each year, in cooperation with IBM, it publishes the e-readiness rankings. One of the factors studied in these reports is the e-readiness of the banking system in various countries.

- Europe's Digital Competitiveness Report 2009 Main achievements of the i2010strategy 2005-2009. European Commission- Europe's Information Society, 2009. ec.europa.eu/i2010.

60.   What financial costs, both hidden and unhidden, of e-commerce should I be aware of?

Because e-commerce is no different, in terms of basic costs, from traditional commerce, it should have no hidden costs. However, as in any business, some costs may be overlooked. The main impact of e-commerce for SMEs has so far been in marketing, as it enables SMEs to reach much larger markets, and in payment methods. For production and delivery, e-commerce does not differ from traditional trade, with the exception of digital products, which can be delivered electronically.

The cost items to be particularly aware of in relation to e-commerce are described below.

Taxes

If you engage in e-commerce, whether locally or internationally, you will usually be liable for income tax and possibly for direct taxes on the value of goods or services sold, in the country where your business premises are located and the income-generating economic activity is carried out. This is usually the country where your business is registered. For companies with ongoing non-electronic businesses, domestic taxes on e-commerce should not differ unless there are specific domestic provisions on e-commerce. Local chambers of commerce or banks should be able to provide advice on e-commerce taxes, if there are any, and how they are applied.

For more information on e-commerce taxation regulations please refer to question 67: "What are some key issues related to the taxation of Internet transactions?"

Cost of credit

Typically, charges for credit, such as interest on loans.

Electronic transaction fees

Credit card companies may charge you a fee to become a credit card merchant. In addition, you must remember that credit card companies and payment service providers impose a charge on every sales transaction, usually a percentage of the value of the transaction.

In addition to transaction fees, some service providers may have recurring costs such as set-up fee, annual fee, monthly minimum fee, gateway access fee.

Fees for ensuring security and for encryption

You may have to pay for installing secure payment facilities for your customers, unless facilities for encryption and authorizing credit card transactions are included in your arrangements with a payment service provider or credit card companies.

Bank charges

It is important to understand how and in what circumstances bank charges apply. An example is the bank fee on each transaction involving a bank, such as payments through SWIFT (Society for Worldwide Interbank Financial Telecommunication).

Insurance

Most companies must have insurance cover for defective products, problems with delivery or production and customer payment fraud. If there are local businesses already exporting to the countries you want to export to, they are likely to have information on liability and insurance requirements. Chambers of commerce both in your country and in your target markets should also be able to provide this information.

Online fraud and chargebacks

Chargeback, or cancellation of purchase, occurs when a customer demands a refund from their credit-card company. The rights of the consumer are quite powerful in this area, as card providers such as Visa and MasterCard have set an international standard period for chargebacks that currently stands at six months [1].

Banks protect themselves against chargebacks and the Merchant Service agreement you have with your bank allows them to transfer liability for payments of chargebacks to you. As an additional security measure, the bank may retain the payment from the customer for a period of time (e.g. 30 days) before crediting your account with the funds [1].

Many Merchant Services also need you to lodge a bond to cover any charges incurred through fraud and chargebacks. This sum will vary depending upon your average transaction value and monthly turnover as well as less tangible features like the time it takes your business to fulfill orders and consequently the exposure to risk of chargeback or fraud [1].

For more information

- Electronic Payments. The Trade Online Project. www.electronic-payments.co.uk.

  This website has information on e-payment benefits, methods, costs, and a directory of e-payment solutions. The Electronic Payments website is sponsored by the Business Link (businesslink.gov.uk), Scottish Enterprise (www.scottish-enterprise.com), and the European Union through their European Social Fund (www.europa.eu)

- Shatz, M. Understanding credit card interchange fees in card-not-present environments, CreateSpace, May 2008.

  The book is a guide on how to manage credit card operations. It provides an overview of the different credit card systems and the fundamental concepts behind merchant discounts, interchange rates commonly applicable to direct merchants, mathematical relationships that make it possible for merchants to understand the impact of interchange on product pricing and other marketing related decisions, and the operational requirements for obtaining the best possible interchange rates.

- Sabri, T. E-payments: A guide to Electronic money and online payments, Tottel Publishing, December 2009.

  This book provides in-depth analysis and guidance on the subject of electronic money and payment systems, and the relevant regulatory systems. Aimed primarily at legal practitioners specializing in banking and finance, it covers the issues and key guidance surrounding e-payments, the technology underlying authentication, confidentiality, credit and debit card payments, electronic money, gift vouchers, emergent payments products, plus many miscellaneous legal issues.

REFERENCES

[1] Electronic Payments Costs. Electronic Payments. The Trade Online Project. www.electronic-payments.co.uk (follow Electronic Payment Costs menu item).

61.   How do I set up payment arrangements with credit card companies?

For a small or medium-sized enterprise using a payment service provider is the best option for online payment. By using a well established and reliable service provider you will reduce the risks and costs of e-commerce substantially.

Options and costs vary considerably from country to country and between service providers so you will need to research this thoroughly for your particular needs before deciding on a solution.

Sources of information online include:

- The Electronic Payments Tool (www.electronic-payments.co.uk). The electronic payment tool is impartial and has been developed by the Trade Online Project, a project sponsored by the Business Link (businesslink.gov.uk), Scottish Enterprise (www.scottish-enterprise.com), and the European Union through their European Social Fund (www.europa.eu) to provide business owners with a clear understanding of what they need to do to take secure online payments.

- **Merchant accounts.** A merchant account is a commercial bank account established by contractual agreement between your business and a financial institution. A merchant account enables your business to accept credit card payments from your customers. Similar to a traditional retail business you need a merchant account to accept credit cards for Internet transactions.

  You can find information on merchant accounts on the following websites:

  - Merchant Account Guide. www.merchantaccountguide.com. MerchantAccountGuide.com is an online merchant account marketplace, bringing business owners and payment processors together. Business owners can compare merchant account offers by category, including retail, wireless, telephone, Internet merchant accounts as well as alternative payment methods and Internet gateway accounts.
  - MerchantSeek. www.merchantseek.com. MerchantSeek offers a free search service to help you search and find a merchant service provider so you can, in return, accept credit card orders from customers. In addition the site offers articles and reviews.

- **Payment service providers.** Payment service providers, such as PayPal (www.paypal.com), RBS WorldPay (www.rbsworldpay.com), and eBill (www.ebillme.com) offer payment facilities similar to credit card companies. Most payment service providers charge a fee on a per-transaction basis. The fee depends on the payment method, and may be lower than credit card fees.

  For more information on payment service providers please refer to question 57: "What are the different methods of payment that can be used with e-commerce?"

- Banks

  For example:

  - HSBC Merchant Services. www.hsbc.co.uk/1/2/business/cards-payments/secure-epayments. The HSBC merchant services gives you the ability to accept all major debit and credit cards as payment from your customers, either online, via the Internet (e-commerce), over the telephone, or by mail or fax.
  - RBS WorldPay. www.rbs.co.uk/corporate/payments/g1/streamline.ashx. RBS WorldPay helps businesses across the world take payments online, face-to-face, over the phone and by mail order.

- Credit Card Companies

  You can find a lot of information on payment arrangements from the credit cards companies' website:

  - MasterCard: www.mastercard.com/us/merchant/index.html.
  - Visa: usa.visa.com/merchants/new_acceptance/accept_online.html.

If your business has a credit card reader on its premises, you will already have a merchant relationship with one or more credit card companies, which can be extended to cover Internet-based transactions. You will probably find that the company that installs card reading machines has the information necessary to help you to set up an online merchant account, or may even do it for you. It may be better to check with the installers before approaching the credit card companies directly to set up arrangements.

If your business does not have a credit card reader on its premises, but you intend to accept online payments by credit cards, you will have to contact the credit card companies or payment service providers to set up an arrangement. You may also choose to do this through a bank.

Anyone who wants to become a credit card merchant must set up arrangements with an approved bank. If you do not already have a commercial bank account, you should contact local traders in your line of business or a local trade association to find out whether there is a local bank specializing in commercial operations. Otherwise, identify several large reputable banks that have known international connections, and discuss your business with them before deciding which one will suit you best.

You should bear in mind the possibility that credit card facilities may not be available in your country. If this is the case, the only realistic option for you is to have your website hosted in a country where these facilities are available. You should ascertain whether there are servicing links between your local bank and a bank in the hosting location and check that there are no legal barriers or excessive taxes that would invalidate this option. A local commercial organization should be able to provide you this information.

62. Do I need to check on my customer's financial status to ensure smooth payment?

Before executing orders from new customers, you should check on their credibility and reputation, including their financial status. This check is essential, except when the buyer pays by credit card, debit card or pre-paid card. In essence, buyers must show that they have a good track record of payments and that they are able to pay for the order, for example, by providing proof that they have sufficient funds deposited with a bank. Clearly this information is more difficult to verify if you are exporting to a distant country but, whatever the buyer's location, you should always work through a reputable bank, preferably one with international connections.

If the buyer pays online with a card, clearing or authorization of the payment will also take place online at the time of payment. In the clearing process, the payment processing company will verify that the card is valid, has not been reported stolen, and that the amount being paid is within the buyers credit limit. It will then either authorize or refuse payment. If payment is authorized, the seller will receive an authorization code to confirm that the payment is valid.

If you accept credit card payments but do not have a direct Internet link with the credit card company for clearing purposes, you will have to seek authorization from the card company by telephone, or through your local bank when you submit the credit card payment slips. It is obvious that not having access to immediate clearing procedures may increase your chances of not being paid. It is therefore in your interest to wait for authorization before dispatching goods, even if this delays the delivery process.

On the whole, the degree of certainty that payment will be made depends on the country and the type of business. For business within your own country, you should check on your customers' credit standing with the country's largest banks and credit-check companies. For exports, the simplest method of payment is by credit card for smaller amounts (usually involving transactions with individual consumers). For larger amounts and business-to-business transactions it is best to avail of the usual payment procedures in conjunction with a reputable international bank. Some of the actions that you can take to help ensure that you will be paid are described below.

For business-to-business transactions in particular, you can request your bank to get in touch with the foreign buyers bank abroad or its correspondent local bank to obtain relevant credit information on the buyer. Some banks subscribe to the services of independent research companies, which provide credit information on companies from all over the world.

Check that the buyer is located at its stated address; verify with the buyers named bank that the buyer has sufficient funds to pay the amount required and that the bank is familiar with the buyer. This can take one, two or more days depending on the banks involved. International clearance can take much longer depending on the commercial connections between your bank and your customer's bank.

Credit information companies may also be able to provide you with information on your buyers. You could obtain the names of relevant credit information companies from a reputable local bank, or through credit-insurance companies such as Euler Hermes (www.eulerhermes.com) or Coface (www.coface.com).

For more information

- Dun & Bradstreet. www.dnb.com.

  This well-known international business and financial services company gives market- and company-specific financial information. Some services are provided free of charge. The website has a special section for small businesses which provides relevant information through an education centre, white papers, and weekly columnists.

63. If payments are made to my company through a credit card transaction, who is liable?

The answer to this question depends on the terms of your contracts with the credit card companies and with your customers.

Customers have the right to contest their credit card bill if the item paid for has not been received, if it arrives damaged and if, on inspection of the bill, the customers realize that they have not ordered the merchandise and want to return it. Such customers will contact their credit card issuer to register a complaint, and will usually not pay the contested amount. When the complaint has been entered into the customer's record, the credit card company will enter into negotiations with the seller.

If stolen cards have been used to pay for goods, there should be no recourse against the vendors. They should not be asked to return the amount received in payment either to the genuine cardholder or to the credit card company. Cardholders may be liable for some, or all, of the amount if they did not inform the credit card company of the theft or loss of the card within a reasonable period. In general, the credit card company will be held liable for fraudulent use of its cards, but it can make a claim for compensation from its insurance company.

However, your contract with a buyer may stipulate that, when goods paid for by credit card are lost or damaged and the buyer contests payment, you may have to accept non-payment or agree to replace the goods. It is possible to reduce the risk of loss by requiring a signature on delivery. The requirement of a signature is usually enough to ensure delivery. Note that most credit card companies have a charge-back fee when a customer demands a refund.

To cover the risk of damage, the goods may be insured. You will have to decide whether or not your liability for the goods is greater than the additional costs of insurance and the special delivery mechanisms required. If you have insurance cover, the insurance company will reimburse you for the cost of sending replacement goods or, if this is not possible, it will reimburse the purchaser.

For more information

- Payment Services. European Commission; Internal Market. ec.europa.eu/internal_market/payments/index_en.htm.
- This site provides legislation and consultation papers on e-money, e-invoicing, fraud and cross-border payments in euro.
- Sabri, T. E-payments: A guide to Electronic money and online payments, Tottel Publishing, December 2009.
- Shatz, M. Understanding credit card interchange fees in card-not-present environments, CreateSpace, May 2008.

64.   What cost items should I include in the calculation of my e-commerce sales price?

The costs of establishing an e-commerce presence will have to be added to the calculation of the sales prices of your goods or services. A large part of these set-up costs needs to be made at the beginning and you will probably recover them only over a period of trading. It is necessary to understand what and how high these costs are before engaging in e-commerce.

Investment and operating costs: These include one-off investment costs such as the costs of a computer, setting up a website, software and ongoing costs, such as line rental, website maintenance, ISP fees and hosting fees. The investment costs need to be apportioned so that they can be recovered over a period of two to three years.

Your website is a series of files that reside on a special computer called a web server, which is connected to the Internet. When customers visit your site, they are actually connecting to the web server via the Internet in order to view your web pages. Web servers and the Internet connections that link them to visitors must be fast and powerful enough to quickly respond to all requests to view your site. They must also be up and running 24 hours a day.

Some large businesses prefer to have complete control of their web infrastructure by purchasing, setting up and managing their own web server hardware and software. However, the cost of doing this is disproportionately high for an SME.

SMEs generally opt to use the services of an ISP or web hosting company to host their website. For a monthly fee, these service providers will provide your site with space on a server, web server software, access to its high-speed Internet connection, tools for managing and maintaining your site, customer support, e-commerce features and so on. There are many ISP and web hosting options to choose from.

In addition to the one time initial set-up expenses, you should also take into account the recurring costs, and costs associated with the regular maintenance of your e-commerce site. The following table lists some of the tasks required to establish, operate and maintain an e-commerce site and the costs associated with them:

Cost item	Fees and charges
Website hosting	Monthly fee
Domain name registration	Annual Fee
Payment Service Provider	Set-up cost, annual fee, minimum monthly fee transaction fees, settlement fees, charge-back fees
Internet Service Provider	Monthly fee, usage fees, telecom charges
Website building tools – to build your website	Free tools, monthly charge or licence fee
Shopping cart software – for enabling online purchases	Free tools, monthly charge or licence fee
Web browser – to view websites	Free
E-mail tool – to communicate with your customers	Free
Security tools such as anti-virus and firewall software – to protect your computers against virus attacks and unauthorised access	Free tools, monthly charge or licence fee
Office software – used to prepare documents for customers	Free tools, monthly charge or licence fee
Supply-chain software – to exchange information with your suppliers and customers	Free tools, monthly charge or licence fee
Other specialized software – B2B systems may have specific requirements for other software	Free tools, monthly charge or licence fee
One computer for each person who needs to access the Internet, send and receive e-mails, or communicate with customers	Purchase or lease
Internet connection – modem, ADSL or other, depending on requirements and what is available	Monthly fee
An expert in dynamic website design, architecture and construction – to set up your site initially and maintain it	Use a specialized firm – fee for what is delivered
An expert in e-commerce and online security	Use a specialized firm – fee for what is delivered
A computer system administrator – to keep your computer hardware running and software up-to-date	Could be an external service provider – monthly fee or call-out charge
A computer-literate person who has experience using the Internet, e-mail and office software	Own staff

Credit card transaction fees: If your business intends to handle credit card transactions, your company will need to enter into an arrangement with one or more credit card companies or a payment service provider. These companies usually charge merchants a percentage of the value of each credit card transaction and charges vary considerably from country to country, so you should adjust the prices of your products accordingly.

Bank charges and foreign exchange: It is important to understand how and when bank charges apply, and have these charges covered in the pricing of your goods or services. If you are accepting payments in currencies other than the currency of the country in which you are receiving the payments you will need to pay particular attention to charges related to foreign currencies and the impact of exchange rate fluctuations.

Insurance: If your goods can be returned for replacement or refund, you need to cover the costs of this eventuality with an insurance policy. You will need to inform your customers under what circumstances the goods can be returned and your return policy statement should cover such details as the period during which return is possible, how the goods should be sent back, who should pay for shipping and handling charges, etc.

Customs duties at point of departure: As customs duties at destination will usually be collected from the purchaser, it is rare to have to pay customs duties at the point of departure. However, you may need to reclaim duties already paid if the goods you are selling do not originate in the country you are distributing them from. This depends on the export destination and the type of goods. A local chamber of commerce or customs office should be able to give you information on whether duties are due or returnable. Goods shipped within the same country or trade area are not liable for customs duties.

Taxes: The current thinking is that taxes should be charged at point of sale. This is less clear for digital content such as digital music, downloadable software, and e-books that can be downloaded directly from a website (i.e. for which delivery can be made through the Internet). As yet, there is no internationally applicable set of rules; however, the World Trade Organization (WTO) is working with a number of governments and trading organizations to bring some order to this situation. WTO members want to have as open a structure as possible to avoid penalizing the countries that could benefit the most from e-commerce. For goods shipped within the same country or trade area, VAT may be imposed. In this case the rules are exactly the same as for non-Internet shopping.

For more information on e-commerce taxation regulations please refer to question 57: "What are some key issues related to the taxation of Internet transactions?"

Packaging: This may be an additional cost item if special packaging is necessary to protect the goods during transport.

Transport of goods to the shipping point: if necessary (costs based on distance plus size and weight of object). If you are selling goods that have to be physically shipped from a storage point to a distribution site, the cost will have to be met locally. This cost needs to be included in the selling price.

Standard shipping charges: If these charges are to be collected from the buyer at the delivery point by an international carrier or express delivery service, you will need to inform the buyer that shipping charges are not included in the sales price. You will also have to ensure that the carrier service agrees to collect its fees at delivery point. If you decide to include shipping charges in your sales price, make sure you use the appropriate charging scale for each customer and destination. The major carrier services have websites through which it is possible to find the nearest local collection point and information on pricing. Some of these companies offer complex logistics services covering the entire supply chain. Most major carriers offer online B2B services to calculate charges and collect shipment information that can be incorporated into your own website. Here are some international courier services with online tools:

- United Parcel Service (UPS):   www.ups.com
- Federal Express (FedEx):   www.fedex.com
- DHL: www.dhl.com

For more information on the financial costs of e-commerce please refer to question 60: "What financial costs, both hidden and unhidden, of e-commerce should I be aware of?"

For more information

- Gregson, A. Pricing strategies for small business (101 for small business), Self Counsel Press, March 2008.

  The book explains how forces within a business environment such as competitors, suppliers, and availability of substitute products can affect pricing. It also includes psychological pricing, price skimming, penetration pricing, cost-plus mark-up strategies and multiple unit pricing.

- Ruskin-Brown, I. Practical pricing for results, Thorogood Publishing, January 2008.

  Ruskin-Brown's book is a practical guide on how to set and manage the pricing of both the products and services. It outlines the process of deriving a pricing strategy first, and then monitoring the profit implications of any pricing decisions made. The book also sets out basic financial tools.

65.   In what currency should I quote a sales price?

Quoting prices in your local currency protects you from the risk of foreign exchange fluctuations between your home currency and a different trading currency. However, your local currency may not be the best one to use from a promotional point of view. There may be a commercial advantage in quoting and accepting payment in the currency of the country in which you would like to sell or in a currency acceptable to your foreign trading partners. Your choice of currency should be guided by the risks you are willing to take in regard to foreign exchange fluctuations.

An acceptable way is to quote prices and accept payment in your local currency and at the same time to quote prices, for comparison purposes only, in another more widely known currency, such as United States dollars, and give a notice of the exchange rate approximation used. This allows buyers to pay in your (the seller's) currency while having a good idea of how your price corresponds to the price of equivalent goods in their home market. It is your responsibility as the seller to make it clear that payment will be accepted only in your local currency, and to use a fair exchange rate approximation so as not to mislead the purchaser. You should be aware that if you use exchange rate approximations that differ greatly from the real exchange rate, this could leave you open to legal proceedings for deception. (An exchange rate of 1:1.615 can be approximated at 1:1.6 but not at 1:1.5). If you want to avoid giving exchange rate approximations, you can provide a direct link from your pricing page to a foreign exchange calculator on the Web, such as the Universal Currency Converter at www.xe.net.

You should also bear in mind the following issues when deciding how to quote prices:

- Some countries, such as Switzerland, have legal restrictions preventing companies from invoicing in currencies other than their home currency. In this case a local price with an equivalent comparison price in another currency, such as the United States dollar, euro or yen, may be the best way to present online pricing of items for export. Your local chamber of commerce or commercial association should be able to provide information as to whether such laws apply in your country.

- The United States dollar is the most used currency for international payments and is acceptable in most, but not all, countries.

- The European Union's single currency, the euro is also acceptable in many countries. If you are trading primarily within the euro zone, you should use the euro for quoting prices (and for accepting payments in, if you wish).

- If you trade in a currency other than your own, not only are you at risk from foreign exchange fluctuations, but you will also have to pay bank charges for currency conversions. You should obtain confirmation from your bank on the most suitable currency for trading with a specific target market.

- Payment by international credit card will allow buyers in other countries to pay you in the currency you advertise your product in. In this case, you, as the payee, bear the risk of currency fluctuations. If you think that this could be the best option for you, you may want to consider setting up a credit card merchant account.

- Some payment service providers and credit card companies now provide the option for the buyer to choose from a selection of currencies at the time of payment using the exchange rate valid at that time.

- Multi-currency websites are difficult to build and require ongoing management of current and past exchange rates, which means that very few such sites exist. Further, if you quote and accept payments in different currencies, there is a possibility that buyers will choose to pay in the currency which provides them with the best exchange rate at any given time. As stated above, it is better to work in only one currency, either your local currency or an international one if possible.

For more information

- Grath, A. The Handbook of International Trade and Finance: The Complete Guide to Risk Management, International Payments and Currency Management, Bonds and Guarantees, Credit Insurance and Trade Finance, Kogan Page, July 2008.
- The Universal Currency Converter. XE. www.xe.com/?ref=ucc.

66.   How do I get information on payment procedures and taxes in different countries?

Payment procedures are the ways in which you receive payment for goods or services sold. These procedures will depend on the banking infrastructure in your country and in your customers' countries.

Information on payment procedures in other countries can be obtained from the following sources:

- **The banking system in your country.** Most central banks have a research department, which should have information on banking and finance in other countries. Alternatively, a local bank with international connections or an international bank should be able to tell you about payment procedures and taxation in your target market, or should know where to get the information you require.

- **The local embassy of your target market** may have a commercial office, which gives this information.

- **Chambers of commerce in your target market** may provide you with information themselves or direct you to an appropriate source.

- **Potential trade partners', importers' associations and trade promotion agencies in your target market** may be able to give you the information or assist you in finding it.

- **The commerce departments** (e.g. United States Department of Commerce- www.commerce.gov) or **ministries of major industrialized countries**, or their **trade support organizations** (e.g. Ubifrance- www.ubifrance.fr), may also compile information on the payment and taxation aspects of trade in foreign countries. You may find it worthwhile to contact the relevant departments of such countries for information, particularly if they have large trade flows with your target market.

The main methods of payment that are likely to be available are as follows:

- **Inter-bank transfers**, which can be handled by any bank with international connections. The bank should be able to tell you what you need to do to use this service, as well as the tax, customs and bank charges that may be incurred.

- **International credit cards**, which provide the easiest payment procedure, if access to the relevant credit card clearing system is available and an agreement with the credit card companies can be established. However, credit card transactions are not always regarded as the best solution by all potential customers or markets, because of a more or less strongly held perception, in spite of advances in encryption technology, that payment by credit card over the Internet entails considerable risk for the card owner.

- **Other Internet payment methods**, customers who do not have credit cards or are reluctant to give credit card information over the Internet, may be willing to use smart cards, prepaid cards or other methods to purchase online.

- **Payment by the buyer on delivery** to the deliverer (usually a post office), which then pays the seller.

For information on taxes, it may be possible to contact the tax authority in the target country. However, if, as is often the case, the authority is not easily accessible to foreign businesses, you should use the sources listed above to obtain information.

General information on taxes that usually apply to foreign trade, including electronic foreign trade, is given below.

- **Import taxes or customs duties** are usually collected at the port (airport) of destination; payment is generally the responsibility of the recipient of goods and will normally be collected by the shipping agency. There is a general consensus, through the World Trade Organization, that taxes are not collected on digital goods, i.e. those that are delivered over the Internet.

- **A value-added tax (VAT)** on imports may be applicable at destination; the buyer normally pays this. For non-imported goods, VAT should be added to the price of the goods and declared to your tax authority as for traditional purchase transactions. If you need specific information on this, a local chamber of commerce or trade association in the target country should be able to provide the information you need.

Please refer to question 14: "Where can I obtain information on foreign markets?"

67. What are some key issues related to the taxation of Internet transactions?

According to a 2005 tax policy study on e-commerce made by the Organisation for Economic Co-operation and Development, the OECD is still endeavouring to achieve an international consensus when it comes to Internet taxation.

World Trade Organization members reached an agreement in November 2009 to recommend a two-year extension of a moratorium on customs duties on electronic commerce [1].

Tax is something that is closely connected to the sovereignty of states due to the nature of tax revenues. In case of double taxation such situations are often resolved through bilateral agreements between states. The OECD agreed in 1998 in Ottawa upon the Taxation Framework Conditions. The Conditions are supposed to guide states when determining a taxation policy for e-commerce. The basic guideline of the conditions is that the same principles should be used for e-commerce as for traditional commerce. There should be no discrimination between the different ways of doing business. Also, OECD countries have agreed that efficiency, certainty, simplicity, effectiveness, fairness and flexibility should underlie any taxation of the Internet or electronic commerce.

Direct taxation

The OECD is currently investigating if the existing treaty rules for taxation of business profits could also be used for e-commerce. The 2005 guidelines are based on the following basic principles:

- Any resident taxpayer may be taxed on its business profits wherever they may have arisen.

- Non-resident taxpayers may only be taxed on their business profits to the extent that these are attributable to a permanent establishment in the country.

- Residence depends on the liability to tax under the domestic law of the taxpayer. A company is considered to be a resident in the State if it is liable to tax in that State by reason of factors (e.g. domicile, residence, incorporation or place of management) that trigger the widest domestic tax liability.

- Since the reference to the domestic factors could result in the same company being a resident of two countries, the treaty's "tie-breaker" rule ensures that a taxpayer will have a single country's residence for the purpose of applying the treaty. The tie-breaker rule provides that a company that is considered to be a resident of two countries is a resident only of the country in which its place of effective management is situated.

The OECD has clarified that it considers the definitions of permanent establishment to apply also to e-commerce activities and has made further clarifications on specific issues. These include that a website cannot in itself constitute a permanent establishment; neither are web hosting arrangements. Servers can be seen as permanent establishments only if the function performed at that place goes beyond what is preparatory or auxiliary. Additionally, only in very unusual circumstances will an Internet service provider be considered to be a permanent establishment.

Consumptions taxes – VAT or GST

A key principle of the Ottawa Taxation Framework Conditions is that the rules for the consumption taxation of cross border electronic commerce should result in taxation in the jurisdiction where consumption takes place.

For consumption taxes such as Value Added Tax (VAT), also referred to by some jurisdictions as Goods and Services Tax (GST), the supplier is responsible for the correct application of tax on each transaction. That means that systems must be able to apply the correct rate of tax, and in the correct jurisdiction, automatically and at the time the transaction is being made, as there is little chance to correct errors later, especially in the business-to-consumer environment.

To apply the correct tax decision, the supplier needs to know the jurisdiction of the customer. In the OECD Consumption Tax Guidance Series ("Verification of Customer Status and Jurisdiction") it is held that the status and jurisdiction of a customer should be based on customer self-identification, supported by a range of other criteria including payment information, tracking/geo-location software, nature of the supply and digital certificates.

The European Union and VAT

For the purpose of exports from European Union to non-member countries, no VAT is charged on the transaction and the VAT already paid on the inputs of the good for export is deducted. As for imports, VAT must be paid the moment goods are imported so they are immediately placed on the same footing as equivalent goods produced in the European Union. For goods moving within the European Union there is no collection of VAT at the internal frontier between tax jurisdictions.

VAT on electronically supplied services

The EU was among the first to develop a framework for consumption taxes on e-services in accordance with OECD guidelines. Under new 2006 rules, EU suppliers of electronic services are no longer obliged to levy VAT when selling on markets outside of the EU. This has removed a significant competitive handicap. Previously, EU suppliers had to charge VAT when supplying digital products even in countries outside the EU. The VAT rules for non-EU suppliers selling to business customers in the EU remain unchanged, the VAT being paid by the importing company under self-assessment arrangements.

In 2008 the New York state legislature passed a new law, as part of the 2008-2009 budget, that forces online retailers to collect taxes from customers referred to them by websites based in this state. The reasoning behind this "Amazon tax" is that New York-based affiliates qualify as a "physical presence" and therefore Internet retailers with New York-based affiliates should be taxed by the state.

For more information

- OECD Tax Policy Studies, E-commerce: Transfer Pricing and Business Profits Taxation. OECD Publishing, 2005. www.oecd.org/bookshop?pub=232005031P1.

- OECD: Implementation of the Ottawa Taxation Framework Conditions, The 2003 Report, available at: www.oecd.org/dataoecd/45/19/20499630.pdf.

- OECD Consumption Tax Guidance Series, available at: www.oecd.org/document/31/0,3343,en_2649_201185_5574623_1_1_1_1,00.html.

- Taxation and Customs Union. European Commission. ec.europa.eu/taxation_customs/taxation/vat/how_vat_works/index_en.htm.

  The site contains background notes on tax and customs policy initiatives as well as the latest speeches and press releases. It also hosts tax and customs consultations. You will find practical information on personal or company tax, VAT, excise duties or car taxation. You will also find explanations about how to calculate customs duties (see value of goods; tariff; origin), customs procedures or customs controls.

REFERENCES

[1] New, W. WTO To Extend Moratorium On Non-Violation Cases, E-Commerce Taxes. Intellectual Property Watch, 6 November 2009. www.ip-watch.org.

Legal issues

68. Are there international or national legal frameworks for e-commerce?

Generally, laws and regulations apply equally to all legal relations, whether paper-based or online. However, since 1995, national laws were enacted in several countries to deal with specific information technology issues. This is because the use of digital techniques brought uncertainty and raised several questions, such as: validity of online transactions, recognition of digital signatures, requirements of evidence and storage of non-paper documents.

The United Nations Commission on International Trade Law (UNCITRAL)

Considering that most countries required some type of adaptation to their legislation, UNCITRAL drafted two "model laws" on e-commerce related issues. A model law is simply a suggested pattern for lawmakers so that they may amend their domestic legislation in accordance with what is universally accepted and recognized. If most countries adopt the model law, national laws are brought closer into line.

As the UNCITRAL model laws have been widely incorporated into domestic laws, it is useful to have an understanding of the gist of these texts.

1) The 1996 UNCITRAL Model Law on Electronic Commerce conveys a key principle: "electronic equivalence", which means that information or documents will not be denied legal effect or enforceability solely because they are in electronic format. In particular, regarding the legal implications of clicking the "I agree" button on a website, the 1996 Model Law removed any doubt that this popular form of online consent is valid, by stipulating that unless the parties agree otherwise, an offer or an acceptance of an offer can be expressed in electronic form.

Legislation implementing provisions of the Model Law has been adopted in: Australia (1999), China (2004), Colombia (1999), Dominican Republic (2002), Ecuador (2002), France (2000), India (2000), Islamic Republic of Iran (2004), Ireland (2000), Jordan (2001), Mauritius (2000), Mexico (2000), New Zealand (2002), Pakistan (2002), Panama (2001), Philippines (2000), Republic of Korea (1999), Singapore (1998), Slovenia (2000), South Africa (2002), Sri Lanka (2006), Thailand (2002), Venezuela (2001) and Viet Nam (2005), Sri Lanka (2006) and United Arab Emirates (2006). This list is updated any time the UNCITRAL Secretariat is informed of changes in enactment of the Model Law. For an updated list please refer to the UNCITRAL website (www.uncitral.org/uncitral/en/uncitral_texts/electronic_commerce/1996Model_status.html).

In the United States, the Uniform Electronic Transactions Act, adopted in 1999, was influenced by the Model Law, as were practically all US state e-laws. The same can be said of Canada's federal legislation and that of its provinces.

2) The 2001 UNCITRAL Model Law on Electronic Signatures applies where e-signatures are used in the context of commercial activities (it does not override rules of law intended for the protection of consumers).

The 2001 Model Law aims at bringing additional legal certainty to the use of electronic signatures. The Model Law treats an e-signature as reliable provided that it meets four criteria: the signature creation data is linked solely to the signatory; it is under the sole control of the signatory; any alteration of the signature is detectable; as is any information as to the integrity of the underlying information. The Model Law follows a technology-neutral approach, which avoids favouring the use of any specific technical solution. The Model Law further establishes basic rules of conduct that may serve as guidelines for assessing possible responsibilities and liabilities for the signatory, the relying party and trusted third parties intervening in the signature process.

Legislation based on this Model Law has been adopted in Thailand (2001), Mexico (2003), China (2004), Viet Nam (2005) and the United Arab Emirates (2006). This list is updated any time the UNCITRAL Secretariat is informed of changes in enactment of the Model Law. For an updated list please refer to the UNCITRAL website (www.uncitral.org/uncitral/en/uncitral_texts/electronic_commerce/2001Model_status.html)

3) In 2005 the United Nations Convention on the Use of Electronic Communications in International Contracts was adopted.

Contrary to the two above-mentioned texts, this is not a "model law" but a treaty. It incorporates most of the solutions found in the two model laws and it allows for electronic communications to satisfy the requirements of other conventions drafted at a time when e-communications were unknown, without need for these conventions to be re-negotiated. In June 2007, the Convention had not yet entered into force.

4) For its part, the European Union has a unified legal framework, which includes:

- Directive 95/46/EC of the European Parliament and the Council of 24 October 1995, Relating to the Protection of Personal Data.

- Directive 1999/93/EC of the European Parliament and the Council of 13 December 1999, on a Community Framework for Electronic Signatures.

- Directive 2000/31/EC of the European Parliament and of the Council of 8 June 2000 on certain legal aspects of information society services, in particular electronic commerce, in the Internal Market ("Directive on electronic commerce").

For more information

- The 1996 and 2001 UNCITRAL Model Laws as well as the 2005 UNCITRAL Convention on the Use of Electronic Communications in International Contracts, together with explanatory texts are available online at UNCITRAL website: www.uncitral.org/uncitral/en/uncitral_texts/electronic_commerce.html.

- LegaCarta. www.legacarta.net.

  LegaCarta is a multilingual web-based system on multilateral trade treaties and instruments designed to assist trade promotion organizations and policymakers in optimizing their country's legal framework on international trade. It is managed by the International Trade Centre.

- EU E-commerce Directive. European Commission. Available online at the EU Single Market thematic website on EUROPA: ec.europa.eu/internal_market/e-commerce/directive_en.htm.

- Uniform electronic transaction act. The United States National Conference of Commissioners on Uniform State Laws. www.nccusl.org/Update/uniformact_factsheets/uniformacts-fs-ueta.asp.

69.   Which national law will cover cross-border electronic transactions between a seller and a buyer?

The question of applicable law arises each time there is a cross-border transaction. Applicable law is the law that the parties to a contract can choose to govern the contract, or the law that is applied when the parties have not made a choice of law.

In general, a distinction is made between transactions involving only businesses (business-to-business) and those with consumers. Where an agreement is entered into between a professional and a consumer (business-to-consumer), the parties involved, in choosing an applicable law, cannot depart from the public laws of the consumer's country, which are meant to protect the consumer.

Business-to-business transactions

The general principle is the autonomy of the parties to a contract, which means that parties have the freedom to choose which law will govern their contract. This principle is recognized in most countries (with some few exceptions), as well as in the Rome Convention of 19 June, 1980 on the law applicable to contractual obligations. It is incorporated into European Union Regulation (No 593/2008) of 17 June, 2008 on the law applicable to contractual obligations. As a consequence, for purposes of legal certainty, parties to a contract are advised to specify which law will govern their transactions.

If the parties have not specified which law will apply to a contract, then the jurisdiction (e.g. State court or arbitral tribunal) responsible for the case will have to decide which law is applicable. Each country has its own guiding rules on choice of law but either one of two following solutions is commonly applied:

- The applicable law is the law of the country of the seller (the party who provides the performance which is characteristic of the contract).

- The applicable law is that of the place of the signing of the contract.

The United Nations Convention on Contracts for the International Sale of Goods (Vienna, 11 April, 1980)

Any professional exporter or importer should have some knowledge of the 1980 Vienna Sales Convention because this Convention sets out the main rules governing international sales contracts, including those done through e-transactions. Some estimates suggest that as much as two thirds of world trade is carried on between parties in states which have ratified the Convention (70 ratifications in 2009).

The UNIDROIT Principles of International Commercial Contracts

The UNIDROIT Principles of International Commercial Contracts, initially adopted in 1994, were enlarged in 2004 to cover a number of additional topics and to cater for the increasing importance of electronic contracting. The UNIDROIT Contract Principles can be chosen by parties to govern their contracts and therefore the disputes that could arise in the context of their contractual relations.

For more information

- United Nations Convention on Contracts for the International Sales of Goods (CISG). Institute of International Commercial Law; Pace Law University. www.cisg.law.pace.edu/cisg/text/caseschedule.html.

  On the 1980 United Nations Convention on Contracts for the International Sales of Goods (CISG), the most complete site is hosted by Pace Law University, with nearly 2000 cases. The CISG Database reflects a collaborative effort between the Institute of International Commercial Law and the Pace Law Library.

- UNIDROIT Principles of International Commercial Contracts 2004. International Institute for the Unification of Private Law. www.unidroit.org/english/principles/contracts/main.htm. (Available in 12 languages).

  The International Institute for the Unification of Private Law (UNIDROIT) is an independent intergovernmental organization with its seat in the Villa Aldobrandini in Rome. Its purpose is to study needs and methods for modernizing, harmonizing and coordinating private and in particular commercial law as between States and groups of States.

- OECD Guidelines for Consumer Protection in the Context of Electronic Commerce. OECD. www.oecd.org/publications, also accessible at: www.oecdbookshop.org/oecd/display.asp?CID=&LANG=EN&SF1=DI&ST1=5LMQCR2K96VC.

70. In the event of a dispute, which court will have jurisdiction over a cross-border e-commerce contract?

Jurisdiction raises the question of which national court or arbitral tribunal will hear the dispute.

In the absence of a term in your contract conferring jurisdiction on a specific court or arbitration panel, a national court will decide if it has jurisdiction over the case in accordance with its national law. Therefore, it is strongly recommended, for the sake of security and predictability that you and the other party stipulate in your contract which court or arbitration panel will have jurisdiction over a dispute arising from your contract. It should be noted, however, that the validity of such a clause depends on national law. For example, in France, such a clause is not valid between non-business parties unless the contract has an international dimension.

The same recommendation is made as regards the applicable law for your contract: business parties are advised to stipulate clearly which law will apply to their contract in case of a dispute.

In international business dealings, arbitration clauses are the usual practice, as they avoid the submission of disputes to a State court and to national rules of procedure that at least one of the two parties will not be acquainted with. Furthermore, arbitral awards can be recognized internationally: the 1958 New York Convention on the Recognition and Enforcement of Foreign Arbitral Awards, ratified by some 142 States, facilitates the recognition of international arbitral awards as if they were national court decisions.

Arbitration may not always be necessary where countries are linked by treaties that facilitate the recognition of State court decisions. For example, in Europe, Council Regulation N° 44/2001 of 22 December 2000 on jurisdiction and the recognition and enforcement of judgement in civil and commercial matters applies in all EU States. Under that Regulation, a judgement given in a European State will be recognized automatically, and special proceedings are not necessary unless recognition is actually contested. The same principles also apply with regard to decisions in Norway, Iceland and Switzerland. As to jurisdiction, EC Regulation N°44/2001 states that the court which has jurisdiction is the court of the defendant's residence, the court of the country where the contract is performed or the court of the country where the event that is the subject of the dispute occurred.

In Central and West Africa, the OHADA Uniform Laws, applicable in 16 States, allow to even a greater extent for recognition of both court and arbitration decisions.

For most countries, however, such regional rules do not exist. Moreover, most countries still accord to their nationals the privilege of submitting disputes to their national courts (in the absence of a contractual clause referring to a State court or to arbitration).

For more information

* Juris International, International Trade Centre. www.jurisint.org.

  Juris International is a multilingual collection (English, Spanish, and French) of legal information on international trade. Juris International aims to facilitate and reduce the work involved in research for business lawyers, advisers and in-house counsel, and state organizations in developing and transition economies, by providing access to texts which have often been difficult to obtain. Juris international contains full texts of some 100 arbitration rules, with model clauses, and a description of the services of arbitration centres.

REFERENCES

EU Regulation N°44/2001 with summary. Europa summaries of EU legislation.
europa.eu/legislation_summaries/justice_freedom_security/judicial_cooperation_in_civil_matters/l33054_en.htm.

OHADA – Business law portal in Africa. www.OHADA.com.

OHADA (Organisation pour l'harmonisation en Afrique du droit des affaires), or the Organization for the Harmonization of Business Law in Africa, was created in 1993 in Port Louis (Mauritius). The OHADA Treaty is made up today of 16 African States.

71. How can I ensure that an agreement made electronically is legally binding?

When parties enter into an electronic commercial contract, the contract is formed by one party making an offer and the other party accepting this offer. The exchange of consents will give legal effect to the contract, without either party having to respect requirements of form, except in such situations where the law requires that a contract be written in a specific form (e.g. for the sale of property, settlements) or where the national law demands a written document (e.g. for the sale of a business, maritime bills of lading).

Nevertheless, for day-to-day transactions, the main legal problem concerns the question of evidence. The existence of a contract can be disputed if you do not have evidence of its formation. Thus, a simple electronic message, which is not signed, can be called into question. Consequently, a message representing an offer or the acceptance of an offer runs the risk of being regarded as simply the initiation of written evidence and not complete documentary evidence.

A vast legislative change has taken place on a global level, recognizing that writing in the electronic medium is the functional equivalent of writing on paper. The legal effect of electronic records is recognized in Articles 6, 7 and 8 of UNCITRAL's Model Law on Electronic Commerce, which is the standard reference for countries wishing to adapt existing laws or to create new laws to deal with electronic transactions. One of the purposes of the Model Law is to promote an understanding of, and confidence in, certain electronic signature techniques when making business transactions. It establishes a presumption that, where certain criteria of technical reliability are met, an electronic signature shall be treated as hand-written signature. The Model Law has a technology-neutral approach. It also offers basic rules for assessing possible responsibilities and liabilities that might bind the parties involved in the process.

In practice, if you use an electronic medium (such as e-mail) during the process of contracting, it is wise to forestall potential problems of evidence by incorporating a reliable, recognized electronic signature into your electronic correspondence. This makes it possible to identify the parties as signatories of the contract, so that they cannot later repudiate the contract on the ground that the agreement was not signed, and the integrity of the contract can be guaranteed. In case of doubt, it may also be wise to confirm the acceptance of an offer by sending a confirmation document by mail, such as an acknowledgement of receipt.

For more information

- Juris International, International Trade Centre. www.jurisint.org.

  Juris International is a multilingual collection (English, Spanish, and French) of legal information on international trade. Juris International aims to facilitate and reduce the work involved in research for business lawyers, advisers and in-house counsel, and state organizations in developing and transition economies, by providing access to texts which have often been difficult to obtain. Juris International contains full texts of some 100 arbitration rules, with model clauses, and a description of the services of arbitration centres.

- International Chambers of Commerce's tools for E-business. www.iccwbo.org/policy/ebitt.

  Business leaders and experts drawn from the ICC membership establish the key business positions, policies and practices on e-business, information technologies and telecommunications through the EBITT Commission.

- Electronic commerce within the WTO. www.wto.org/english/tratop_e/ecom_e/ecom_e.htm.

  The WTO work programme on electronic commerce was adopted by the General Council on 25 September 1998. Under this programme issues related to electronic commerce are being examined by the Goods, Services and TRIPS (intellectual property) Councils, and the Trade and Development Committee. This website provides progress reports, member proposals, and WTO electronic commerce activities and publications.

- For information about UNCITRAL's Model Laws, go to www.uncitral.org.

- Exporting FAQs. U.S. Small Business Administration.
  www.sba.gov/smallbusinessplanner/start/getlicensesandpermits/SERV_BP_EXPFAQ.html.

  The Exporting FAQs has been developed by the United States Small Business Administration (SBA). SBA is an independent agency of the Federal Government.

72.   If a buyer accepts online my online offer of goods for sale, am I legally bound by a contract?

The following answer only applies to business-to-business contracts, and not business-to-consumer contracts.

In countries with a common law system (e.g. India, New Zealand, Nigeria, the United Kingdom), when sellers offer products for sale, they are, as a rule, entitled to revoke their offer at any time before it is accepted by a buyer. This applies to online and offline offers of sale.

In countries with a civil law system (e.g. Brazil, France, Germany, Indonesia), when sellers offer products for sale, they are bound to maintain their offer open (i.e. they cannot revoke their offer as long as they have sufficient stocks of products to meet any order). This principle applies to online as well as offline offers of sale.

In view of the above, potential buyers may wish to provide evidence of their order. The best means for this are:

- To sign the order electronically; or

- To print a copy of the acceptance of the order; or

- Perhaps even to store the exchanges electronically (e.g. by saving them in a folder or database).

A crucial text for business-to-business transactions is Article 14 of the Vienna Convention on the International Sale of Goods of 1980, which defines the terms offer and invitation to make offers, and specifies that an offer must be made to the persons concerned.

1) A message constitutes an offer if it is sufficiently definite and indicates the intention of the offer or to be bound in the case of acceptance. A proposal is sufficiently definite if it indicates the goods and expressly or implicitly fixes or makes provision for determining the quantity and the price.

2) A proposal other than one addressed to one or more specific persons is to be considered merely as an invitation to make offers, unless the contrary is clearly indicated by the person making the proposal.

On the basis of Article 14, a fundamental question arises as to whether an offer should be considered binding where a seller makes a general offer (i.e. not to a specific person or group of persons) on its website and a foreign buyer accepts the offer. On this issue, the United Nations Centre for the Facilitation of Procedures and Practices for Administration, Commerce and Transport (UN/CEFACT), in Article 3.2.1 of its Electronic Commerce Agreement (see appendix V), which was approved in March 2000, provides an answer that can be incorporated into contracts: a message constitutes an offer if it includes a proposal for concluding a contract addressed to one or more specific persons which is sufficiently definite and indicates the intention of the sender of the offer to be bound in case of acceptance. A message made available electronically at large shall, unless otherwise stated therein, not constitute an offer.

Another important question when it comes to e-commerce is when an offer or a response to an offer should be considered to have reached the corresponding party. According to the Advisory Council of the United Nations Convention on Contracts for the International Sale of Goods, CISG-AC, (a private initiative from the Pace University School of Law) an electronic message should be considered to have reached the other party when it has entered that party's server.

For more information

- Juris International, International Trade Centre. www.jurisint.org.

  Juris International is a multilingual collection (English, Spanish, and French) of legal information on international trade. Juris International aims to facilitate and reduce the work involved in research for business lawyers, advisers and in-house counsel, and state organizations in developing and transition economies, by providing access to texts which have often been difficult to obtain. Juris international contains full texts of some 100 arbitration rules, with model clauses, and a description of the services of arbitration centres.

- The Advisory Council of the United Nations Convention on Contracts for the International Sales of Goods (CISG). Institute of International Commercial Law; Pace Law University. www.cisg.law.pace.edu/cisg/text/caseschedule.html.

- Exporting FAQs. U.S. Small Business Administration. www.sba.gov/smallbusinessplanner/start/getlicensesandpermits/SERV_BP_EXPFAQ.html.

  The Exporting FAQs has been developed by the United States Small Business Administration (SBA). SBA is an independent agency of the Federal Government.

73.   How do I sign a contract electronically? Is an electronic signature as binding as a written signature?

Most countries recognize that it is perfectly valid to sign a contract electronically, especially when this occurs in a closed electronic system, such as an electronic data interchange system.

The digital signature is a well-known technology for electronic signatures. This technology, as well as being widespread, is also recognized as being secure. The signatory generates a pair of asymmetrical digital keys: a public and a private key. The key is basically a long number that comes from a cryptographic algorithm. The public key is freely distributed to the public at large, i.e. anyone interested in communicating securely with the holder of both keys. The public key is used to encrypt messages using one of several different encryption algorithms. The second key, a private key, belongs to the key owner, who keeps the key secret. The owner uses the private key to decrypt all messages received. Anyone with the same public key can encrypt information that only the holder of the private key can read.

In order to make sure that the public key used to which you are encrypting data is actually the public key of the intended recipient you could add a digital certificate. The digital certificate is a public key with one or two forms of ID attached. A certification authority, a trusted third party, creates and signs a digital identification certificate, which establishes a link between the signatory and his or her pair of keys, so that the signatory cannot later disclaim the signature.

To sign a document, the key holder creates a message digest, which is a number that summarizes the original information. The message digest is then encrypted with the private key. The encrypted message digest, which can be deciphered by anyone who has the public key, is called a digital signature. Upon receipt of the signed message, the message digest is decrypted and compared with the digest created from the received document. If the two match, then the document has not been altered during transmission. In addition, a match guarantees that the document has been sent by the key holder, and hence authenticates the sender, because only the key holder's private key would yield an encrypted message that could be decrypted by the associated public key. The following figure illustrates how a digital signature and a signed message are created and sent.

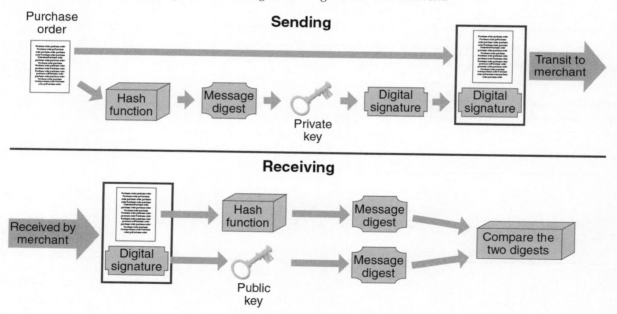

Sending and receiving a digitally signed message [1].

Electronic signatures can be used on anything recorded digitally, for example an e-mail, a picture or a document. The intervention of a third party is indispensable to establishing confidence and security in electronic exchanges, as the contracting parties are never physically present to sign their contracts.

The development of e-commerce relies, to a large extent, on the trust and security that users feel in electronic communications. Applications related to or requiring electronic signatures are numerous. Examples are payments, contracts, administrative declarations and procurement operations.

The Council of Europe since 1981 and UNCITRAL as of 1985 have been recommending that countries should take all necessary measures to eliminate legal requirements imposing paper-based documents and handwritten signatures to the detriment of their data-processing or electronic equivalents.

Article 7 of UNCITRAL's Model Law on Electronic Commerce of 1996 specifies that where the law requires a signature of a person, that requirement is met in relation to a data message if:

- Method is used to identify that person and to indicate that person's approval of the information contained in the data message; and

- That method is as reliable as was appropriate for the purpose for which the data message was generated or communicated, in the light of all the circumstances, including any relevant agreement.

The above applies whether the requirement therein is in the form of an obligation or whether the law simply provides consequences for the absence of a signature.

For more information

- The International PGP homepage, a non-profit initiative provides "The Basics of Cryptography", available online at www.pgpi.org.
- Electronic Signature Factsheet. Department for Business Innovation and Skills. www.berr.gov.uk/files/file34339.pdf.

REFERENCES

[1] Schneider, Gary P. Electronic Commerce. Seventh Edition. Course Technology, a division of Thomson Learning, Inc., 2007. From Chapter 10, page 473.

74.   How can I guarantee that the terms I actually see on my computer are valid?

From a technical perspective, it is impossible to guarantee that the electronic document being displayed on one's computer screen is identical to the document sent. A guarantee can be provided to some extent by having the document or the originating site labelled (certified) by an independent third-party entity such as an auditing firm and a chamber of commerce. Alternatively, cryptographic methods could be used, please refer to question 73: "How do I sign a contract electronically? Is an electronic signature as binding as a written signature?"

75. How can I protect my business, brand name, domain name and published material from being copied?

Brand names (Trademarks and Company names)

The laws of most countries protect brand names (trademarks) when they are distinctive and non-deceptive. Protection for trademarks is usually obtained through registration in a government office. The minimum period of protection for trademarks under the World Trade Organization's Agreement on Trade-Related Aspects of Intellectual Property Rights (TRIPS) is seven years from the date of initial registration. Registration is renewable indefinitely.

A brand name can also be deposited for registration at the international level, with the World Intellectual Property Organization (WIPO). Protection of the brand will then last 20 years in Member States of the Madrid Agreement.

In Europe, the business community can file to register a Community Trademark under European Council Regulation No. 40/94 of 20 December 1993.

The protected brand name can cover one or more classes of products, and its holder has the right of ownership. It should be noted that a design can be protected by both copyright and trademark law at the same time. Manifestly known brand names, even if they are not the subjects of an application for registration, are protected. The illegal copying of a trademark can be the subject of an infringement proceeding.

The illegal registration of a brand name counterfeiting an existing trademark can be the subject of an action in cancellation or of an action in claim to determine the rightful owner of the mark.

Protecting your website's domain name

A company domain name can be registered in a number of different ways, through so called 'top-level domains' (TLDs). You can choose from:

- Generic top-level domains, such as .com, .net, .org and .info;

- Specialized and restricted top-level domains, which you need to qualify to be able to use, for example .aero (air travel and transport business);

- Country code top-level domains, for example .cn for China, .se for Sweden and .ch for Switzerland.

The awarding and registration of a domain name for your website is carried out by organizations that have been delegated this responsibility by the Internet Corporation for Assigned Names and Numbers (ICANN). For example:

- .org is operated by Public Interest Registry;
- .com is operated by the VeriSign Global Registry Services;
- .aero is sponsored by Société Internationale de Télécommunications Aéronautiques SC (SITA).

As domain names are granted on a first-come first-served basis, conflicts often arise between existing brands or trade names and domain names. Hence, the best protection is a simultaneous registration of your brand name (trademark or company name, see above) and your domain name (of the type ending in .com, .fr, .net) with the national organization that manages patent and trademark rights in your country.

It is possible to register your site's domain name as a trademark (if your brand name is already registered with your national intellectual property institute or with WIPO) by justifying your ownership of the trademark. It is thus possible to obtain and register a domain name such as HILTON.tm.fr, if you are the holder of HILTON.

These precautions will ensure effective protection against a possible third party's fraudulent application to register a similar brand name, and later allotment of a domain name. For example, the holder of the mark HILTON will be able to oppose use by, or attribution to, others of HILTTON.fr as a brand or domain name. However, ownership of the HILTON mark alone may not be sufficient (except by invoking some clear offence of unfair competition, of parasitic dealing and of abuse of the right of reservation of the domain name just added) to ensure withdrawal of a domain name such as HILTTON.fr.

ICANN in 2001 implemented a Uniform Domain Name Dispute Resolution Policy (UDRP) upon recommendation from WIPO. Any person or company can file a complaint about a domain name concerning a generic top-level domain name using the UDRP Procedure. For country code top-level domains, which are registered at national authorities, the procedure can still be used as long as the registration authority has adopted the UDRP Policy voluntarily. The disputes still have to follow certain criteria in order for the UDRP Policy to apply:

- The domain name registered by the domain name registrant is identical or confusingly similar to a trademark or service mark in which the complainant (the person or entity bringing the complaint) has rights; and

- The domain name registrant has no rights or legitimate interests in respect of the domain name in question; and

- The domain name has been registered and is being used in bad faith.

Protecting published material on the Web

According to the Berne Convention, which was signed in 1886 and last revised in 1996, any original intellectual creation that is subject to ownership, confers on the owner a monopoly over exploitation, and provides the following exclusive rights: representation, reproduction, translation, broadcasting, adaptation, recording, public reciting, right of continuity, moral rights. The protection lasts for the lifetime of the author and 50 years after his or her death. According to the World Trade Organization's TRIPS Agreement, computer programs should be considered literary works, and protected under national copyright laws.

Legal precedent in several European countries and in North America has established that digitalization of an intellectual creation without the right to do so constitutes illegal reproduction.

In addition to the symbols for copyright and for registered trademark, which inform the user that a work is protected, one of the most common protections currently in use is electronic tattooing (watermarking) and citing of a third party, agent and identifier of work. Hence the work protected by copyright law can freely circulate on digital networks insofar as watermarking reinforces the right of ownership of its author, the author being identified. It also makes it possible to know the methods used to manage any royalties, and thus to whom rights must be paid.

Know-how, commercial secrets and ideas

You should be aware that know-how, commercial secrets and ideas are not protected by patent or copyright laws. They are difficult to protect, except by means of a confidentiality agreement. It is necessary to have such an agreement to prevent any collaborators, partners, subcontractors or customers from exploiting ideas that a company wishes to protect.

In practice, protection is ensured by undertakings of confidentiality and non-competition clauses in contracts, together with penalty clauses in the event of any violation of the agreement.

In addition, several countries provide protection facilities such as the possibility for depositing sealed, date-stamped envelopes containing details of trade secrets at the national industrial property institute. A virtual equivalent is the InterDeposit Digital Number system (IDDN), which identifies the owner of digital works and lays down conditions for their use. It provides right holders the possibility of protecting and exercising their rights over their digital creations.

Under the system, an IDDN identifying a specific digital work is assigned by the international federation InterDeposit. As the IDDN website says, a right holder obtains an IDDN certificate to be attached to the work, containing in particular the IDDN, the title of the work, the special conditions of use and exploitation and any original sources of creation. Chain uses of digital works may then be made in compliance with intellectual property rights, thanks to the identification at each stage of the right holders, their respective creative contributions and the conditions they have stipulated for the use of their work. The international IDDN is designed to accompany the work in all its reproductions and representations, and the right holder can thus always be identified. InterDeposit carries out checks for any unlawful use or reproduction on the Internet

The Internet and its content (images, sounds, designs, models and text) are multimedia by nature. This, in conjunction with its international character, makes traditional distinctions between works of the mind, designs or models less and less relevant. It is not possible here to go into greater detail of the various rights concerned.

For more information

- Intellectual property issues related to e-commerce. World Intellectual Property Organization. www.wipo.int/sme/en/e_commerce/index.htm.

  The purpose of these pages is to provide non-lawyers with a quick guide on IP issues related to E-Commerce. You can use these pages to link to other websites where you can get more in-depth information.

- The Trade Marks and Designs Registration Office of the European Union; The Office for Harmonization in the Internal Market. oami.europa.eu.

  OHIM is the European Union agency responsible for registering trademarks and designs that are valid in all 27 countries of the EU.

- Domain Name Dispute Resolution. WIPO Arbitration and Mediation Center. www.wipo.int/amc/en/index.html.

  Based in Geneva, Switzerland, the WIPO Arbitration and Mediation Center was established in 1994 to offer Alternative Dispute Resolution (ADR) options, in particular arbitration and mediation, for the resolution of international commercial disputes between private parties. Developed by leading experts in cross-border dispute settlement, the procedures offered by the Center are widely recognized as particularly appropriate for technology, entertainment and other disputes involving intellectual property.

- Trademark Database Portal. World Intellectual Property Organization. www.wipo.int/amc/en/trademark/index.html.

  WIPO has a Trademark Database Portal where you can search and find out if the domain name you have chosen is a registered trademark in a particular country.

- InterDeposit Digital Number. www.iddn.org.

  InterDeposit, an international federation for data-processing and information technologies, set up in Geneva on 10 January, 1994, is made up of the various organizations concerned by the protection of intellectual property rights over digital works. This website has information and links related to IDDN, and International protection of author's rights.

76. What guidelines and regulations exist for the protection of the confidentiality of electronic exchanges?

The exchange of files by e-mail, FTP (File transfer protocol, a system for transferring files between computers over the Internet.), or other means without any specific protection does not offer any guarantee of confidentiality. The exchanged data can easily be intercepted (and read) and even modified.

One should also take into account the fact that most electronic exchanges (telephone, fax, e-mail, etc.) with other countries can be intercepted and read (or heard) by the new supercomputers. This means that all significant data from an industrial or commercial point of view can be intercepted and redistributed to rival companies. For instance, a fax or an e-mail originating from an aeronautical manufacturer on a commercial bid for an airline could, in theory, become known to competitors who could then rapidly realign prices on their first offers and win the bid.

Confidentiality of electronic exchanges is therefore crucial, not only for the security of electronic trade, but also for the commercial survival of companies and the privacy of their personnel.

At the international level, the following guidelines and regulations exist:

- Guidelines for Cryptography Policy, adopted by the OECD Council on 7 March, 1997.

- Wassenaar Agreement of 11-12 July, 1996, in force in September 1996 (covering 40 countries) and amended in 2001.

- Council Regulation (EC) No. 3381/94 of 19 December 1994 setting up a Community regime for the control of exports of dual-use goods; and Council Decision 94/942/CFSP of 19 December 1994 on the joint action adopted by the Council of the basis of Article J.3 of the Treaty on European Union concerning the control of exports of dual-use goods.

Nevertheless, as the cryptography system affects the internal and external security of countries, each sovereign State applies its own policies to serve its strategic interests.

For more information

- Intellectual Property in the Global Marketplace (Valuation, Protection, Exploitation, and Electronic Commerce, vol.1). *By* Simensky, M. *and others.* John Wiley & Sons Inc., 1999.

- The Wassenaar agreement. www.wassenaar.org.

  The Wassenaar Arrangement seeks to promote transparency and greater responsibility in transfers of conventional arms and dual-use goods and technologies.

- OECD Cryptography Guidelines: Recommendation of the Council. OECD Directorate for Science, Technology and Industry. 1997. www.oecd.org/document/34/0,3343,en_2649_201185_1814690_1_1_1_1,00.html.

77. Why should I consider intellectual property issues in undertaking e-commerce?

IP is a crucial element of e-commerce. More than other business systems, e-commerce often involves selling products and services that are based on IP and its licensing. Music, pictures, photos, software, designs, training modules, systems, etc. can all be traded through e-commerce, and IP is the main component of value in the transaction. IP is also important because the things of value that are traded on the Internet must be protected, using technological security systems and IP laws, otherwise they can be stolen or pirated and whole businesses can be destroyed.

IP is also involved in making e-commerce work. The systems that allow the Internet to function – software, networks, designs, chips, routers and switches, the user interface, and so on – are often protected by IP rights. Trademarks are an essential part of e-commerce business because branding, customer recognition and goodwill – the essential elements of a web-based business – are all protected by trademarks and unfair competition law.

E-commerce and Internet-related businesses may also be based on product or patent licensing. This is because so many different technologies are required to create a product that companies often choose to outsource the development of some components, or share technologies through licensing arrangements. If every company had to develop and produce all the technological aspects of its products independently, the development of high-tech products would be impossible. The economics of e-commerce depends on companies working together to share, through licensing, the opportunities and risks of business. Many of these companies are SMEs.

And finally, a great deal of the value of e-commerce-based businesses is usually held in the form of IP – so the valuation of an e-commerce business will be affected by whether it has protected its IP rights. Many e-commerce companies, like other technology companies, have patent portfolios, trademarks, domain names, software or original databases that are by far their most valuable business assets.

For more information

- Intellectual Property on the Internet: A Survey of Issues. WIPO. 2002.
  www.wipo.int/export/sites/www/copyright/en/ecommerce/pdf/survey.pdf.

  Discusses the far-reaching impact that digital technologies, the Internet in particular, have had on intellectual property (IP) and the international IP system.

- eBusiness lex.net. www.ebusinesslex.net.

  Portal offering European companies, in particular SMEs, information on all legal aspects of e-business.

- A Legal Guide to the Internet; 4th edition. Merchant & Gould and the Minnesota Department of Trade and Economic Development. 2002. www.merchantgould.com/attachments/11.pdf.

  Discusses IP issues that arise when operating on the Internet. Covers IP and legal issues in use of e-mail and e-video, e-commerce, related to domain names, use of trademarks, patents and copyright on the Internet, with other contractual and employment related issues, mainly from a United States perspective.

78.   What are the intellectual property issues involved in choosing and registering domain names?

Domain names are Internet addresses, and are commonly used to identify and find websites. For example, the domain name 'wipo.int' is used to locate the WIPO website at www.wipo.int. Over time, domain names have come to constitute business identifiers, thereby coming into conflict with trademarks. It is important, therefore, to pick a domain name that is not the trademark of another company, or a well-known mark.

The choice of a domain name (or Internet address) has become one of the most important business decisions a company can make. A domain name is registered by you to enable Internet users to locate your company's site on the World Wide Web. Company domain names may be registered in any number of top-level domains (TLDs). You can choose from the generic top-level domains, such as .com, .net, .org and .info. Or you can choose from the specialized and restricted top-level domains if you qualify (such as .aero for air travel and transport businesses, or .biz for commercial enterprises).

You can also register your domain name under a country specific top-level domain, for example: .bn for Bulgaria, .cn for China, .ch for Switzerland.

The technical management of the domain name system is in the hands of the Internet Corporation for Assigned Names and Numbers (ICANN). However, for generic top-level domains, the registrations themselves are handled by a number of Internet registrars accredited by ICANN. These can be found at ICANN's site at www.icann.org. You can also check whether a domain name has already been registered, either by searching a registrar's site, or by using a 'Who is' search, such as that at www.uwhois.com.

For registrations in the country specific top-level domains, you will need to contact the registration authority designated for each country domain name. For this, consult a country code top-level domain database set up by WIPO, that links to the websites of 243 domains, where you can find information about their registration agreement, the 'Who is' service and dispute resolution procedures.

For further information on domain names you may refer to question 0: "What is a domain name and why do I have to register it?", and question 25: "How do I register or buy a domain name?".

For more information

- A Legal Guide to the Internet; 4th edition. Merchant & Gould and the Minnesota Department of Trade and Economic Development. 2002. www.merchantgould.com/attachments/11.pdf.

  Discusses IP issues that arise when operating on the Internet. Covers IP and legal issues in use of e-mail and e-video, e-commerce, related to domain names, use of trademarks, patents and copyright on the Internet, with other contractual and employment related issues, mainly from a United States perspective.

- The Internet Corporation for Assigned Names and Numbers (ICANN). www.icann.org/faq.

  Answers to frequently asked questions on domain name registrations, including IP issues.

- Domain name disputes. WIPO. http://arbiter.wipo.int/center/faq/domains.html#b.

  A range of documents on domain name disputes and how to resolve them.

79.   What should I consider when choosing a domain name?

Depending on where you register, you may pick a commonly used generic name, but if you choose a name that is distinctive, users are more likely to be able to remember and search for it more easily. Ideally, it should be distinctive enough also to be protectable under trademark law, because domain names can be protected as trademarks in some countries. If you pick a very common phrase as your domain name (e.g. 'Good Software'), your company could have difficulty in building up any special reputation or goodwill in this name and even more difficulty in preventing others from using your name in competition.

You should pick a domain name that is not the trademark of another company, particularly a well-known mark. This is because most laws treat domain name registration of another person's trademark as trademark infringement (also known as 'cybersquatting') and your company might have to transfer or cancel the domain name, as well as pay any damages. All domain names registered in the generic top-level domains category, such as .com, and many registered in the 'country code top-level domain' are subject to a dispute resolution procedure (described below) that allows a trademark or service-mark owner to prevent 'cybersquatting' of their trademark.

There are various databases that you can search on the Web to determine if your choice of domain name is a registered trademark in a particular country. WIPO has established a trademark database portal (ecommerce.wipo.int/databases/trademark) to help you carry out this search.

If you find that someone else is using your trademark or service mark as a domain name, there is a simple online procedure you can go through where an independent expert will decide whether the domain name should be returned to you, and the registrars are required to follow this decision. You can find information on this Uniform Administrative Dispute Resolution Policy (UDRP) at the WIPO site http://arbiter.wipo.int/domains.

In addition to trademarks, it is wise to avoid domain names that include certain other controversial words such as geographical terms (e.g. Champagne, Beaujolais), names of famous people, generic drug names, names of international organizations and trade names (e.g. name of another person's business) that might interfere with the rights of others or international systems of protection.

For further information on domain names you may refer to question 24: "What is a domain name and why do I have to register it?", and question 25: "How do I register or buy a domain name?".

For more information

- The Internet Corporation for Assigned Names and Numbers (ICANN). www.icann.org/faq.

  Answers to frequently asked questions on domain name registrations, including IP issues.

- Frequently Asked Questions: Internet Domain Names. WIPO. http://arbiter.wipo.int/domains.

  Provides links to a number of domain name-related articles, publications, frequently asked questions, news items and information on domain name disputes.

- The Universal 'Who is' for Internet Domain Names. www.uwhois.com.

  Search engine to identify the registered holder of a domain name.

80.   What intellectual property issues should I consider when I design and build my company's website?

One of the basic elements of e-commerce is the design and function of the company website. In designing and building your website, the first thing to be aware of is whether you own the website presentation and content and every aspect of IP in it. You may not, but this is not necessarily a problem. What is important is to know what you own, what you have rights to use, and what you do not own or have rights to use. If you are using a consultant or specialist company to design your website, check out the provisions in the agreement concerning ownership and IP rights. Who owns the website design and text? Check out exactly what obligations the company has and ensure it does not use, in the course of its work, any IP that belongs to a third party.

If you are using a database, software, a search engine or other technical Internet tools licensed to you by another company, check the terms of the licence agreement to see who owns the system, whether you are allowed to make modifications to the system and who owns such modifications. Make sure that you have a written agreement, and get it checked by a lawyer before you sign it and before any design, custom work or installation of the site begins.

You will need written permission (also referred to as a licence, a consent or an agreement) to use any photos, videos, music, voices, art work or software, etc. that belong to someone else. Just because you find material on the Internet does not mean that it is in the public domain. You may have to pay for permission to use this material. In many countries you will need to communicate with a collecting society or association of artists in order to get permission.

Do not distribute from, or download onto, your website any content or music that does not belong to you, unless you have obtained written permission from the owner to distribute it on the Internet.

Hyperlinks

Take care when linking to other websites. Links are a great e-commerce tool, and a useful service to your customers, but in many countries there is no clear law on when and how you can use links. The safest practice is to seek and obtain permission from the other site before putting in the link, especially if you are 'deep-linking' i.e. linking to a page on another website that is not the homepage.

Framing

Framing is a practice that is more controversial than linking. It means including parts of another website in your website in a way that makes it look as though it is part of your site. Always get written permission before doing this.

For more information

- A Legal Guide to the Internet; 4th edition. Merchant & Gould and the Minnesota Department of Trade and Economic Development. 2002. www.merchantgould.com/attachments/11.pdf.

  Discusses IP issues that arise when operating on the Internet. Covers IP and legal issues in use of e-mail and e-video, e-commerce, related to domain names, use of trademarks, patents and copyright on the Internet, with other contractual and employment related issues, mainly from a United States perspective.

- Intellectual Property on the Internet: A Survey of Issues. WIPO. 2002. http://ecommerce.wipo.int/survey.

  Discusses the far-reaching impact that digital technologies, the Internet in particular, have had on intellectual property (IP) and the international IP system.

81. How can I protect my intellectual property rights on the Web? What precautions can I take to avoid violating the intellectual property rights of others?

In recent years, there has been much publicity about the unlawful distribution of IP-protected music, films, art, photos, scripts and software ('content') on the Internet. These unauthorized downloads often violate national laws of copyright.

It is important to protect your IP rights on the Internet. This can be done in a number of ways. Always clearly identify your content, with either a copyright notice or some other indication of ownership. You may wish to simply tell users what they can and cannot do with your content. Never distribute or permit downloads of third party content that does not belong to your company, and put in place programmes to make sure that your employees understand your company policies in this regard.

The Napster case in the United States puts an international spotlight on the unauthorized downloading of music files. The case, which resulted in the court issuing a permanent injunction preventing Napster from operating its file-sharing system, was a 'contributory infringement' case because the claim was that Napster facilitated illegal copying by users of the system, not that Napster copied the files itself. Other cases will continue to test the law in this area, and there may be different issues and different results in different jurisdictions, but the lesson of Napster is that it is important for an e-commerce company to make sure it has a clear policy against unauthorized copying of files, or any actions that encourage or facilitate such copying.

Increasingly, some companies are using technical means to protect content on the Internet by watermarking, encrypting or otherwise creating identification and tracking systems. Electronic copyright management systems are being proposed by business consortia and individual companies, which see these systems as a way to use technical means to control use of content.

For more information

- A Legal Guide to the Internet; 4th edition. Merchant & Gould and the Minnesota Department of Trade and Economic Development. 2002. www.merchantgould.com/attachments/11.pdf.

  Discusses IP issues that arise when operating on the Internet. Covers IP and legal issues in use of e-mail and e-video, e-commerce, related to domain names, use of trademarks, patents and copyright on the Internet, with other contractual and employment related issues, mainly from a United States perspective.

- Dusollier, S. Legal Aspects of Electronic Rights Management Systems. Research Center for Computer and Law (CRID), University of Namur. www.droit.fundp.ac.be/Textes/Dusollier%204.pdf.

  Discusses the importance of and need for regulatory mechanisms for electronic rights management systems.

Trust, security and encryption

82.   How can consumers shop online with confidence?

Here are some of the questions that you should ask yourself any time you visit an unknown e-commerce website: How do you know you are dealing with a reputable merchant? Do you have enough product information to make a decision to buy especially when you cannot touch or sample the product? How do you buy something on the Internet, and what do you do if something goes wrong? How can you ensure that your personal and financial information is secure and will be treated confidentially?

Some tips to help you answer these questions and shop online with confidence are given below [1].

Shopping online

- **Think about security**, starting with your connection. Information sent over the Internet can be intercepted. If this information includes your credit card number, for example, then you should take steps to ensure that your credit card details are protected. One common method by which online merchants can offer acceptable levels of security to their customers is to set up a secure server. This server uses a modification of the hypertext transfer protocol (HTTP) to ensure that communications between it and web browsers are encrypted, using strong encryption methods. Most popular browsers are capable of participating in this encrypted exchange protecting the information you exchange with the server. When you connect to a server using a secure connection, the web address starts with 'https://' instead of the regular 'http://'. This is also highlighted in most browsers by showing lock logo at the bottom of the page.
  You should be wary, however, of the further use of information sent over the Internet. Although the exchange with a secure server using the secure communications protocol is protected, the data stored on the server after the exchange (your credit card number, for example) is not encrypted. It may be retransmitted, without your knowledge, on the open Internet, or even stolen by some person with physical access to the server computer. Ultimately, the only guarantee of security is to use encrypted communications and to deal with a reputable company, which will respect your privacy and the need for secure treatment of your private data once they have acquired it.

- **Know the merchant you are dealing with.** Look for websites that are professionally designed and display the company name and address prominently along with detailed contact information. You may even want to call the telephone number to verify it. In addition, you can check a company's standing with organizations such as the Better Business Bureau (www.bosbbb.org, covers North America) and consumer agencies.

- **Look for detailed product information.** Look for websites that offer detailed information on their products and services in plain, understandable language.

- **Read the contractual terms and conditions and save them.** This should include the full price, delivery options, return policies, warranties and methods of transaction. If necessary, ask about shipping charges so you will know in advance what you will be expected to pay. Before ordering, make sure you understand what the company's return policy is.

- **Check for quality assurance certificates or seals.** The agencies that issue approval ratings and certifications of online businesses verify that the business exists at its claimed address and provide results of audits and other checks.

- **Verify that the merchant has a fair and clear complaints-handling process.** A merchant's website should include a simple process for handling complaints, concerns and inquiries.

- **Some Internet sites ask you to create an account with a password.** To protect yourself, do not use the password you use for other accounts or sites.

Credit card caution

- **Ensure that you are comfortable with the merchant's purchasing process** and that you know how to cancel your order. Most websites allow you to complete an order form or fill a shopping cart with the items you are considering buying. Only after you complete and confirm your list and transaction arrangements should you finalize the sale by clicking the send button. Make sure the full price, terms and conditions and methods of transaction are clearly set out and that you print or save a copy of the transaction.

- **Make sure the website has a secure transaction system to protect your financial information**. Ensure that the merchant has a security system in place before you send your credit card number over the Internet. Merchants who use secure transaction systems will advertise this fact.

- **Before giving out your credit card number online, look for the graphic that indicates that the business is operating with a secure server**. If you are not sure that the connection is secure, you may not wish to transmit your credit card information. Also, be aware that the web server is not the only point from which your data could be fraudulently acquired.

Personal information

- **Be cautious if you are asked to supply personal information**, such as your national identification number or personal bank account information. This information is not required for a purchase.

- **Not all personal information is equally important**. Personal information that most people do not know about you, such as a national identification number or mother's maiden name, is far more sensitive than a name and address that can be found in a telephone book. In many countries, a mother's maiden name is used to confirm identity and is especially sensitive information.

- **Review the merchant's policy for protecting personal information**. Reputable websites will post a privacy policy on their website telling you how they will treat information you submit while making a purchase. If you cannot find the privacy policy, contact the site and ask to see its policy on privacy protection. Be aware that if you consent to allow your name to be used by other organizations you may receive more marketing information or solicitations.

General

- **Remember that buying internationally involves risk**. Check that products meet your governments health and safety standards, know how much money you are willing to risk if something goes wrong owing to complicated and costly redress and different laws, check on the limits to guarantees on foreign products, and in which currency the prices are quoted.

- **Be on your guard against mass-market e-mail**. If you receive junk or unsolicited commercial e-mail from a merchant, do not reply even to ask to be removed from the sender's e-mail list.

- **Watch out for scams**. Be especially wary of any offer that sounds too good to be true, a site that asks you to send personal or financial information before disclosing an offer, promises of a valuable prize in return for a low-cost purchase, or glittering investment schemes.

  When receiving a suspicious e-mail you may check the possibility of a scam on sites such as PC Magazine's Security Watch blog (http://blogs.pcmag.com/securitywatch).

For more information

- Canada's Office of Consumer Affairs (OCA). www.ic.gc.ca/eic/site/oca-bc.nsf/eng/h_ca02132.html.

  OCA's website has a section on e-commerce where in addition to the Canadian code of practice for consumer protection in electronic commerce, you can find an Internet sales contract template and ways to earn consumer trust on the Internet. The identity theft section of the website provides information on how to reduce the risk of identity theft, tips on how to protect yourself and what to do if identify theft happens.

- Guidelines for consumer protection in electronic commerce. Consumer protection commission; Executive Yuan, Republic of China.
  www.cpc.gov.tw/KnowledgeBase_Query/ShowFAQ_English.asp?ID=5015&CID=652.

REFERENCES

[1] Principles of consumer protection for electronic commerce: A Canadian framework. Consumer Measures Committee-Industry Canada. cmcweb.ca/eic/site/cmc-cmc.nsf/eng/fe00113.html.

83.   Is e-commerce safe? If it is, why are many people afraid of making payments through the Internet?

E-commerce can be a safe way to conduct business. If it were not, e-commerce would not be continuing to grow at the rate that it is.

Safety is never an absolute state, only a relative one. Compared to the level of fraud affecting other forms of consumer purchasing, the Internet appears to be safe. Every shopper who hands a credit card across a shop counter, gives it to a waiter in a restaurant or reads the number over the telephone to make a purchase, is taking a greater risk that the card will be fraudulently used than a consumer on a secure Internet connection.

For merchants, the overall risks of e-commerce are probably lower than they are for a traditional business. An e-merchant can dramatically reduce such commercial risks as inventory risk and the risks of fire, theft and employee pilfering.

Customers need to be aware of the risks and to be cautious about electronic transactions in the same way, as they would be with any other type of payment. If a deal sounds too good to be true then it probably is.

There are people who eagerly embrace new ideas. Others will consider using innovations only when these have been proven to be effective. They will become repeat users if they find the new ways satisfactory. Eventually, the new ways will become routine and the old ways will disappear.

The Internet has been found to be workable and effective. Many individuals purchasing through the Internet have become comfortable with the process. Unfortunately, however, some websites are not secure and there are people who have been defrauded. The media gives widespread coverage to problems arising from the lack of security on the Internet.

At the same time, it reports on the explosive use of the Web, citing the rapidly rising numbers of users around the world and increased sales of consumer goods. They focus on ongoing research and relate how companies are developing new strategies to take advantage of the Internet. The positive stories encourage greater use of the Internet.

There are many institutes and companies that are constantly working to increase awareness, develop the underlying technology for a secure communication over the Internet and offer the required components for safer online commerce. Some of them are also a good source of security information on the Internet for both buyers and sellers. Some examples are:

- National Fraud Information Center. www.fraud.org. The mission of the National Fraud Information Center is to give consumers the information they need to avoid becoming victims of telemarketing and Internet fraud and to help them get their complaints to law enforcement agencies quickly and easily.

- RSA Fraud Center. www.rsa.com. The RSA Online Fraud Resource Center provides information and expertise on the latest threats and trends in online fraud including that supplied by the RSA Anti-Fraud Command Center. This website publishes a monthly online fraud report.

- Verisign. www.verisign.com. Verisign's SSL, identity and authentication, and domain name services allow companies and consumers all over the world to engage in trusted communications and commerce.

- eTrust. www.etrust.org. The Electronic Trust foundation (eTrust) is an organization dedicated to the promotion of online privacy through the establishment of best practice and policy. eTrust is also responsible for the Safe to Shop e-commerce certification.

- WISeKey. www.wisekey.com. WISeKey is a known source of encryption and identification products and services, which enable public and private organizations to identify individuals and assets and engage in safe, secure and confidential electronic communications and transactions.

- The Center for Internet Security. www.cisecurity.org. The Center for Internet Security (CIS) is a not-for-profit organization that helps enterprises reduce the risk of business and e-commerce disruptions resulting from inadequate technical security controls, and provides enterprises with resources for measuring information security status and making rational security investment decisions.

- Community Emergency Response Teams (CERT). www.cert.org. The CERT Programme is part of the Software Engineering Institute (SEI), a federally funded research and development centre at Carnegie

Mellon University in Pittsburgh, Pennsylvania. The CERT coordination centre (CERT/CC) is in charge of coordination communication among experts during security emergencies and to help prevent future incidents. In addition CERT offers public training courses for technical staff and managers, some of which are offered online: www.vte.cert.org.

- Information Warfare Site (IWS). www.iwar.org.uk. IWS is an online resource that aims to stimulate debate on a variety of issues involving information security, information operations, computer network operations, homeland security and more. It is the aim of the site to develop a special emphasis on offensive and defensive information operations.

84. How do I inspire confidence in my trustworthiness as a supplier through my website?

Surveys show over and over again that customers consider the trustworthiness of a supplier the most important determinant of their decisions to buy: they must have confidence that the supplier will deliver the goods described, of the quality specified and within the expected period. Even to make your first sale, you should specifically address the issue by:

- Being professional in your use of text and graphics.

- Making the content of your site easy to understand, perhaps by providing an option for viewing the site in a second language.

- Informing visitors, through the use of text and symbols, of the certifications you have earned for your products and services.

- Providing information on your firm (turnover, trading history, principals) and verifiable recommendations from recent customers.

- Providing references, such as evidence of membership of business or professional associations (particularly associations with an international presence), together with their contact details.

- For sites offering consumer goods that can be ordered immediately, asking prospective buyers for appropriate billing information, including their e-mail addresses.

- Providing security symbols where you outline payment procedures.

- Providing buyers an opportunity to confirm their purchases.

- Providing your address, telephone and fax numbers and enabling the viewer to click on your e-mail address to send you an e-mail.

- Stating your privacy policy for information that visitors may provide.

- Asking visitors for information (contact details, preferences, experience of your products or competitive products, product suggestions). Do not expect to get a response unless you provide some incentive such as a small prize, a discount on a purchase or an item of value that can be transmitted online.

- Offering an Internet escrow service to give customers assurance of satisfactory performance before they transfer funds.

- Recognizing that potential customers are likely to visit a site several times before making a purchase. A hit counter is not convincing evidence of such activity. Testimonials from customers, a feedback facility for customers and visitors (where comments are visible online) are better, as is up-to-date news of company activity and sales.

Legitimacy should be built into your website. However, trust is also dependent upon how well you treat the viewers who contact you after they have been to your site.

Respond quickly to any inquiry. The verification of credit cards can be automated so that confirmation of receipt and acceptance of orders can be sent by e-mail within minutes. The confirmation should carry a brief mention of all the pertinent details of the purchase: the name of the product(s) and the payment method.

Factors affecting Internet purchasing:

The customers most likely to make the transition to online buying are your existing customers, who already trust you.

Other factors, which will affect the willingness of the customer to pay online, include:

How much they know about your company

- Company name or brand name recognition
- Ease of contact: availability of street address, e-mail, phone and fax numbers
- Pictures or location maps that show you really exist
- Customer lists and references
- Testimonials from current customers
- Affiliations with known and respected organizations

How much they are planning to spend

- The size of the transaction – people are more willing to risk small amounts
- Incentives
- Discounts for online payment
- Loyalty programmes

Security

- A secured site
- A trusted payment service provider

Image

- The reputation of your company
- The reputation of the country in which you are located
- The reputation of the payment service you are using
- The reputation of the Internet service provider or web hosting service that you are

Blogs are examples of how companies can use the Web to engage in communications with customers that more closely resemble the personal contact mode of communication. Typically a personal contact inspires a higher level of trust, compared to mass media communication modes such as the Internet.

Trust seals

Companies such as TRUSTe (www.truste.com) offer a web privacy seal programme. The TRUSTe privacy seals help businesses promote online safety and trust, and guide consumers to websites that protect their privacy online.

Trust Guard (www.trust-guard.com) is another company that offers security, privacy, and business seals.

For more information

- Furman. S. Building Trust, Usability.gov, September 2009. www.usability.gov/articles/092009news.html.

  Online trust is important whether you are trying to distribute information or initiating online business transactions. Users decide whether they are going to 'buy' your information or your goods and services based on trust.

85.   What is being done to reassure consumers about the increased safety and privacy of Internet transactions?

Individual firms, computer system vendors, trade associations and governments are taking steps to ensure safety and privacy and to assure their partners of this.

Individual firms

Firms setting up websites are:

- Purchasing more sophisticated versions of software applications that include encryption, firewalls and other security devices.
- Including statements on privacy and security in their website text and graphics.
- Establishing order confirmation procedures.

The firms with established websites are:

- Upgrading their current computer systems.
- Including statements on privacy and security in their website text and graphics.
- Establishing order confirmation procedures.

Vendors of computer systems

Recognizing that they should be part of the solution to security problems, vendors are developing new techniques and new products to address current and future problems of fraudulent use of computer systems.

Trade associations

Individual industries are educating their members about problems and solutions, and training them on how to incorporate safety measures into their websites.

Governments

The nature of cyber crime and its gravity changes every day, as more and more people rely on computers and the Internet in their daily life, and because the technology is constantly changing. That is why many governments have started to educate people on common security issues and to provide up-to-date information on how to protect themselves from attacks. The United States Computer Emergency Readiness Team (US-CERT) is one example. In addition to supporting the Federal Civil Executive branch, US-CERT (www.us-cert.gov) interacts with federal agencies, industry, the research community, state and local governments, and others to disseminate reasoned and actionable cyber security information to the public. US-CERT also provides a way for citizens, businesses, and other institutions to communicate and coordinate directly with the United States government about cyber security.

An integral component of any national cyber security strategy is the adoption of appropriate legislation against the misuse of ICTs for criminal or other purposes, including activities intended to affect the integrity of national critical information infrastructures [1]. As threats can originate anywhere around the globe, the challenges are inherently international in scope and it is desirable to harmonize legislative norms as much as possible to facilitate regional and international cooperation.

In the United States, after massive attacks in February 2000 on the security of several major websites, the White House held a meeting with industry leaders to address the issue and the Federal Bureau of Investigation became involved. Criminal law were examined to determine its applicability to events that disrupt Internet transactions of all kinds and to identify what new laws may be required.

In April 1999, the Telecommunications Ministers of the then 15 European Union countries agreed a draft directive to govern the use of electronic signatures.

In March 2000, officials of the United States Government and the European Commission announced that they had reached preliminary agreement on new regulations to safeguard consumer privacy, ending several years of differences on the approach to such rules. Online businesses that fail to meet standards of consumer privacy protection will be liable for prosecution under existing laws governing deceptive practice.

In May 2009 the International Telecommunication Union (ITU) released a Toolkit for Cybercrime Legislation [2]. The toolkit was developed by a global, multidisciplinary team of policy experts, industry representatives, academicians, attorneys, technical experts and government personnel from around the globe. The toolkit aims to provide countries with sample legislative language and reference materials that can assist in the establishment of harmonized cybercrime laws and procedural rules.

Generally, businesses are expected to follow these principles when dealing with personal information:

- Companies conducting business online are usually required by law to disclose clearly how they collect and use information.
- Consumers must be given control of how their data are used.
- Web surfers should have the ability to inspect that data and to correct any errors they discover.
- When companies break the rules, the government must have the power to impose penalties.

The OECD Working Party on Information Security and Privacy (WPISP) develops policy options to sustain trust, information security and privacy in the global networked society, www.oecd.org/sti/security-privacy. The OECD Guidelines for the Security of Information Systems and Networks are downloadable from the OECD website: www.oecd.org/dataoecd/16/22/15582260.pdf.

There has been considerable international recognition of the OECD security guidelines, international cooperative security initiatives among governments, and some information security initiatives by international/regional organizations. The OECD website has compiled a collection of these security initiatives, as well as some online tools at: www.oecd.org/site/0,3407,en_21571361_36139259_1_1_1_1_1,00.html.

In 2003, the European Commission adopted a proposal for a regulation establishing a European Network and Information Security Agency (ENISA), europa.eu/agencies/community_agencies/enisa/index_en.htm, to help increase information exchange and cooperation between different stakeholders in Europe. The aim is to ensure a high level of network and information security within the EU and to contribute to the development of a culture of network and information security.

Measures to achieve a culture of security include:

- Raising ICT users' awareness and responsibility
- An advisory and coordination role to ensure international functions are provided
- Public/private cooperation, more specifically an information exchange between public and private units, to accelerate legislation, standardization and certification procedures
- Regular review and updating of the legal framework for e-security to adapt to changing requirements
- A European Warning and Information System incorporating Computer Emergency Response Teams to react directly to possible e-security threats
- Ensuring that necessary research and development into security components is carried out and that security products, such as encryption software, are freely available and affordable

For information on ways to inspire confidence in customers please refer to question 84: "How do I inspire confidence in my trustworthiness as a supplier through my website?"

For more information

- The OECD Working Party on Information Security and Privacy (WPISP). Organisation for Economic Co-operation and Development (OECD). www.oecd.org/sti/security-privacy.
- ICT Security and e-payments. E-business w@tch; Cross-sector studies on specific ICT topics, September 2005. www.ebusiness-watch.org/studies/special_topics.htm.

REFERENCES

[1] ITU-D ICT Applications and Cybersecurity Division. International Telecommunication Union. www.itu.int/ITU-D/cyb/.

[2] ITU Toolkit for Cybercrime Legislation. International Telecommunication Union. www.itu.int/ITU-D/cyb/cybersecurity/projects/cyberlaw.html.

86.   How is an online privacy statement formulated?

A Privacy statement is a legal document. The purpose of a privacy policy is to inform your customers how their personal information will be used by your company. It also describes how this information and other data are retained by the website, how they will be processed, and whether they will be disclosed to third parties. It is strongly recommended that all small and medium-sized enterprises, government agencies and national organizations post a privacy statement on their websites. The statement should be easy to find by customers (e.g. the first page of the website should provide a link to the statement).

According to the OECD's report and recommendations, privacy notices are an excellent tool to disclose an organization's privacy practices and policies [1]. Research suggests, however, that many notices are too lengthy, confusing, and contain complex legal language. This report recommends that privacy notices be short, simple and usable to make it easier for individuals to assimilate the information they contain and to compare the privacy practices of the organizations processing their personal data.

The contents of the privacy policy will depend upon the applicable laws of your country. You should check your national websites for examples of privacy statements conforming to national law.

Websites may define their privacy policies using the following standards, allowing browsers to automatically asses the level of privacy:

- The Platform for Privacy Preferences (P3P) project (www.w3.org/P3P): P3P is a protocol developed by W3C that enables websites to express their privacy practices in a standard format that can be retrieved automatically and interpreted easily by user agents. P3P user agents will allow users to be informed of site practices (in both machine- and human-readable formats) and to automate decision-making based on these practices when appropriate.

- The Internet Rating Association (ICRA), www.fosi.org/icra: ICRA (formerly the Internet Content Rating Association) is part of the Family Online Safety Institute (www.fosi.org), an international, non-profit organization working to develop a safer Internet. The centrepiece of the organization is the descriptive vocabulary, often referred to as "the ICRA questionnaire." Content providers check which of the elements in the questionnaire are present or absent from their websites. This then generates a small file containing the labels that is then linked to the content on one or more domains. Users can then use filtering software to allow or disallow access to websites based on the information declared in the label.

Privacy seal programmes

For more information please refer to question 84 "How do I inspire confidence in my trustworthiness as a supplier through my website?"

For more information

- Sample Privacy Notice. Council of Better Business Bureau. www.bbbonline.org/privacy/sample_privacy.asp.

  The Council of Better Business Bureau has prepared a sample privacy notice that describes the basic practices for websites in the United States.

- Safe Harbor Framework. www.export.gov/safeharbor.

  While the United States and the European Union share the goal of enhancing privacy protection for their citizens, they have taken different approaches. In order to bridge these different privacy approaches and provide a streamlined means for United States organizations to comply with the Directive, the U.S. Department of Commerce in consultation with the European Commission developed a "Safe Harbor" framework."

- Privacy Notices Code of Practice, Information Commissioner's Office, June 2009. www.ico.gov.uk.

  This code helps organizations to draft clear privacy notices and to make sure that they collect information about people fairly and transparently.

REFERENCES

[1] Making Privacy Notices Simple: an OECD Report and Recommendations. Organisation for Economic Co-operation and Development (OECD) Digital Economy Papers. July 2006. www.oecd.org.

87. What else can be done at the national and sectoral level to protect online customers?

National governments and organizations can foster consumer confidence in e-commerce by ensuring effective consumer protection online. They should explore opportunities for global cooperation in the enforcement of consumer protection laws and for facilitating partnerships between industry and consumer advocates to develop redress mechanisms for online consumers.

Overall, the electronic marketplace is a safe and secure place to purchase goods, services and digitized information. Yet, to encourage more online sales, consumers must be confident that the goods and services offered online are of good quality, and that merchants will deliver goods on time, without fraud or deception.

The private sector must develop codes of conduct for business-to-consumer e-commerce and alternative, easy-to-use mechanisms for consumer dispute resolution and enforcement.

Exporters must offer customers privacy assurances on their websites.

For example, in an attempt to raise confidence in online purchases and to quell European fears over the trans-Atlantic flow of sensitive information, several companies now offer certification services in the United States. One service under discussion by United States and European negotiators is the Better Business Bureau, which has developed a code of Online Business Practices. BBBOnline (www.bbbonline.org), works with industry, consumer representatives and government to develop guidelines for online merchants in implementing consumer protection mechanisms, such as disclosure of sales terms, data privacy, dispute resolution methods and non-deceptive advertising. BBBOnLine allows businesses with websites to display the BBB Accredited Business seal online following confirmation of their adherence to the BBB Code of Business Practices, including its online standard.

The International Marketing Supervision and Enforcement Network (www.icpen.org) shares information and cooperates in law enforcement investigations with consumer protection agencies in more than 36 countries, most of which are members of the Organisation for Economic Co-operation and Development (OECD). One of the activities of ICPEN is a yearly global web-surfing exercise to search for sites that may potentially be deceiving and defrauding consumers. The Sweep's objective is to improve consumer confidence in e-commerce by demonstrating a global law enforcement presence online. ICPEN has also established a website (www.econsumer.gov) to gather and share cross-border e-commerce complaints of consumer protection agencies from 24 countries.

In December 1999, the OECD Council approved Guidelines for Consumer Protection in the Context of Electronic Commerce. According to the OECD website [1], these are:

"...designed to help ensure that consumers are no less protected when shopping online than they are when they buy from their local store or order from a catalogue. By setting out the core characteristics of effective consumer protection for online business-to-consumer transactions, the Guidelines are intended to help eliminate some of the uncertainties that both consumers and businesses encounter when buying and selling online. The result of 18 months of discussions among representatives of OECD governments and business and consumer organizations, the Guidelines will play a major role in assisting governments, business and consumer representatives to develop and implement online consumer protection mechanisms without erecting barriers to trade."

Here are some measures you can take to inspire confidence in your customers:

Tell customers who you are. Display your company name and address on your home page, along with detailed contact information. Consumers like using methods other than e-mail to contact companies, such as telephone, fax and regular mail.

Provide detailed information. As online shoppers cannot inspect your wares, offer as much detailed information as you can about your products and services. Describe them in simple language.

Provide customers with a clear, multi-step, purchasing process. Set up a clear page for an order form or shopping cart, which allows consumers to identify the items they are thinking about buying. The page should list the items in the shopping cart and ask the customer to click on the send button to finalize the order. If you do not have a multi-step purchasing process, you should provide a period during which customers can change their minds. Show full prices, terms and conditions, and transaction methods.

Allow a quick-buy option for repeat customers. Repeat customers may want a convenient way to order products. A quick-buy feature provides customers with a clear and simple purchasing process for future orders.

Provide clear terms and conditions. Indicate full prices, the currency in which prices are calculated and paid, shipping charges, taxes, customs duties, customs brokerage fees, delivery schedules, and state your return and exchange policies. A link to the terms and conditions page should be at all the stages of the purchasing process.

Tell customers about the security of your transaction system. State who provides the security and how it works.

Post a privacy policy on your website. The privacy policy should inform your customers how their personal information will be used by your company. It also describes how this information and other data are retained by the website, how they will be processed, and whether they will be disclosed to third parties. For more information on how to formulate a privacy statement please refer to question 86: "How is an online privacy statement formulated?"

Have your website certified. One way to reassure consumers is to have a reputable third party endorse your business. A number of Internet approval programmes are emerging. They range from those that simply verify that your business exists at its claimed address to comprehensive auditing services. For more information on privacy and trust seal programmes please refer to question 84: "How do I inspire confidence in my trustworthiness as a supplier through my website?"

Other companies, such as Verisign (www.verisign.com) certify the level of security of your website. The Verisign Secured Seal will show the visitors that your site is secured using an SSL technology.

Respond to customer complaints. Provide a simple and effective process for handling customer complaints, concerns and inquiries. There are third-party dispute resolution services, which act as mediators or arbitrators.

For more information

- The International Consumer Protection and Enforcement Network (ICPEN/RICPC). www.icpen.org.

  The International Consumer Protection and Enforcement Network is a network of governmental organizations involved in the enforcement of fair trade practice laws and other consumer protection activitie. The ICPEN/RICPC website has compiled a list of other organizations concerned with e-commerce consumer issues.

- National Consumer Policy and Consumer Protection Authorities. Organisation for Economic Co-operation and Development (OECD). www.oecd.org/countrylist/0,3349,en_2649_34267_1783507_1_1_1_1,00.html.

  Links to the consumer protection authority (or authorities) of the countries represented on the OECD Committee on Consumer Policy.

- Canada's Office of Consumer Affairs (OCA). www.ic.gc.ca/eic/site/oca-bc.nsf/eng/h_ca02132.html.

  OCA's website has a section on e-commerce where in addition to the Canadian code of practice for consumer protection in electronic commerce, you can find an Internet sales contract template and ways to earn consumer trust on the Internet. The identity theft section of the website provides information on how to reduce the risk of identity theft, tips on how to protect yourself, and what to do if identify theft happens.

=== **REFERENCES** ===

[1] OECD Guidelines for Consumer Protection in the Context of Electronic Commerce. Organisation for Economic Co-operation and Development (OECD), 1999.
www.oecd.org/document/51/0,2340,en_2649_34267_1824435_1_1_1_1,00.html.

88.   How do I protect myself from e-commerce fraud?

Internet fraud is international. According to a 2009 report by Forrester, 40% of those surveyed have seen an increase in fraud incidents in the past 12 months and, as a result, are intensifying efforts to combat it [1]. The report found that, on average, e-business leaders plan to spend $23 million on technology on their customer-facing online sites to detect and combat fraud, and they estimated losses to fraud at 0.6% of sales.

For the most part, the precautions you need to take to avoid fraud are the same precautions that you would take in any other business environment. Above all, be prudent in your purchases and investments and satisfy yourself about the good faith and reputation of your suppliers and your trade debtors including your customers if you extend credit.

The anonymity of online transactions is frequently used as a cover for fraud, but you can protect yourself from most of this fraud by taking ordinary precautions:

- Check your correspondent's bank and business references before entering into substantial commitments.
- Verify credit cards and clear checks through a bank before providing a product or service.

Merchants who sell products or services that are delivered online must be particularly careful of the risk of fraudulent use of credit cards. Many merchants invest in online credit card clearance services that establish their identity with their customers but do not verify the identity of these customers. They therefore continue to be at risk from customer use of stolen or cancelled credit cards. Unless you are prepared to accept a level of loss from fraudulent use, always wait for the authorization of credit card transactions before delivering your products.

Online fraud has increased in sophistication and intensity, making protection against it a top priority for almost any organization. Be sure to check the following sites to stay up-to-date on the latest scams involving e-commerce, the Internet or e-mail marketing.

- National Fraud Information Center: www.fraud.org
- Ontario Provincial Police PhoneBusters: www.phonebusters.com
- RCMP's Scams and Fraud: www.rcmp-grc.gc.ca/scams-fraudes/index-eng.htm
- Econsumer.gov: www.econsumer.gov

Credit Card Fraud

Fraud comes in many forms, but in general it usually involves shipping an order to you, and only later finding out the card was stolen. This usually results in a credit card chargeback to your business. According to an article by Merchant Accounts Express the following are some of the measures you can take to reduce, even eliminate credit card fraud [2]:

- Understand that an authorization code on a transaction does not mean that the card is not stolen.
- Use AVS – Address Verification Service.
- Only ship to the card's billing address.
- Use CVV2 / Card Code.
- Scrutinize unusually large orders and those customers in a super rush.
- Use other fraud prevention tools.
- Obtain the customer service number on the back of the credit card.

Many of these fraud prevention tools and steps can be implemented for little or no cost, through e-commerce payment gateways, such as Authorize.net (www.authorize.net). The US government portal "On Guard Online" (www.onguardonline.gov) also offers useful advice on these topics.

For more information

- The Internet Crime Complaint Center (IC3). www.ic3.gov.

  The Internet Crime Complaint Center (IC3) was established as a partnership between the United States Federal Bureau of Investigation (FBI) and the National White Collar Crime Center (NW3C) to serve as a means to receive Internet related criminal complaints and to further research, develop, and refer the criminal complaints to federal, state, local, or international law enforcement and/or regulatory agencies for any investigation they deem to be appropriate. The IC3 website has tips on preventing Internet crime, and a list of current and ongoing Internet crime schemes.

- DirectGov. www.direct.gov.uk.

  DirectGov is the website of the United Kingdom government for its citizens, providing information and online services for the public. The website has a section, under "Home and Community", on how to shop and bank safely online.

- Australian High Tech Crime Centre. www.ahtcc.gov.au.

  One of the main roles of AHTCC's high tech crime operations, officially launched on 1 March 2008, is to provide a national coordinated approach to combating serious, complex and multi-jurisdictional technology enabled crimes, especially those beyond the capability of single jurisdictions. The AHTCC has a special section on online fraud.

- SpamLaws.com. www.spamlaws.com.

  SpamLaws.com is dedicated to providing accurate and up-to-date information on issues affecting Internet security.

- National Fraud Information Center. www.fraud.org.

  The mission of the US-based National Fraud Information Center is to give consumers the information they need to avoid becoming victims of telemarketing and Internet fraud and to help them get their complaints to law enforcement agencies quickly and easily.

REFERENCES

[1] Johnson, C. The State of Fraud in eBusiness, Forrester, 17 August 2009. www.forrester.com.

[2] How to reduce credit card fraud. Merchant Accounts Express. www.merchantexpress.com.

89.   How do I build firewalls for system integrity, virus protection and protection from intruders?

The Internet is a constantly changing network. New vulnerabilities may arise, and new services and enhancements to other services may represent potential difficulties. Despite advances in security systems, fraudulent users, including hackers, frequently succeed in targeting sites and disrupting operations. Therefore, protect your website information and transmitted data with a security system that is flexible enough to adapt to changing needs. Discourage fraudulent users to the point that it would not be worth their time and effort to defraud you.

For electronic communication platforms, applications and services to contribute to economic and social development, they must be reliable, efficient and trustworthy. Today, however, e-mail and other electronic communication tools, and consequently users' trust and confidence in these tools, may be threatened by unsolicited, unwanted, and harmful electronic messages, commonly known as spam. In view of the wide impact of spam, the OECD brought together policy-makers and industry experts in the OECD Task Force on Spam (www.oecd-antispam.org) to develop a framework aimed at tackling spam using a broad multi-disciplinary range of solutions.

The Task Force developed the Anti-Spam Toolkit (the "Toolkit"), which recommends a range of policies and measures which should be key elements of a comprehensive public policy framework for addressing the problem of spam.

Dealing with and preventing security problems

There are a number of ways of preventing and dealing with security problems: firewalls and routing filters, anti-malware programs, browser security and e-mail security. Authentication devices, such as log-in names and passwords, smart cards and biometric measuring devices, can also be used in connection with access to sensitive data or servers.

The National Institute of Standards and Technology of the US Department of Commerce provides guides and up-to-date security information on its Computer Security Division website (www.csrc.nist.gov).

Large and reputable Internet service providers and web hosting services usually provide enough security to the sites they host. Within your own organization all servers, personal computers and mobile devices that connect to the Internet must be protected with firewalls and software to protect against viruses and other types of intrusion. The nature of threats is constantly changing and both hardware and software suppliers update their products on an ongoing basis to deal with new threats.

Some of the major suppliers of security software, listed bellow, offer a variety of software options for small businesses.

- Firewall guides: www.firewallguide.com
- Computer Associates: www.ca.com
- Sophos :   www.sophos.com
- Trend Micro: www.trendmicro.com
- McAfee: www.mcafee.com
- Symantec :   www.symantec.com
- Zone Labs: www.zonealarm.com

It is also possible to obtain free anti-virus protection. A search for "free anti-virus" will provide a list of the most popular ones. Here are some examples:

- Avast Home Edition: www.avast.com
- Avira Personal: www.free-av.com
- AVG Free Edition: free.avg.com

Firewalls and routing filters. A firewall is a device located between a host computer and a network to block unwanted network traffic while allowing other traffic to pass through.

Although you can develop a firewall for your Internet host computer, doing so can be expensive in terms of the time required to build and document the firewall, to maintain it, and to add features to it as required. It is more economical to purchase a firewall. Most vendors of Internet hardware, such as routers and network hubs, can provide specialized firewall hardware and software packages that you can install between your local network and the Internet. Dedicated hardware firewalls provide greater protection. Operating both a software firewall and a separate device provides the opportunity to screen out intruders and to identify any rogue software that attempts to transmit messages from the user's computer to an external system.

Web browsers

Web browsers should be configured to limit vulnerability to intrusions. Because they represent a threat of compromise, web browsers require some additional configuration beyond the default-installed configuration. Browser plugins should be limited to only those required by the end user. Active code, such as ActiveX and Java applets, should be disabled or used only in conjunction with trusted sites. The browser should always be updated to the latest or most secure version. Privacy is always a concern with web browsers, particularly the use of cookies and monitoring of web browsing habits of users by third parties. The range of options for addressing cookies includes disabling or selective removal using a variety of third-party applications or built-in browser features. Internet proxies that encrypt all data protect web surfers from monitoring and allow them to use both the Web and e-mail anonymously.

Operating system protection and Anti-Malware

Malware is software designed to infiltrate or damage a computer system without the owner's informed consent. It is a blend of the words "malicious" and "software". The expression is a general term used by computer professionals to mean a variety of forms of hostile, intrusive, or annoying software or program code.

Software is considered malware based on the intent of the creator rather than any particular features. It includes computer viruses, worms, trojan horses, spyware, adware and other malicious and unwanted software [1].

The default configuration of most operating systems is generally inadequate from a security standpoint, although operating systems are now beginning to be delivered with security turned on rather than off, as was the case in the past. File and printer sharing should almost always be disabled. The operating system and major applications should be updated to the latest and most secure version or patch level. All computers should have an anti-virus program installed and configured to scan all incoming files and e-mails. The anti-virus program should have its virus database updated on a regular basis. Another concern is the surreptitious installation of spyware by certain software applications. There are now a variety of programs available for detecting and removing this spyware.

- **Anti-virus.** A virus is a string of computer commands that may severely affect your computer hardware and software. Viruses are generally distributed by disc transfers and through e-mail and the Internet. A virus that has infected your system may remain dormant for a time and become active when triggered by certain conditions.

  You may already be using anti-virus software, but to be effective, the software must be updated daily with the latest virus definition files. If you are unsure how to do this, you should refer to the program's help function.

- **Anti-Spyware**. A spyware reports information on a user (generally without their knowledge) back to a third party. This information could be information about their system or their web browsing habits.

Networks

Selection of wireless and other networking technologies should be in accordance with security goals. A variety of networking technologies have become available. While most of these technologies are secure, several represent a threat to security of both the home network and, sometimes, the office network. In particular, wireless networking has several vulnerabilities that should be carefully considered before any installation. More detailed information on wireless network security is provided in NIST Special Publication 800 series (csrc.nist.gov/publications/PubsSPs.html).

A virtual private network (VPN) serves as an encrypted "tunnel" between two organizations (or hosts) that makes it possible for secured communication to occur over public networks. This tunnel allows a variety of different types of traffic, rather than a single encrypted connection such as an e-commerce credit card transaction using a web server. To ensure correct operation, the VPN must be carefully configured on both the organization's central office systems and the remote system. Users should also be educated on VPN operation, since current implementations are not as simple or "transparent" as some other security applications. Organizations considering a VPN should thus proceed with caution, first ensuring that security goals cannot be achieved with less complex mechanisms. If a VPN is used, the organization's system administrators should be responsible for correctly configuring the VPN and for providing users with properly configured software for their offsite systems.

E-mail security. Most workers need to be able to send and receive e-mail at either their main office or offsite. E-mail can be handled in a number of ways, with varying security considerations. Some approaches can affect the vulnerability of main office systems.

- **Remote login.** The most common method of receiving e-mail offsite is to log in remotely and receive e-mail messages from a central server just as at the office. This approach requires the organization to be especially careful in password management and in blocking access between mail servers and other critical organization computers. If several hundred users have remote login access, there is a significant chance that a few will be careless with passwords, making it possible for intruders to gain at least some access to the e-mail server. Also note that many remote e-mail tools use the POP3 protocol, so passwords may be sent unencrypted.

- **E-mail forwarding.** One simple approach is to set up the e-mail system on the user's main office computer to automatically forward a copy of each e-mail received to the user's ISP account. Although this method does not protect the privacy of messages through encryption, it avoids the need for users to log in to a computer at the main office. This option may be appropriate if privacy of e-mail messages is not a significant concern, but the organization wants to minimize the chance that an intruder could gain access to main office systems by compromising a user's offsite computer.

(Source: based on Security for Telecommuting and Broadband Communications [2])

Updates and patches

From time to time, vulnerabilities are discovered in programs running on your computer. The publisher will then release a "patch" to correct this weakness. Virus writers and hackers regularly exploit these weaknesses, to gain unauthorised access to computers that have not been patched. To check for patches and updates you should visit the publisher's website, typically in their download section. Microsoft patches can be found at: windowsupdate.microsoft.com.

Passwords

Passwords are the key to your online information, so avoid using the same password for different systems. Doing so puts you at risk should anyone discover this single password. Here are more tips on improving password security:

- Do not use passwords that can be easily guessed, e.g. children's or pet's names, birth dates.

- Do not use real words, make your password a combination of numbers and letters or a meaningless string of letters. Passwords can be "guessed" by programs that try every word in a dictionary or other list.

- Never write passwords down. If you feel that you must, write it in a way that cannot be understood by somebody else.

- Change your password frequently.

- Never disclose your Internet login details anywhere online except at your usual website, which you have accessed in the normal way, and never via a link sent in an e-mail.

For more information

- Special Publications (800 series). National Institute of Standards and Technology; Computer Security Division. csrc.nist.gov/publications/PubsSPs.html.

  Special Publications (SP) in the 800 series present documents of general interest to the computer security community. This SP 800 series reports on ITL's research, guidelines, and outreach efforts in computer security, and its collaborative activities with industry, government, and academic organizations.

- Get Safe Online. www.getsafeonline.org.

  The Get Safe Online site helps you protect yourself against Internet threats. The site is sponsored by government and leading businesses working together to provide a free, public service.

- SecurityFocus. www.securityfocus.com.

  SecurityFocus is a vendor-neutral site that provides objective, timely and comprehensive security information to all members of the security community, from end users, security hobbyists and network administrators to security consultants, IT Managers, CIOs and CSOs.

- Information Security Essentials for Small Business. Australian e-business guide. www.e-businessguide.gov.au/protecting/tips.

REFERENCES

[1] Malware. Wikipedia. en.wikipedia.org/wiki/Malware.

[2] Security for Telecommuting and Broadband Communications. Recommendations of NIST, August 2002.

90.   How do I provide a secure credit card payment system on my website?

When designing your website for payment transactions, make sure that it is secure for these transactions.

Secure Electronic Transaction (SET) payment-card protocol

Advanced by Visa and MasterCard, SET provides confidentiality of payment and order information, ensures the integrity of transmitted data, authenticates the identities of cardholders and merchants and allows for the reversal of transactions if this should be necessary. SET was heavily publicised in the late 1990s as the credit card approved standard, but failed to win market share, mostly due to its high cost and complexity for merchants compared to other alternatives.

Secure Socket Layer based methods

To provide a secure payment platform, you will need authentication and encryption services. Authentication validates identity or proves the integrity of information. This can be implemented using a public key infrastructure and digital signatures (for more information on digital signature please refer to question 73: "How do I sign a contract electronically? Is an electronic signature as binding as a written signature?"). Encryption converts information into a form unintelligible to all except holders of a specific cryptographic key. It protects information between the encryption process and the decryption process (the inverse of encryption) against unauthorized disclosure. The Secure Sockets Layer (SSL) is a cryptographic protocol that provides security for communications over networks such as the Internet.

Companies such as Verisign (www.verisign.com), and RSA (www.rsa.com) offer a variety of services such as SSL certificate, identity and authentication, helping organizations to engage in secure and trusted communications and commerce.

PGP Corporation (www.pgp.com) provides e-mail and data encryption software for enterprise data protection. A trial version of its Pretty Good Privacy encryption application can be downloaded free from the PGP website.

Escrow services

An alternative to charge card services is an escrow service, under which money is held in trust (in escrow) by a trusted third party until certain agreed conditions are met. Because no merchant account is needed, buyers are not charged until they receive the product, providing them with a level of confidence that the transaction is legitimate. Your cost to use the escrow service can be added to the price of the product.

Under the procedures of iEscrow.com (www.iescrow.com), one of the providers of this service, buyers pay iEscrow with a credit card, personal check, business check, money order, cashiers check or wire transfer. iEscrow will then ask the seller to ship the merchandise to the buyers. The latter must notify iEscrow of their satisfaction with the merchandise before iEscrow can pay the seller.

Payment Services Providers (PSPs)

For a small or medium-sized enterprise using a Payment Service Provider is the best option for online payment. By using a well established and reliable service provider you will reduce the risks and costs of e-commerce substantially.

Advantages

- Relieve you of the administrative burden of managing customers' card details and running a merchant account.

- Relieve you of the responsibility of keeping customer's payment details secure and confidential. You as the merchant will never see these details.

- Save you the cost of setting up a secure payment system.

- Have slightly less strict application procedures than a merchant account.

- Some offer insurance policies or other protection to cover you against the cost of fraudulent use of cards.

Disadvantages

- Customers can see that the payment is not going directly to you even though they may be conducting the transaction through your website. This can also be an advantage, if the payment service provider is perceived as being honest and well established.

- They tend to hold on to your money. Some don't release funds from transactions for up to eight weeks, which could have cash flow implications for your business.

- Charges are generally high. You may have to pay a set-up fee and an annual fee, plus a percentage of each transaction. For credit-card payments, the transaction fee is in addition to the percentage charged by the credit-card company.

To find a Payment Service Provider, talk to your own bank first: they may offer a service themselves or work closely with one of the service providers. If they are unable to advise you, look at what other sites are doing. The most popular services are also likely to be the best. Information about payment service providers can be found on their websites, and this will usually be sufficient for an initial comparison. However, before you make a final decision, you must obtain a proposal from them for your specific case and a copy of the terms and conditions that you will be asked to sign.

If your site is going to process online payments choose a Payment Service Provider before starting to build your website for the following reasons:

- There is no guarantee that you will find a Payment Service Provider which will accept your business.

- You may find that their charges are too high for your business to support.

- You will have to integrate your website with theirs: there are different methods in use and they will tell you what you need to do.

Here are some well-known payment service providers:

- PayPal. www.paypal.com. PayPal allows members to send money without sharing financial information, with the flexibility to pay using their account balances, bank accounts, credit cards or promotional financing. With more than 78 million active accounts in 190 markets and 19 currencies around the world, PayPal enables global ecommerce. PayPal is an eBay company and is made up of three leading online payment services: the PayPal global payments platform, the Payflow Gateway and Bill Me Later.

- RBS WorldPay. www.rbsworldpay.com. RBS WorldPay, part of the Royal Bank of Scotland Group, provides a globally connected, locally coordinated payment processing service for all sorts of businesses, big and small.

- eBill me. www.ebillme.com. eBillme is an alternative payment option that allows consumers to securely pay cash when they are shopping online.

- First Data. www.firstdata.com. First Data helps businesses, such as merchants and financial institutions, safely and efficiently process customer transactions and understand the information related to those transactions.

For more information on payment service providers please refer to question 57: "What are the different methods of payment that can be used with e-commerce?"

For more information

- The Electronic Payments Tool (www.electronic-payments.co.uk).

  The electronic payments tool has been developed by the Trade Online Project, a project sponsored by the Business Link (businesslink.gov.uk), Scottish Enterprise (www.scottish-enterprise.com), and the European Union through their European Social Fund (www.europa.eu) in order to provide business owners with a clear understanding of what they need to do to take secure online payments.

Policy and country issues

91. When is a country ready for e-commerce?

The Economist Intelligence Unit has published the annual e-readiness rankings of the world's largest economies since 2000, using a model developed together with the IBM Institute for Business Value. A country's e-readiness, according to this model, is a measure of its e-business environment, which is measured by a number of factors that indicate how amenable a market is to Internet-based opportunities.

According to the 2009 report [1], in part because of the wide-scale deterioration of countries' business environments over the previous 12 months, the e-readiness scores of all but nine of the 70 countries in the study declined in 2009. Some of the findings in this report are:

- Emerging markets continue to rack up the biggest advances in connectivity, or the extent to which people are connected to communications networks.

- The Governments of Mexico (40th), Jordan (50th) and Viet Nam (64th) have made substantial progress in recent years in making digital channels available to citizens for information provision and consultation ("e-participation").

- Broadband and mobile connectivity levels continue to increase for almost all countries, notwithstanding the downturn.

- Access to ICT does not mean usage of it, but when connectivity increases usage tends to increase with it, in rich and developing worlds alike.

- Of the 70 countries ranked in 2009, Denmark has reclaimed its top position, followed by Sweden, the Netherlands, and Norway.

Another source of information is the e-business readiness index published by the European Commission.

For more information

- e-Business readiness index. European Commission; Enterprise and Industry.
  ec.europa.eu/enterprise/sectors/ict/competitiveness/ebi/index_en.htm.

  The "e-Business readiness indicator" gives a broad picture of the level of ICT adoption, ICT use and e-business development at country level in the European Union.

REFERENCES

[1] E-Readiness rankings 2009 – The usage imperative. The Economist Intelligence Unit. 2009. www.eiu.com/sponsor/ibm/e-readinessrankings2009.

92. What are some of the positive and negative implications of e-commerce for SMEs in developing countries?

E-commerce provides lots of opportunities for small and medium-sized enterprises (SMEs) to compensate for their traditional lack of access to national and international markets. It helps them expand their market share and enter into newer markets. At the same time, however, the opportunities opened up by e-commerce can be dangerous to your company, because new competitors can enter into your existing markets.

The Internet removes the restrictions of geography. Shopping locally is no longer the only choice, and goods can be ordered from anywhere. This is another opportunity for smaller businesses, which can extend their customer base to everyone with Internet access, rather than being restricted by a local or regional market. Once again, if exploited by your competitor this becomes a serious challenge.

Research by Chong found that communication methods employed, government support, external pressure from customers and suppliers were very important for Australian SMEs in driving them towards e-commerce [1]. This also applies to the rest of the world, including developing countries. In the past decade, e-commerce has lead to the emergence of new business models. E-commerce enables companies to re-evaluate their value chain and reduce costs. Electronic commerce can also turn into a serious threat for your company, if your suppliers start bypassing you using the Internet to access your customers directly.

Security and confidentiality is a major concern for many companies doing business online. Each year, millions of dollars are spent on security efforts to ensure that transactions are safe and that customers will feel comfortable conducting business online. Beyond day-to-day transactions, major security threats such as hackers, viruses, and cyber crime mean that providing security online requires an added expenditure that simply doesn't exist elsewhere. Breaches of security, such as the highly publicized theft of credit card data, lead customers to question the safety of doing business online, which can hurt a business further by lowering confidence levels.

How does this relate to SMEs in developing countries? Kartiwi and MacGregor have examined the underlying barriers to adopting e-commerce, as perceived by SMEs in developing countries [2]. According to their study some of these barriers can be summarized as:

- High cost of e-commerce implementation
- Complexity of e-commerce implementation
- Low level of existing hardware technology incorporated into the business
- SMEs need to see immediate ROI, while e-commerce generally is a long-term investment
- Organizational resistance to change because of the fear of new technology among employees
- Lack of technical skills and IT knowledge among employees
- Lack of time to implement e-commerce
- E-commerce is not deemed to be suited to the way the SME does business
- E-commerce is not deemed to be suited to the products/services offered by the SME
- Lack of awareness about business opportunities/benefits that e-commerce can provide
- Concern about security of e-commerce
- Lack of critical mass among customers, suppliers, and business partners to implement e-commerce
- Lack of e-commerce standards

REFERENCES

[1] Chong, S. Success in electronic commerce implementation; a cross-country study of small and medium-sized enterprises, Journal of Enterprise Information Management, vol. 21, no.5, 2008.

[2] Kartiwi, M., MacGregor, R. C. Electronic commerce adoption barriers in small to medium-sized enterprises (SMEs) in developed and developing countries: A cross-country comparison, Journal of Electronic Commerce in Organizations, vol. 5, no. 3. 2007.

93. What are the constraints to developing countries in regard to e-commerce?

According to UNCTAD's Information Economy Report 2009, in both developed and developing countries, large enterprises use Information and Communication Technologies (ICTs), such as computers and the Internet, more than SMEs. This may partly be a result of their greater financial and human resources and partly of their greater need for such technologies [1]. According to the 2008 European e-Business report, which highlights similar trends, large companies in the chemical, rubber and plastics industries are advanced users of ICT and e-business in all business areas. They are increasingly replacing paper-based, manual processes by electronic exchanges [2].

UNCTAD´s Information Economy Report 2007-2008 found, however, that Internet access by enterprises in developing countries continues to grow, as does the number of employees using the Internet in their daily work [3]. Nevertheless, the way these companies use the Internet is mostly limited to sending and receiving e-mails; few companies in developing countries use it as a marketing tool or to make banking transactions [1].

The 2007-2008 UNCTAD report cites a firm-level survey by the World Bank which indicates that service-sector enterprises use websites and computers more than the manufacturing sector, and have a higher proportion of employees who use computers regularly. The report also indicates that within the service sector, firms in the telecommunications and information technology industries are the main users of ICT; they are followed by real-estate companies, hotels and restaurants.

This could be explained by the fact that marketing and sales functions can be carried out with a relatively basic level of Internet access and usage, while supply chain management, which is important in manufacturing, requires higher levels of systems integration. Integrating business functions by using ICT is hard for SMEs in any environment, but much more so in developing countries [3].

SMEs typically represent the backbone of developing economies and employ a large majority of the workforce. Despite recent progress in infrastructure and connectivity, many bottlenecks still prevent entrepreneurs and small firms from using ICTs efficiently. The 2009 Information Economy Report indicates that even if companies have access to basic ICT infrastructure, its use is often limited by low levels of ICT literacy, slow speed of connection, a lack of local content and high costs of use [1].

Moreover, in rural areas of many developing countries, even basic connectivity remains a challenge. Countries in which the business sector has been keen to adopt ICTs have typically shown a strong policy commitment towards such technologies, emphasized the development of competitive ICT infrastructure, at least in urban areas, taken steps to build a workforce with the necessary skills and technological capabilities and sought to create an enabling regulatory environment. Important areas of government intervention to encourage greater adoption and use of ICT in the business sector include making it a core element in a national ICT strategy, improving ICT infrastructure in under-served areas, building relevant skills, promoting the development of local content and strengthening the legal and regulatory framework [1].

E-Business Opportunities for Small Firms in Developing Countries

- Flexibility: SMEs can be more flexible in decision-making and implementing organizational changes than larger firms.
- Internal communication processes are often 'smoother' in smaller organizations.
- Used to cooperation: Out of necessity, SMEs tend to be used to cooperating with other companies, for example in tendering. Online cooperation can further enhance this attitude

E-Business Challenges for Small Firms in Developing Countries

- **Access.** Many enterprises still have no access to the Internet. Once this overriding constraint is resolved, other barriers can be addressed.
- **Lack of ICT strategy and skills**: Smaller firms often lack a coherent ICT investment strategy or the related skills.
  Many enterprises find it difficult to design sites that generate sales. Without effective strategies, firms will not recoup their investments in their websites.
- **Standards:** The lack of e-standards and interoperability increases risk in technology decisions and investments.
- **Pressure on prices and margins:** Sophisticated e-procurement schemes of large buyers increase the pressure on supply companies, many of which are SMEs.

- **Cost:** Many enterprises find the cost of doing business on the Internet much higher than they anticipated. This has been due to a misunderstanding of the factors involved in Internet marketing, lack of employee training, inadequate or inappropriate website content, and the lack of funds for updating websites. Cost items include basic computer equipment; Internet access, for which fees vary considerably from country to country; website design; website maintenance; and advertising and promotion of the website on television, radio, newspapers, billboards and other venues.

- **Security:** Problems of customer fraud, access by hackers to vulnerable information and security of Internet service providers, as well as the need for privacy and confidentiality of information, still require government and commercial solutions.

- **Lack of success:** Insufficient marketing, inability to meet costs, staffing constraints and competition are factors that contribute to the lack of hits, leads and sales for most enterprises transacting on the Internet.

- **Lack of computer equipment:** The personal computer ratio per 100 inhabitants gives an indication of the information technology gap.

- **Lack of telecommunications infrastructure:** Access to basic telephone services remains a prerequisite for e-commerce.

- **Limited connectivity:** Although the number is growing rapidly, according to a recent ITU report, only a little more than a quarter of the world's population are using the Internet [4].

- **Limited use of the Internet to buy products:** Only a small percentage of Internet use among enterprises and consumers has to do with the actual purchase of goods and services. The Internet is mainly employed for e-mail, research, customer support and Intranet communications.

- **Conflict with traditional buying practices:** Consumers and enterprises want to comparison-shop, find good-quality pictures of products that are described well, and be able to ask questions and get answers online quickly and securely. Consumers often do not buy for the following reasons:

  - They are uncomfortable about sending credit card data over the Internet
  - They prefer to see the product before purchasing
  - They need to talk to a sales representative
  - They cannot obtain enough information to make a decision
  - The cost of the product
  - The transaction takes too long
  - They have to download special software
  - The website is difficult to navigate
  - The process is confusing and product information is not current

For more information

- The European e-Business Report 2008. 6th Synthesis Report of the Sectoral e-Business Watch. www.ebusiness-watch.org.

  The Sectoral e-Business Watch (SeBW) studies the impact of ICT and e-business on enterprises, industries and the economy in general. It highlights barriers to a wider or faster uptake of ICT and identifies public policy changes.

REFERENCES

[1] Information Economy Report 2009: Trends and outlook in turbulent times, UNCTAD, 2009. www.unctad.org.

[3] Information Economy Report 2007-2008 – Science and technology for development: the new paradigm of ICT, UNCTAD, 2008. www.unctad.org.

[4] The World in 2009: ICT Facts and Figures, International Telecommunication Union, 2009. www.itu.int/ITU-D/ict/.

94. How can government and national organizations facilitate e-commerce in developing countries?

The core of any national e-commerce strategy should be to offer an integrated array of products, publications and services that can be provided to small firms when they need it, where they are (i.e. from their computers) and in a format that is user-friendly, comprehensive and cost effective. National organizations (including trade support institutions) and government ministries can provide technical assistance services that focus on the following, among others:

- Online mentoring services
- Online classrooms for small businesses
- Counselling by e-mail
- Web publications and tutorials on e-commerce, laws, regulations, taxes
- Information network on environmental, health and safety regulations
- Identifying best practices in e-commerce
- Profiles of successful e-commerce strategies
- Providing answers to the most commonly asked e-commerce questions
- Online review and assessment of the websites of small firms
- Online exhibitions of products available for export
- Programmes for matching online exporters and importers
- One-stop virtual marketplace for buying from, and selling to, the government (public procurement).
- Virtual marketplace for posting offers, bids, reply to bids; awarding contracts; and tracking invoices
- Online tools on how to sell to government, businesses and consumers
- Online tools on how to win contracts
- Online equity lending and matchmaking
- Online processing and approval of loan pre-qualification forms
- Securing e-loans
- Online complaints ombudsman

According to UNCTAD's Information Economy Report 2009, countries in which the business sector has been keen to adopt ICTs have typically shown a strong policy commitment towards such technologies, emphasized the development of a competitive ICT infrastructure, at least in urban areas, taken steps to build a workforce with the necessary skills and technological capabilities and sought to create an enabling regulatory environment. Important areas of government intervention to encourage greater adoption and use of ICT in the business sector include making it a core element in a national ICT strategy, improving ICT infrastructure in underserved areas, building relevant skills, promoting the development of local content and strengthening the legal and regulatory framework [1].

In a survey conducted by the International Trade Centre (www.intracen.org) to identify the information, training, publication and technical assistance needs of developing countries in e-commerce, the respondents suggested the following actions to be carried out by government ministries and national organizations:

- **Identify the needs of enterprises**. Establish focus groups of enterprises to identify general and country-specific needs in sales, marketing and communication.

- **Identify the needs of buyers, whether individuals or businesses**. Carry out research into why online purchases remain limited and what can be done to encourage increased online sales to consumers and businesses.

- **Identify country-specific technological, infrastructural and political barriers to e-commerce**. For example, some countries prohibit access to the Internet and e-mail, and some countries require websites set up by enterprises to be approved by their governments.

- **In each country, find out the percentage of companies that have e-commerce sites and track their usage of the Internet**. Establish how many companies have sites, whether they allow their customers to purchase online, and the extent to which they use the Internet themselves to make purchases.

- **Determine the return on investments in websites**. Determine to what extent enterprises are achieving a return on their investments in their websites. Prepare case studies of what works, what does not and why. Profile successful e-marketing strategies. Carry out industry-specific research into the relationship between website visits, leads generated and sales made.

- **Develop strategies for putting as many enterprises as possible online and develop a website template for customization by individual enterprises.**

- **Take an active role in developing e-commerce**. Establish a national cybermall or portal to serve as an entry point for those interested in sourcing products from a particular country. The cybermall should carry a listing of enterprises by industry.

- **Organize the Web for business**. Developing countries should participate in discussions with other countries, firms providing search engines and international organizations on improving the organization of the Web for business-to-business and business-to-consumer e-commerce use.

- **Develop a checklist of issues to be addressed by enterprises or organizations before contacting vendors.**

- **Run workshops for supply-chain managers on how to apply Internet technology to improve the efficiency and effectiveness of private-sector supply chain operations.**

- **Train enterprises on how to source products and services through search engines and how to evaluate suppliers over the Internet.**

- **Produce a manual on Internet search techniques.**

- **Offer training programmes on the design, development and maintenance of websites**. An inside e-business seminar could showcase best practices in e-commerce and supply-chain applications.

- **Stimulate competition in the development of e-commerce projects among SMEs, industry sectors, and e-commerce development organizations to raise awareness of what it takes to succeed in e-commerce.**

- **Create blue pages or online catalogues of SME products and services.**

- **Create or support a "geeks for development" community** of volunteers that provides Internet-based online assistance for the formulation of e-commerce solutions for developing countries.

- **Create national business search engines or directories**. Businesses and consumers need a well-organized business search engine or directory to speed up their search for products and services.

- **Encourage competition**. Encourage competition among Internet service providers to lower costs to subscribers and increase Internet access.

For more information

- ITU's E-Strategies. International Telecommunication Union. www.itu.int/ITU-D/cyb/estrat/index.html.

  With the acute need to establish and support the development of national e-strategies in developing and least developed countries as well as emerging economies, the ITU-D ICT Applications and Cybersecurity Division aims to assist these countries.

- Internet Governance Forum. www.intgovforum.org.

  The Internet Governance Forum (IGF) is a multi-stakeholder forum for policy dialogue on issues of Internet governance. One of the mandates of the IGF is to discuss public policy issues related to key elements of Internet governance in order to foster the sustainability, robustness, security, stability and development of the Internet.

- The OECD Information Economy Group. Organisation for Economic Co-operation and Development (OECD). www.oecd.org/department/0,3355,en_2649_33757_1_1_1_1_1,00.html.

  The OECD information economy group examines the economic and social implications of the development, diffusion and use of ICTs, the Internet and e-business. It analyses ICT policy frameworks shaping economic growth, productivity, employment and business performance.

- Internet Governance for Development. South Centre Analytical Note, August 2006. www.southcentre.org.

  This South Centre Analytical Note provides a brief discussion of the link between Internet governance and development. It suggests that focus on development, capacity building, and increasing the level of democracy and transparency of Internet governance will contribute toward improving equity among Internet governance stakeholders and successfully bridging the digital divide.

REFERENCES

[1] Information Economy Report 2009: Trends and outlook in turbulent times, UNCTAD, 2009. www.unctad.org.

95.   What policy and technical issues must be dealt with at the national level?

There is no doubt that there are unprecedented opportunities for small and medium-sized enterprises to participate in the e-commerce revolution. However, a number of policy and technical issues must be dealt with at the national level to enable SMEs to participate fully in e-commerce.

Policy issues

- International legal issues
- Dealing with fraud
- Consumer protection
- Intellectual property protection
- Access to telecommunications infrastructure
- Improvement of telecommunications infrastructure
- Development of national e-commerce strategies

Technical issues

- Encryption
- Security of payment
- Certification of buyers
- Authentication of buyers
- Digital signatures
- Data protection
- Privacy protection

Current problem areas

- E-commerce concentration in the North American and European markets
- Difficulties of locating small suppliers in developing countries
- Credibility issues for unknown small and medium-sized enterprises
- Cost of developing websites
- Misunderstanding website design
- Low online sales by small enterprises throughout the world
- Lack of equipment
- Poor telecommunications infrastructure
- Limited connectivity
- Cost of Internet service providers

For more information

- ITU's E-Strategies, International Telecommunication Union. www.itu.int/ITU-D/cyb/estrat/index.html.

   With the acute need to establish and support the development of national e-strategies in developing and least-developed countries as well as emerging economies, the ITU-D ICT Applications and Cybersecurity Division aims to assist these countries.

- ITU-D Cybersecurity, International Telecommunication Union. www.itu.int/ITU-D/cyb/cybersecurity/index.html.

   Enhancing cybersecurity and protecting critical information infrastructures are essential to each nation's security and economic well-being.

- Digital Economy in Canada, Industry Canada. www.ic.gc.ca/eic/site/ecic-ceac.nsf/eng/home.

   Canada is a world leader in the adoption, use and development of e-business. The Electronic Commerce Branch of Industry Canada aims to build on this foundation to support and facilitate continued growth of e-business in the Canadian economy.

96. How have some developed countries formulated their national e-commerce strategies?

Most developed countries have identified the opportunities of e-commerce for business and consumers early on, and have outlined a strategy to promote and support it. Through time, these strategies have been updated to incorporate new technologies and priorities.

If your country does not currently have an e-commerce strategy, you should contact the relevant national ministry, national industry association and business assistance organization to encourage them to move towards the adoption of a national strategy in collaboration with each other and with other groups.

Some examples of national e-commerce strategies from developed countries follow.

North America

- *Canada*

In September 1998, the Government of Canada released the Canadian Electronic Commerce Strategy to encourage the development and use of electronic commerce. Developed in consultation with the federal, provincial and territorial governments, the private sector, consumers and public interest groups, the strategy sets out challenges and opportunities, priority issues and an action plan. The overall goal of this strategy was to make Canada a world leader in the development and use of e-commerce. Here are some of the elements that were recognized as high priority:

- Building trust in the digital economy.
  - The government released a cryptography discussion paper in February 1998.
  - The strategy for the protection of privacy is to put the Canadian Standards Association National Standard into effect through light legislation, complemented by private sector action and consumer awareness.
  - The strategy for consumer protection in electronic commerce was based on a balance of voluntary and legislative measures, education and the application of technology.

- Clarifying marketplace rules
  - The Government of Canada's autumn 1998 electronic documents legislation allows departments to adopt a set of general provisions authorizing the use of electronic communications.
  - The Minister of National Revenue's Advisory Committee on Electronic Commerce issued a report in April 1998 titled Electronic Commerce and Canada's Tax Administration that examines how existing taxation systems apply to electronic commerce.
  - The protection of content, balanced with the needs of users, was determined vital to the growth of electronic commerce.

- Strengthening information infrastructure
  - Growth of electronic commerce is underpinned by the strength of information infrastructure.
  - Along with Internet access, stable and efficient functioning of the network is of fundamental importance to the future of electronic commerce.
  - For electronic commerce to be globally adopted, common standards for interoperability are required.

- Realizing the opportunities
  - Governments will play a key role in demonstrating the advantages of electronic service delivery, building critical mass and trust among users, and piloting new technologies.
  - Digital literacy is required for businesses and consumers to use and develop electronic commerce.

In its business plan for 2009-2010, Industry Canada has determined the following key strategies and business objectives:

- Advancing the marketplace through economic framework policies.
- Fostering the knowledge-based economy through enhanced research and innovation, training and skills.
- Supporting business through policies and programs that promote competitiveness and productivity.

Currently, the Electronic Commerce Branch of Industry Canada is responsible for encouraging the development and adoption of e-business in Canada. This is accomplished through three main lines of business:

- Policy development and implementation

    - By facilitating the establishment of an orderly marketplace and providing a favourable legal and regulatory environment for e-commerce.

- International development

    - By promoting the use of e-commerce as an enabler to trade in a global environment and as a catalyst for development.

- Strategies for e-business development

    - By developing strategies, building private and public sector partnerships, and developing research and statistical data to promote the deployment of e-business across the Canadian economy.

▪ *United States*

In June 1997, the Clinton Administration released a report titled: "A Framework for Global Electronic Commerce". In this report the United States administration advocated a wide range of policy prescriptions. These included calling on the World Trade Organization (WTO) to declare the Internet to be a tax-free environment for delivering both goods and services; recommending that no new tax policies should be imposed on Internet commerce; stating that nations develop a uniform commercial code for electronic commerce; requesting that intellectual property protection (patents, trademarks and copyrights) be consistent and enforceable; that nations adhere to international agreements to protect the security and privacy of Internet commercial transactions; that governments and businesses cooperate to more fully develop and expand the Internet infrastructure; and that businesses self-regulate e-commerce content.

The United States Government's initiatives were directed by the Working Group on Electronic Commerce, which was guided by the following principles:

- The private sector should lead.
- Governments should avoid undue restrictions on e-commerce.
- Where governmental involvement is needed, its aim should be to support and enforce a predictable, minimalist and consistent legal environment.
- Governments should recognize the unique qualities of the Internet, and e-commerce over the Internet should be facilitated on a global basis.

The Working Group developed strategies to help small businesses overcome barriers to the use of the Internet. It also ensured that no new taxes were imposed on electronic transactions. Initially the group set its goal to expand the Government's online shopping service for the federal community to cover 4 million items by December 2000.

Most states in the United States have developed their own strategies. Key issues in most of these strategies include leadership, governance, education, infrastructure investment, organizational competency, technology and access [1].

European Union

The i2010 strategy was presented in the i2010 Communication in June 2005. Since then, it has been reviewed through annual reports and most recently updated through Europe's Digital Competitiveness Report. Work has started on identifying policy issues for a post-i2010 agenda [2].

According to Europe's Digital Competitiveness Report 2009, the following actions were undertaken from 2005 to 2009 as part of the i2010 strategy [3]:

- Review of the regulatory framework for electronic communications.
- Strategy for a secure European Information Society; increasing trust and confidence.
- Strengthening European research through the Framework Programmes
- Promoting e-Business solutions
- Promoting ICT-enabled public services (e-Government and e-Health).

Asia

There are a number of similarities between IT strategies in key Asian countries. The most obvious is the governments' efforts to build legal and regulatory structures, provide IT training, and deploy IT in the public sector. E-government is viewed as important for enhancing efficiency and providing a progressive and leading model for the private sector. Countries have enacted laws on electronic signatures, protection of software programs, computer privacy and other fundamental legal safeguards necessary for the spread of e-commerce. Most have emphasized information technology education beginning in elementary school.

For more information

- Digital Economy in Canada, Industry Canada. www.ic.gc.ca/eic/site/ecic-ceac.nsf/eng/home.

  Canada is a world leader in the adoption, use and development of e-business. The Electronic Commerce Branch of Industry Canada aims to build on this foundation to support and facilitate continued growth of e-business in the Canadian economy.

- E-Policy Resources, Canadian e-Policy Resource Centre (CePRC). www.ceprc.ca/ecomm_e.html.

  The e-commerce policies section of the e-Policy resources of the CePRC website provides an overview of Canada's domestic and international approach and resources to electronic commerce policy and strategy.

REFERENCES

[1] Hong, M.J. World Class e-Commerce Strategies, California Research Bureau, October 2000. www.library.ca.gov/crb/00/07/crb-00-007.pdf.

[2] Priorities for new strategy for European information society (2010–2015). European Commission – Europe's Information Society. ec.europa.eu/i2010.

[3] Europe's Digital Competitiveness Report 2009; Main achievements of the i2010 strategy 2005-2009. European Commission – Europe's Information Society. 2009. ec.europa.eu/i2010.

97. How have some developing countries formulated their national e-commerce strategies?

Malaysia

Through its National E-Commerce Council which consisted of sub-committees on trade (coordinated by the Ministry of International Trade – MITI), and electronic infrastructure (coordinated by the Ministry of Energy, Communications and Multimedia – MECM), the Government conducted an in-depth study. This resulted in the National E-Commerce Strategic Directions Plan (NESDP). The objectives of this plan were [1]:

- To understand and assess the full potentials of e-commerce and anticipate their various ramifications
- Recommend options for national strategy
- Recommend programmes for developing local capability to exploit e-commerce for national competitiveness

The outcome was five recommendations and 22 sub-recommendations [1]. The five recommendations were:

- To build critical mass
- To build trust on the Web
- To attract inbound consumers
- To transform organization in Malaysia to be e-commerce ready
- To establish ground rules: a policy and regulatory framework

The Government of Malaysia has already initiated efforts to lay the foundation for e-commerce in the country. The Government in consultation with the private sector has initiated a legal and regulatory framework of cyber laws and intellectual property laws to create a predictable environment for the implementation of e-commerce. Six cyber laws have been enacted. They are the Digital Signature Act 1997, the Copyright (amendment) Act 1997, the Computer Crimes Act 1997, the Telemedicine Act 1997, the Communications and Multimedia Act 1998 and the Communications and Multimedia Commission Act 1998.

South Africa

Individual government departments had been formulating their own information and communication technology (ICT) policies for several years, before the development of a coordinated ICT strategy was approved by the Government in March 1998.

In August 2002, South Africa passed the Electronic Communications and Transactions Act (ECT Act), after much consultation with stakeholders. The aims of the act were:

- To provide for the facilitation and regulation of electronic communications and transactions
- To provide for the development of a national e-strategy
- To promote universal access to electronic communications and transactions and the use of electronic transactions by SMEs
- To provide for human resource development in electronic transactions
- To prevent abuse of information systems
- To encourage the use of e-government services

Venezuela

Business leaders and public officials head the Venezuelan Chamber of Electronic Commerce (Camara Venezolana de Comercio Electronico, or CAVECOM-e). This independent body has been assigned the following tasks:

- Promoting e-commerce activities by Venezuelan enterprises at home and abroad
- Establishing e-commerce as a recognized sector of economic activity at home and abroad
- Contributing to reforms in legal and regulatory frameworks
- Strengthening research, development and training activities on e-commerce
- Acting as interlocutor for private and public players in e-commerce, nationally and internationally, and participating in discussions with these players.

CAVECOM-e (cavecom-e.org.ve) has held workshops, published a book on Electronic Commerce: Legal Frontiers (Comercio Electronico: Fronteras de la Ley), and actively promoted tools (such as the Venezuelan Electronic Invoice) through the Venezuelan Federation of Chambers of Commerce (Fedecamaras).

Thailand

Electronic commerce in Thailand has been an agenda of the National Information Technology Committee since its formation in 1992. At that time, Electronic Data Interchange (EDI) for international trade was starting.

National-level bodies joined forces to develop Electronic commerce. A national level committee for E-Commerce Policy was appointed by the cabinet to oversee this development process.

In March 2002, the government endorsed an information technology framework for 2001–2010, referred to as IT 2010. As one of the main flagships of IT 2010, the national e-commerce vision aims to strengthen the competitive advantage of Thai entrepreneurs, especially SMEs by using e-commerce as an opportunity for exporting goods and services as well as for domestic trade. This policy framework was initially developed by both public and private stakeholders since October 2000, and later incorporated within the national IT 2010 and ICT Master Plan.

According to the e-commerce framework, the Government must put forward the following eight strategies:

- Declare e-commerce as the national trade strategy and proactively engage in international trade
- Raise public awareness and understanding
- Create trust and confidence by developing legal frameworks
- Promote interoperable payment systems and security
- Promote and facilitate SME e-commerce development
- Develop human resources
- Collect indicators and create the databases necessary for measuring and monitoring e-commerce development
- Provide adequate and affordable IT infrastructure

Islamic Republic of Iran

The Iranian National Electronic Commerce Policy was approved in 2002. The objectives of this policy were:

- To provide a nationwide secure network for businesses and government agencies to conduct electronic commerce
- To remove barriers to the use of the Internet for electronic commerce
- To support non-governmental organizations (NGOs) through policies and programmes that promote competitiveness and productivity
- To enhance awareness through training and by promoting electronic business
- To provide a favourable legal and regulatory environment for e-commerce

The Iranian electronic commerce law was enacted in 2003. The first Iranian e-commerce development plan was approved in 2005. Since then an annual report is prepared by the public and private sector that outlines the developments, and challenges of each sector.

For more information

- Electronic commerce strategies for development: The basic elements of an enabling environment for e-commerce, UNCTAD, July 2002. www.unctad.org/en/docs/c3em15d2.en.pdf.
- UNCTAD programme of work on Information and Communication Technologies (ICT). r0.unctad.org/ecommerce.

  The UNCTAD programme of work on Information and Communication Technologies (ICT) carries out policy-oriented analytical work on the implications for developing countries of the adoption of ICT, Internet and e-business technologies.

REFERENCES

[1] National e-commerce strategic directions, MDC Knowledge Sharing Forum, April 2003.

98. What are the essential elements of a national e-commerce strategy?

In the past two decades, the Internet has changed the way we work, live, play and learn. These changes have created an Internet economy, in which technology connects everyone to everything and where open communications, open standards and open markets prevail. Governments, like industry, must adopt as a core business process the use of technology, particularly e-commerce, to deliver information and services faster, cheaper, and to wider groups of constituents. In addition governments must prepare the technical and legal frameworks for the private sector. Organizations not using e-commerce will become uncompetitive and will eventually fail.

To succeed, governments must have a clear national e-commerce strategy. Here are some of the suggested elements of this strategy.

The overall goal

A national e-commerce strategy should attempt to create an Internet-based gateway to serve small entrepreneurs when and where they need help, deliver SME-assistance products and services electronically, and educate small firms on the importance of using e-commerce services.

Strategic components

Networks: Today, many people believe that the Internet is the hottest marketing channel, advertising medium, research tool and mechanism for quick transactions. National organizations should change their service delivery, customer service approach and culture to be successful in this new Internet-based, information-now medium. Networks that emphasize electronic services from the government, at federal, state and local levels, and from industry partnerships must be emphasized.

Electronic transactions: Information technology and communications will be used in e-business transactions to replace the current paper-intensive processes. Computerized application review systems will help banks evaluate a borrower's creditworthiness, verify a firm's eligibility for credit programmes, and match small businesses with procurement opportunities.

Training: Small firms will be trained in the use of e-commerce through Internet-based tools produced to help them buy and sell to the government, find funding, commercialize technology and secure trade leads.

Wider access to information: Much business assistance can be conducted on the Internet. This can range from elementary business guidance for prospective business owners, to online counselling and education, to brokering networks of buyers and suppliers of trade leads, innovation and research grants, equity capital and contract opportunities. The national organization should provide access to government information and services through its own website and develop cross-agency gateways and portals so that anyone can access the information at any time and from any place.

Access to networks and matchmaking: The national organization should help create markets, fix market imperfections where possible, and provide a platform for buyers and suppliers to connect and transcend the boundaries of time and distance. Some call this function electronic brokering.

Access to transactional assistance: National organizations should aim to conduct most of their business online: approving loan guaranties, providing eligibility and certifying minority businesses, getting government contracts, finding grants, and providing answers, not to mention creating business assistance tools to help the small firm find appropriate solutions.

Organizations and government agencies and ministries must ask themselves:

- How can our organization foster e-commerce among small businesses?
- What programmes and services can be offered?
- How can the private sector be involved?
- How can partner organizations within the country become more involved?
- How can organizations within the country provide better counselling, training, research and information?
- How can small enterprises be encouraged to use the Internet as a sales, marketing, research, communication and supply management medium?

For more information

- U.S. Small Business Administration. www.sba.gov.

  The U.S. Small Business Administration (SBA) was created in 1953 as an independent agency of the Federal Government to aid, counsel, assist and protect the interests of small business concerns, to preserve free competitive enterprise and to maintain and strengthen the overall economy of our nation.

- ITU's E-Strategies. www.itu.int/ITU-D/cyb/estrat/index.html.

  With the acute need to establish and support the development of national e-strategies in developing and least developed countries as well as emerging economies, the ITU-D ICT Applications and Cybersecurity Division aims to assist these countries.

99. What should governments take into account when developing a national e-commerce strategy for SME's?

A national e-commerce strategy should address the following issues:

- How the Internet will benefit SMEs
- How to increase awareness among SMEs of what the Internet is and what it can do
- How to answer the technical questions posed by enterprises
- How to train enterprises on the use of the Internet as a sales, marketing, communication and supply management medium
- Profiling products and services that will benefit from sales on the Internet

To encourage greater use of the Internet among small businesses, government ministries, agencies, trade development organizations, private-sector industry associations and non-profit groups must address a number of financial, legal, connectivity and other policy issues such as:

- Effective marketing techniques
- Encryption
- Security of payments
- Taxation
- Certification and authentication
- Confidentiality
- Protection of intellectual property
- Dealing with fraud and ensuring consumer protection
- Access to telecommunications facilities

To ensure the success of national e-commerce strategies, countries should develop specialized services for both the goods and services sectors. These should result from a joint effort of SMEs, trade associations, universities, government ministries and other lead organizations collaborating through some form of working group on small business e-commerce. Such a group should coordinate SME e-commerce activities to prevent duplication of efforts and enhance use of programmes and services.

Among the specialized services that could be provided are the following:

- Virtual trade shows or online exhibitions to supplement trade missions
- Delivering timely market research and trade leads via e-mail to SMEs
- Nationwide e-commerce seminars for exporters
- Video-conference capabilities to facilitate export transactions by electronically linking exporters with potential customers
- Specialized programmes to match exporters and importers
- Virtual business centres on the Internet
- Developing partnerships with credit card companies to increase the number of small businesses certified to conduct card transactions with government and private card holders
- Online e-mail assistance and counselling to small firms
- Profiling successful e-commerce strategies
- Online exhibitions of export products
- Providing answers to the most commonly asked e-commerce questions
- Carrying out research to guide the development of e-commerce outreach materials and services for the following purposes:
  - Educating SMEs on the benefits of using e-commerce tools throughout the business process
  - Providing examples of SMEs that have utilized e-commerce tools
  - Improving understanding of e-commerce business models
  - Guiding SMEs to information sources and technical support services

For more information

- Europe's Digital Competitiveness Report 2009; Main achievements of the i2010 strategy 2005-2009. European Commission, 2009. ec.europa.eu/i2010.

  The EU's i2010 is the union's policy framework for the information society and media. It promotes the positive contribution that information and communication technologies (ICT) can make to the economy, society and personal quality of life.

- Exchange, Valorisation and Transfer of regional best policy measures for SME support on IT and e-business Adoption (EVITA). www.evita-interreg4c.eu.

  EVITA builds upon various good practices developed under different regional or interregional development programmes. In addition to the exchange of know-how, EVITA proposes the pilot implementation of these practices, together with the development of new approaches, such as the integration of e-learning techniques and methodologies for reaching SMEs in remote areas.

Other issues

100. How does the International Trade Centre (ITC) provide assistance in the area of e-commerce?

Topics currently covered	Resources
Technology (e-business)	

E-commerce
E-mail and messaging
Internet
Web hosting
Managing IT projects
Web design and development
	ITC possesses the relevant expertise in ICT-related issues, and has developed the following modules to build e-commerce capacities:
	
	• Two comprehensive publications that act as a directory of technologies categorized under more than 70 business and management areas of any micro, small and medium-sized enterprise.
	
	• "Online2Export" training modules on Internet marketing, e-commerce strategies, e.marketplaces and digital contents: trade in sounds, relying on a course book and visual aids (PowerPoint presentations). In conjunction with the above two publications, these modules build a directory of web-marketing and e-commerce solutions, with a practical "How To" approach.
	
	• The above mentioned "Online2Export" training modules are also accompanied by an advisory methodology on e-commerce, with a particular emphasis on building and expanding web shops, relying on checklists for easy implementation of the recommendations.
	
	• Training modules cover the use of e-mail, Internet, web-hosting, hardware, etc. They are practical and include step-by-step and/or multimedia-based instructions on:
	
	   – How to search the web using major search engines such as Google, Yahoo, Bing;
	
	   – How to use major software packages such as MS Office, Open Office in the form of online interactive training;
	
	   – How to use e-mail services such as Gmail, Yahoo, etc. and software packages such as MS Outlook, Lotus Notes, etc.;
	
	   – How and when to use third-party web-hosting services;
	
	   – How to design and develop a customer-focused website. The modules also list online and desktop tools for designing and developing websites.

Diagnostic tools

ITC has developed a series of self- and/or expert-based checkers and diagnostic tools which are destined to assess the performance of SMEs in the field of web marketing and e-commerce:

• Are you Online2Export? Website assessment tool. This diagnostic tool evaluates the main features of a website in the context of international trade. Results are presented automatically with recommendations for corrective measures.

• Are you Online2Export? Web Strategy assessment tool. This diagnostic tool reviews the main aspects of an SME web strategy and evaluates them according to a best-practice benchmark. Results are presented automatically with recommendations for corrective measures.

• Are you Online2Export? Hospitality industry web strategy assessment tool. This diagnostic tool reviews the main aspects of an SME web strategy in the hospitality industry. It evaluates them according to a best-practice benchmark. Results are presented automatically with recommendations for corrective measures.

101.   What other international bodies carry out programmes and services to facilitate e-commerce?

In this section, you will find some of the international bodies which offer special programmes to promote e-commerce or provide related services:

International Telecommunication Union (ITU)

ITU has coordinated the World Summit on the Information Society (WSIS- www.itu.int/wsis). The first phase was held in Geneva in December 2003, where foundations were laid through agreement on a Declaration of Principles and a Plan of Action. The second phase was held in Tunisia in November 2005, adopting the Tunis Commitment and the Tunis Agenda for the Information Society. The latter includes chapters on financing mechanisms, Internet governance and implementation and follow-up. The latest summit was held in Geneva in May 2009.

One of the programmes put forward at the first summit was the ICT for Development platform (ICT4D). Its objective was to showcase the development dimension of information and communication technologies in a unique multi-stakeholder gathering. The platform was organized by the Swiss Agency for Development and Cooperation jointly with the Global Knowledge Partnership. A similar platform, called ICT for all (ICT4all) was organized during the Tunis Summit, by the Tunisian authorities.

In addition, as part of its ICT Applications programme, ITU has activities to promote and implement e-services and e-applications such as e-government, e-business, e-learning, e-health, e-employment, e-environment, e-agriculture, and e-science, in developing countries.

On the associated resource pages (www.itu.int/ITU-D/cyb/app/index.html) you can find more related information and supporting documents.

International Chamber of Commerce (ICC)

Under the ICC's (www.iccwbo.org) commission on E-Business, IT, and Telecoms (EBITT), business leaders and experts drawn from the ICC membership establish the key business positions, policies and practices on e-business, information technologies and telecommunications. With members who are users and providers of information technology and electronic services from both developed and developing countries, ICC provides a platform to develop global voluntary rules and best practices for these areas.

One of the objectives of EBITT is to provide a business interface on telecommunications, ICT and e-business issues, with all relevant intergovernmental and technical organizations.

Through its BASIS (Business Action to Support the Information Society) initiative, ICC represents business at the post-WSIS (UN World Summit on the Information Society) global meetings. These meetings include:

- Internet Governance Forum (IGF)

- UN Global Alliance for ICT and Development (GAID)

- WSIS action lines and follow-up process within the UN system, notably via the UN Commission for Science and Technology for Development (CSTD)

ICC is a founding institution of the World Chambers Network (www.worldchambers.com), which puts chambers around the globe on the Internet. The WCN is the chamber portal for international trade and offers key trust, verification and business intellectual property protection services.

United Nations Commission on International Trade Law (UNCITRAL)

UNCITRAL (www.uncitral.org) produces legislative norms, which are of interest mainly to legislators. However, some of the explanatory material accompanying UNCITRAL texts and some of the provisions of its Model Law on electronic commerce may be useful reading for anyone wishing to learn more about the legal issues of e-commerce.

United Nations Conference on Trade and Development (UNCTAD) Information and Communication Technologies Programme

UNCTAD's ICT programme (http://r0.unctad.org/ecommerce) carries out policy-oriented analytical work on the implications for developing countries of the adoption of ICT, Internet and e-business technologies.

Internet Governance Forum (IGF)

The Internet Governance Forum (www.intgovforum.org) is a multi-stakeholder forum for policy dialogue on issues of Internet governance. One of the mandates of the IGF is to discuss public policy issues related to key elements of Internet governance in order to foster the sustainability, robustness, security, stability and development of the Internet.

Global Alliance for ICT and Development

The Global Alliance for Information and Communication Technologies and Development (UN GAID, www.un-gaid.org) is an inclusive, cross-sectoral, multi-stakeholder platform promoting the use of information and communication technologies for enhancing the achievement of the internationally agreed development goals, notably the reduction of poverty.

It has launched five Flagship Partnership and Advocacy Initiatives – to accelerate connectivity and access for Africa, enhance and scale up the telecentre movement, a Cyber Development Corps based on south-south and triangular cooperation, promote assistive technologies for persons with disabilities and advocate for free Internet accessibility for schools – and a number of Communities of Expertise.

OECD

The committee for Information, Computer and Communications Policy (ICCP, www.oecd.org/sti/ict) of the Organisation for Economic Co-operation and Development (OECD), develops policies to maximize the benefits of the Information Society. ICCP addresses issues arising from the digital economy, the developing global information infrastructure and the evolution towards a global information society.

102. What areas of e-commerce require further research and inquiry?

The concept and practice of e-commerce are evolving as new technology and software are introduced to facilitate transactions, communication and marketing. Such changes make research into the practical aspects of e-commerce necessary at the national level, in sector-specific areas, and in collaboration with business, government, associations and universities. The following are suggested areas for research:

- The extent to which SMEs in developing countries can successfully promote and sell their products and services using websites, e-mail, and integrated communication, ordering and payment processing systems.

- The extent to which the supply chains have been modified by the Internet. In other words, what distinct technological changes have been made to the traditional supply chain, and in what ways are developing countries participating in the modified chain?

- The extent to which small suppliers in developing countries are more easily integrated into the supply chain as a result of web-based business transactions.

- Sector-specific case studies or case studies that focus on particular technological applications (e.g. order processing, marketing, inventory control, project monitoring, information dissemination) to illustrate to SMEs in developing countries how to learn from first movers in developed countries.

- Brief case studies of how industries have been changed by e-commerce.

- The ways in which SMEs can use the Internet to obtain efficiencies and economies of scale.

- From an international marketing perspective, how to organize the Web for SMEs from a developing country or groups of developing countries. The current industry portals are dominated by multinationals. International or regional trade support organizations could take the lead on this matter. What is needed is a coordinated strategy to make the Web more business friendly for SME vendors, and provide buyers in other countries with a simple, easy-to-use mechanism for identifying SME suppliers in developing countries. The major search engines should be brought in as partners in any discussion of such a strategy.

- How national organizations in developing countries can take a proactive role in helping SMEs to exhibit their products and services more effectively by establishing sector- and product-specific national portals for SMEs. Such portals could carry directories (sometimes referred to as blue pages) on which SMEs can post brief descriptions of themselves to achieve a small but coordinated visual presence on the Internet.

- How developing countries can encourage the use of e-commerce by showcasing successful programmes and services, highlighting how they did it.

- How to encourage the free flow of ideas among e-commerce experts to identify cutting-edge issues in e-commerce in regard to SMEs in developing countries. A roster of experts has been set up by ITC.

- Developing new secure payment methods for countries where the technological infrastructure is less developed.

- Working on new business models for under-developed markets.

- What will it take for SMEs to be successful in achieving mass customization, as one of the tools to increase customer perceived value.

- How SMEs can benefit from the innovations of Web 2.0, in particular in the area of social networking.